AF842469

Omnipresence of Advertising

Studies in Philosophy, History of Ideas and Modern Societies
Edited by Jan Hartman

Volume 27

Joanna Iwanowska

Omnipresence of Advertising

PETER LANG

Berlin - Bruxelles - Chennai - Lausanne - New York - Oxford

Bibliographic Information published by the Deutsche Nationalbibliothek
The Deutsche Nationalbibliothek lists this publication in the Deutsche Nationalbibliografie; detailed bibliographic data is available in the internet at http://dnb.d-nb.de.

Library of Congress Cataloging-in-Publication Data
A CIP catalog record for this book has been applied for at the Library of Congress.

Cover illustration: Courtesy of Benjamin Ben Chaim.

ISSN 2191-1878
ISBN 978-3-631-90583-8 (Print)
E-ISBN 978-3-631-92023-7 (E-Book)
E-ISBN 978-3-631-92024-4 (E-PUB)
DOI 10.3726/b21913

© 2024 Peter Lang Group AG, Lausanne
Published by Peter Lang GmbH, Berlin, Deutschland

info@peterlang.com - www.peterlang.com

All rights reserved.
All parts of this publication are protected by copyright.
Any utilization outside the strict limits of the copyright law, without the permission of the publisher, is forbidden and liable to prosecution.
This applies in particular to reproductions, translations, microfilming, and storage and processing in electronic retrieval systems.

This publication has been peer reviewed.
www.peterlang.com

Content

Acknowledgments

For intellectual inspiration, I wish to express my gratitude towards Atty. Mirosław Sajewicz, Prof. Paweł Łuków, Prof. Marcin Poręba, Prof. Magdalena Borowska, Frédéric Pallu.

For other kinds of inspiration and support, I would like to thank Prof. Ryszard Iwanowski (†), Prof. Zdzisław Naniewicz (†), Jolanta Naniewicz, Gregory Szczurek, Lilia Sajewicz-Iwanowska, Jolanta Sajewicz-Świackiewicz, as well as the tea artisans of Hoshino-mura, Yame District, Fukuoka Prefecture, Japan.

0 Setting the Scene

> "Advertising is a pervasive presence in society—on television, radio, magazines, newspapers, handbills, posters, billboards, direct mail and on the Internet. Advertising is everywhere. We are besieged with commercials at airport baggage carousels, on corporate telephone lines, on flashing screens at the local market, etc."
> J.A. Cohan "Towards a New Paradigm in the Ethics of Women's Advertising" (2001)

0.1. The Omnipresence of Advertising: Vignettes

A primary school kid is writing a mathematics test. On the bottom of the test sheet there is an advertisement of the local pizza restaurant.

A classic music fan reads a book about the life of one of her favorite cellists: to her surprise, she finds that the back cover of the book has been used as advertising space for a textile manufacturer.

A person enters a taxi they have ordered. On the back of the driver's seat, just in front of the passenger's eyes, there is a television screen playing advertisements adjusted to the gender and age of the freshly seated passenger. More advertising, in the form of an advertising poster, is visible below the screen.

A woman who has given birth enters a hospital room. On the windowsill, she finds a breastfeeding manual written by medical professionals: alongside medical information and health advice, the manual features an advertisement of a lactation-boosting supplement, accompanied by a few samples of the product. When leaving the hospital, the woman also receives a sampling package from the hands of a medical professional: inside are different product samples with advertising leaflets, as well as a postnatal health manual where medical information is interspersed with advertisements.

At a jail lobby, a person is waiting to visit a detained relative. The lobby is equipped with a large television screen that keeps playing advertisements.

In an airplane, a passenger is seated for a three-hour flight. On the back of the seat—just in front of the passenger's eyes—there is an advertisement sticker. All along the airplane aisle, there are multiple monitors hanging from the cabin ceiling, playing air flight information interspersed with advertisements.

At a parent-teacher meeting at school, a parent receives a report card that communicates the academic performance of their child. The report card is wrapped in a special colorful jacket with a logo of a fast-food chain.

Sitting on a bench, a man watches a leaf fall of a tree. He sees a woman who raises her arm, trying to catch the leaf. A small advertisement is stamped onto the skin of the woman's armpit.

A person goes for a swim in the ocean. As they enter the beach, they notice imprints on the sand. All across the beach, commercial logos are stamped into the sand.

0.2. The Omnipresence of Advertising: An Introduction

The short vignettes from the previous section paint a preliminary sketch of a bourgeoning trend within contemporary advertising: to be everywhere, or—in the words of Jay Walker-Smith, President of the Marketing Firm Yankelovich—"to cover every blank space with some kind of brand logo or a promotion or an advertisement" (Johnson, 17 Sep 2006). The advertisers themselves openly admit that reaching the consumer anywhere and everywhere is something they strive for. Linda Kaplan Thaler, chief executive at the Kaplan Thaler Group, explains it in the following manner: "We never know where the consumer is going to be at any point in time, so we have to find a way to be everywhere. Ubiquity is the new exclusivity" (Story, 15 Jan 2007). Walker-Smith, on the other hand, admits that striving for the omnipresence of advertising is a self-propelling advertising strategy which makes the advertisers keep raising the bar and crossing the limits: "Everywhere we turn we're saturated with advertising messages trying to get our attention (…) All of this marketing saturation that's going on is creating this kind of arms race between marketers where they have to up the ante the next time out because their competitors have upped the ante the last time they were out. And the only way you can win is to have more saturation" (Johnson, 17 Sep 2006).

As a result, the omnipresence of advertising seems to be characterized by the advertisers respecting no boundaries as to *where* or *when* advertising might appear: in Chapter 1, I will illustrate this tendency by providing plenty of real-life examples of types of space and events that used to be free from advertising—often for a good reason—but have lost this status. This lack of respect for boundaries displayed by advertising that aims to be ubiquitous has been noted by such philosophers as Michael Sandel or Edward Spence. Sandel writes about the "boundlessness" of the proliferation of advertising we have been experiencing since the 1990s (2013, 186). However, he also underscores that "it is not easy to explain what is wrong with the proliferation of advertising we have witnessed in the last two decades" (185). In a similar vein, Spence (in collaboration with Brett Van Heekeren) talks about "the pervasiveness and unrestricted proliferation of advertising that threatens to engulf all aspects of our private and public domains" and refers to it as "the biggest ethical problem in advertising" that remains unsolved (Spence, Van Heekeren, 2005, 122). As the empirical material in Chapter 1 will make clear, this is a "problem" in the sense that advertising which aims to be ubiquitous and respects no boundaries is perceived by people as inappropriate, invasive, and intrusive.

This book has a double purpose: to elucidate the nature of the omnipresence of advertising and to show why it is ethically problematic. Chapter 1 is devoted to completing the first task, and Chapter 2—the second one. In Chapter 3, the final version of the definition of the omnipresence of advertising is presented and the possibility of finding solutions is discussed.

0.3. Focus on Personal Autonomy

In order to show why the phenomenon in question is ethically problematic, I have decided to focus on the friction between the omnipresence of advertising and the value of personal autonomy. In a nutshell, I argue that the omnipresence of advertising produces conditions that are adverse to an agent being able to effectuate their decision not to be exposed to advertising (Section 2.3.1.1), as well as to the cultivation of critical reasoning which is an important autonomy skill (Section 2.3.2.1). Furthermore, the omnipresence of advertising has a negative impact on interpersonal trust that plays an important role in the development, maintenance, and exercise of autonomy competency (Section 2.3.2.2).

Constructing the three arguments that discuss these infringements upon personal autonomy has not been easy as there already exists some philosophical argumentation concerning the value of autonomy in the context of the contemporary proliferation of advertising (see the Philosophical Appendix for a more detailed account). Spence and Van Heekeren (2005), as well as Sandel (2013), make some interesting points concerning the proliferation of advertising being a threat for people's autonomy of choice. Andrew Sneddon (2013), on the other hand, consciously departs from discussing autonomy of choice in favor of focusing on the overwhelming amount of advertising being detrimental to the autonomy of persons (for more about the distinction between the autonomy of choice and the autonomy of persons, see Chapter 2). With this already existing pool of arguments, it was not obvious that something new and autonomy-relevant could be said regarding the topic of the pervasiveness of advertising.

Nevertheless, I was able to provide a fresh perspective on this subject for two reasons. The first is my openness to an eclectic mixture of inspirations, most notably coming from feminist ethics and the American legal doctrine, but also from urban studies (more on this in the next section). The second reason is my emphasis on the need for a definition of the phenomenon: to my best knowledge, nobody has yet attempted to provide a definition of the omnipresence of advertising, which makes this book pioneer.

0.4. Sources of Inspiration

0.4.1. American Legal Doctrine

An important extra-philosophical source of inspiration for this book is the American legal doctrine due to its pioneering work on commercial speech that includes two areas of high relevance to the subject of the omnipresence of advertising: the topic of a captive audience and the topic of pervasiveness of commercial speech (see the Legal Appendix for a more detailed account).

The captive audience doctrine is relevant because it is concerned with freedom from unwanted speech—a topic which includes freedom from unwanted *commercial* speech and naturally connects to a discussion of the value of autonomy. I have been especially inspired by reading about the so-called "impracticality standard," which serves as a guide in defining an audience as captive to unwanted speech—it has propelled me to rethink the nature of obstacles that may stand in the way of making an autonomous choice. Consequently, the definition of the American legal term "captive audience"—along with the accompanying impracticality standard—has proven to be a useful tool in an attempt to identify how the omnipresence of advertising diminishes the autonomy of choice of contemporary individuals, not so much by making the avoidance of exposure to advertising *entirely impossible*, but by making it *highly impractical* and thus disruptive of these individuals' everyday functioning (see the argument from a captive audience in Chapter 2, Section 2.3.1.1).

As to the second area of relevance to this book, I have been inspired by R. George Wright whose work on the pervasiveness of commercial speech contains important intuitions that I have been trying to further develop. It is noteworthy that already in the late nineties Wright had planted the seeds for the 21st century philosophical argumentation concerning the omnipresence of advertising, construed by Spence, Sandel, and Sneddon. Importantly, Wright pointed out that the pervasiveness of commercial speech and commercial values affects personal autonomy (1997, 11, 34–54) and the way we construct personal relationships

(6, 40, 199–202). Many years after these concerns were voiced, I am offering an argument from non-benign objectification and the erosion of trust (see Chapter 2, Section 2.3.2.2), which somewhat echoes Wright's intuitions, but considers the problem of undermining interpersonal (as well as intrapersonal) trust in a very specific context of personal relationships with autonomy-promoting others. Also, another argument I present—the argument from hindering critical thinking (see Chapter 2, Section 2.3.2.1)—resonates with Wright's conviction that certain types of space, like schools, for example, should serve as a refuge from commercial advertising (1997, 10–11).

Moreover, although Wright does not explicitly define what he refers to as "the pervasiveness of commercial speech" (40), or "near ubiquity of commercial speech" (38), or "the pervasiveness of the culture of commercial speech" (5), I have profited from trying to interpret the meaning that he implied. This process made me realize that more than one interpretation is possible and recognize the importance of spelling out my own definition of the phenomenon in an explicit fashion (see Chapter 1, Section 1.4, and Chapter 3, Section 3.1).

0.4.2. Feminist Ethics

Following the guidelines of Alison Jaggar, the philosophical work in this book should not be classified as belonging to feminist ethics, as it does not satisfy two out of three "minimum conditions of adequacy for any approach to ethics that purports to be feminist" (1989, 910): namely, this book does not focus on the experiences of (all) women and does not contribute—in any direct or explicit way—to subverting the subordination of women. Rather, this volume aims to critically consider the experiences of a considerable amount of contemporary human beings, who are faced with the omnipresence of advertising, and to contribute to the defense of these individuals' personal autonomy, regardless of their gender. However, even though this book cannot be classified as feminist, I would not have been able to produce the argumentation in Chapter 2 without adopting the relational (contextual) approach to personal autonomy, trust, and self-trust, conceived and further developed by feminist scholars who are philosophers, jurists, and medical professionals (e.g. Meyers, 1987, 1989, 2005; Barclay, 2000; McLeod, Sherwin, 2000; McLeod, 2002; Kukla, 2005; Benson, 2005; Atkins, 2006; Goldberg, 2003, 2008; Goering, 2008; Kong, 2017; Brison, 1997/2018). Similarly, Martha Nussbaum's work on objectification has been very helpful in composing the argument from non-benign objectification and the erosion of trust (Section 2.3.2.2), while in constructing the argument from hindering critical reasoning (Section 2.3.2.1) I have referred to some of Nel Noddings' remarks concerning the role of schools in training "ad-resistance" in young people. Interestingly, the fact that my work does not classify as feminist and yet makes productive use of certain ideas and intellectual tools developed by feminist thinkers suggests that these tools are applicable not only to feminist research, but also beyond it. All in all, defining autonomy relationally has proven indispensible in arguing that the omnipresence of advertising is hostile to autonomy; in contrast, substantive definitions of autonomy, for instance, would not have been as effective for that task.

0.4.3. Urban Studies and Spatial Thinking

As an underlying theme of this book—not at the forefront, but always somewhere in the background—is the theme of *spatiality*, because the spatial dimension of human existence is of high relevance to the discussion of the omnipresence of advertising.[1] As rightly observed by Edward Soja, a philosophizing urbanist, human beings are "intrinsically spatial beings" and "the spatial dimension of our lives has never been of greater practical and political relevance than it is today" (1996, 1). Incidentally, Soja expressed this view in the 1990s, at the time when the phenomenon I refer to as "the omnipresence of advertising" was beginning to gain substance.

Significantly inspired by Henri Lefebvre, a spatially thinking philosopher, Soja entertained a firm belief that it is not merely geographers, architects, and urbanists who are capable of thinking spatially: indeed, he was encouraging a transdisciplinary discourse that would involve spatial thinking (3). This book follows that suggestion. Therefore, not only have I allowed myself to be influenced by the research of some geographers, architects, and urban scholars—such as Jan Gehl (2010, 2011), Marek Czyński and Marek Ostrowski (2011), Karolina Listwan-Franczak and Paweł Franczak (2015)—but I have also tried to employ spatial thinking in theorizing the omnipresence of advertising (Chapters 1 and 3), in the formulation of argumentation pertaining to personal autonomy in the context of omnipresence of advertising (Chapter 2), as well as in some of the final conclusions of this book (Chapter 3).

---

1 As first emphasized by Spence and Van Heekeren (2005, 93–94).

0.5. The Spatial and Temporal Aspects of the Omnipresence of Advertising

0.5.2. The Spatial Aspect

The empirical data within this book come from many different types of locations—city parks, natural reserves, schools, police stations, hospitals, means of transport, etc.—but also from many different countries. This is motivated by the fact that just like advertising is a worldwide phenomenon, the omnipresence of advertising is also not restricted to any particular country or continent.

However, although the author made sure to include empirical examples from across the globe, it is also true that a relatively large proportion of the examples comes from the American and British contexts. This can be succinctly explained in the following manner. First, even though advertising has a multilocation history dating back to ancient times,[2] the United States and the United Kingdom have a special relationship with advertising in its professional form (which is most relevant to the analysis in this book), since it is in these two countries that the first advertising agencies were set up, and consequently this is where advertising became a profession.[3] Second, the Unites States and the United Kingdom are both countries that seem to have established many precedents in terms of turning an advertising-free type of space into an advertising space. For these reasons, having a larger proportion of empirical examples from these two countries is justified.

0.5.3. The Temporal Aspect

The omnipresence of advertising can be said to have a temporal aspect in two senses. First, in the sense that it affects many different types of *events* in people's lives, just like it has been discussed to affect different types of *spaces* in the

2 The earliest advertisements are said to have been discovered in the form of stenciled inscriptions on bricks made by the Babylonians (Presbrey, 1927; Beard, 2017). Using trademarks and advertising mottos to help customers differentiate between brands goes back to potters from Iron Age Greece (Beard, 2017). "Point-of purchase advertisements (…) visible on the walls of Pompeii and Herculaneum" are another famous early instance of commercial messages (Beard, 2017, 240).

3 For information about the first British advertising agencies in the late 18th and early 19th centuries, see Mackay, 2004, 70. For information about the first American advertising agencies in the second half of the 19th century, see Mendelová, 2018, 11–12; Hower, 1949, 185.

everyday reality of human beings (see Section 0.5.2; see Chapter 1, Sections 1.4, 1.5). The omnipresence of advertising is not a purely spatial phenomenon, but rather a spatio-temporal phenomenon, or—theorizing it in a more trialectic fashion in the spirit of Lefebvre (1974/1991) and Soja (1996)—it could even be called a spatio-tempo-*relational* phenomenon, as will be discussed later within the book (Chapters 2 and 3).

Second, the omnipresence of advertising has a temporal aspect in the sense that it is stretched over time. As mentioned above (Section 0.4.3), I identify the time when the omnipresence of advertising was beginning to gain substance with the last decade of the 20th century. However, this identification calls for an explanation. It is not easy—and expectedly so—to pinpoint the exact moment when the omnipresence of advertising can be said to have begun, because its seeds or beginnings (with an s at the end to make the word "beginning" plural) are spread all over the 20th century and some even at the end of the 19th century. This will be reflected in Chapter 1, where some empirical data I give come from before (or way before) the 1990s (see also Sandel, 2013, 185).

Nevertheless, as rightly observed by Sandel on the basis of his study, it was in the 1990s and early 2000s that people began to be faced with a particularly intense proliferation or even "explosion of naming rights and advertising" (2013, 184–186): apart from giving empirical examples to justify his thesis, Sandel points to a significant amount of journalists reacting to that phenomenon with article titles such as *Nowhere to Run, Nowhere to Hide from Ad Barrage* (Los Angeles Times), *Ad Onslaught* (The Sunday Times, London), *Ads Infinitum* (The Washington Post), *Anywhere the Eye Can See, It's Now Likely to See an Ad* (The New York Times), *Ads Here, There, Everywhere* (USA Today) (Sandel, 2013, 184). Sandel's thesis could be further corroborated by the fact that it was in the 1990s that the famous Yankelovich Monitor poll was conducted, according to which an average American was supposedly exposed to as many as 5000 ads per day (13 Nov 1995, ADWEEK-W.EDITION; Ayres, Funk, 2003, 95, ftn 71). Also, Wright's book, written in 1997 as a commentary on the reality at that time, speaks about the pervasiveness of commercial speech as an important up-to-date topic that should be addressed by legal scholars. Finally, in their book from the early 2000s, Spence and Van Heekeren say that *lately* there has been an observable trend of ambience and 360-degree advertising strategies to try "to permeate all aspects of the consumer's life" (2005, 85).

Therefore, even though the seeds of the omnipresence of advertising might have been sown before the last decade of the 20th century, it is the 1990s which witness an unparallel proliferation of advertising messages in our everyday reality. Thus, it is the last decade of the 20th century that constitutes the beginning of the phenomenon I refer to as the omnipresence of advertising.

0.6. Important Definitions

As far as the "omnipresence of advertising" goes, it is a conscious choice of the author to let the complex definition of this term evolve throughout the book. This process might be called definitional exploration and it will be summarized in Chapter 3.

However, there are two terms—"commercial values" and "noncommercial values"—that I wish to introduce early on. These will appear throughout the book and it seems imperative that the reader understands their intended meaning from the start. The term "commercial values" shall be used to refer to commercial brand recognition (i.e., consumers' ability to correctly identify a particular commercial product or service through visual or auditory cues such as a logo, a slogan, a jingle, packaging, colors), commercial brand loyalty (i.e., consumers' dedication to continuously repurchase one brand's products or services over another), commercial brand resonance (i.e., the intensity of the psychological connection consumers have with a particular commercial brand), commercial brand revenue (i.e., the revenue generated by a brand for a commercial organization), commercial brand-expression (understood as the expression of a brand's identity and history); to avoid needless repetition I will hereafter use these terms without the addition of the adjective "commercial," nevertheless continuing to refer to commercial brands. In turn, the term "noncommercial values" will be employed to refer to such values as trust, loyalty, care, devotion, honesty, dependability, self-expression, exchange of thoughts, ideas, and opinions.

Another term that I wish to define early on is "commercial advertising," and I credit the American legal doctrine for inspiring me in this respect (see the Legal Appendix). Importantly, I am taking into account Wright's doubts about defining commercial speech as speech that proposes a commercial transaction (Wright, 1997, 55; see the Legal Appendix for details) and also the reservations of advertisers that advertising does not constitute an offer in the legal sense of the word (this is often written in small print below the advertising message). Even though Wright's reasons for not being content with using the word "proposal" may not be as relevant to the attempt to define the term "commercial advertising" as they are to the definition of "commercial speech," his doubts are inspiring because many contemporary commercial advertisements also manage to escape being easily classified as messages that simply "propose" to buy a commercial product (sometimes, for instance, they may rather seem to encourage a certain lifestyle).

Therefore, I will shun using the word "proposal" or "offer" in my definition of commercial advertising. Instead, I will define commercial advertising—which I shall hereafter refer to as "advertising," in order to avoid needless repetition—as speech and/or image and/or sound, meant to promote the sales of commercial products (for instance, by encouraging a certain lifestyle). I believe it to be a broad enough definition to encompass the multitude and sometimes ingenuity of forms in which contemporary advertising occurs, as will be empirically illustrated in Chapter 1.

0.7. How to Read This Book and How It Came to Be

The book that you are reading was initially a PhD thesis, defended (*cum laude*) at the University of Warsaw in 2023. In its primary form, my work was meant to be read in a linear way and contained two additional chapters which summarized what has been said so far by other scholars; these chapters paved the way to my original input. In the process of turning the PhD thesis into a book, I realized that these two chapters could appear uninteresting to the general reader. Indeed, the "heart" or the core of my original thoughts was elsewhere in the thesis: hence, the key chapters have become chapters 1, 2, and 3 of this book, while some information from the more redundant chapters has been kept in the form of two appendices: the Legal Appendix and the Ethical Appendix. This way, the appendices can be consulted at any time, but they no longer "stand in the way" of accessing the original input. As far as the current Chapters 1, 2, and 3 go, I would like to further encourage the reader to approach them in a nonlinear way. For example, you might feel the need to read first about the ethical problems caused by the omnipresence of advertising, or maybe a particular ethical problem, like the erosion of trust, piques your interest the most. Should this be case, feel free to begin the book by reading Chapter 2, or even a particular section of Chapter 2. There is no right or wrong way to start reading this book. Let your curiosity be your guide.

1 Portraying the Omnipresence of Advertising

> "In a communication environment where messages and brands are placed on gas pumps, at automatic tellers, in elevators, on taxi seat-backs, on sporting celebrity's attire, in the sky, in films and TV series, in camouflaged editorial content, it requires a creative strategy to stand out in this omnipresent clutter. But when is a point of contact with consumers appropriate, and when have advertisers overstepped the mark?"
> Spence, Van Heekeren, *Advertising Ethics* (2005)

1.1. Introduction

Nowadays advertising seems to be everywhere. We notice it, we talk about it, and we seem to intuitively grasp what this "everywhereness" is about. However, (to my best knowledge) nobody seems to have defined what the omnipresence (or "everywhereness") of advertising really is. Is it even possible to define it? Or is the phenomenon too elusive for that? In this chapter, I try to sketch a portrait of the omnipresence of advertising: a theoretico-empirical one. First, I analyze the scholarly usage of the term "omnipresence" in contexts not pertaining to the topic of advertising—this is a way of exploring what the term "omnipresence" means. Second, I present a wealth of empirical material that illustrates how the omnipresence of advertising manifests in the contemporary reality. Combining these two steps has allowed me to offer the first approximation at a definition of this phenomenon. I end this chapter with a conclusion (drawn from the empirical material) that in the contemporary reality the omnipresence of advertising manifests in two ways: on a global scale and on a more local scale.

1.2. What Does the Term "Omnipresence" Mean?

In the contexts not connected with advertising, the term "omnipresence" is used in two ways, indicating two somewhat different meanings of the term. The first meaning is very literal: "omnipresence" is understood as signifying the presence of a certain person or phenomenon literally everywhere. This meaning is typical in many religious contexts. For example, when John Milton gives a voice to the Christian God, the God says: "Boundless the Deep, because I AM who fill Infinitude, nor vacuous the space" (1667/1821, 206). In his book *Milton's*

Ontology, Cosmogony, and Physics, Walter C. Curry describes Milton's God as "an all-pervading Spirit who is everywhere in total space at the same time" (1957, 18), by which Curry means that Milton's theopantic God is present—in an immaterial way—in the finite space of our universe, but also in the vacuous space which extends indefinitely beyond our universe and in which no material thing exists (19–20). This meaning of omnipresence, as being literally everywhere, is also implied in the concept of a pantheist God, like the Stoic *Logos*. As Massimo Pigliucci says: "The Stoics believed in God, though theirs was a material God immanent in the cosmos" (2017, 22). Intriguingly, Tiantai Buddhism, for instance, applies the same meaning of omnipresence to the notion of experience of sentient beings. In his book *Emptiness and Omnipresence: An Essential Introduction to Tiantai Buddhism*, Brook Ziporyn writes that "Tiantai philosophy tells us that every fleeting moment of experience of any sentient being persists eternally through all time, pervades all space, and is experienced constantly by all other sentient beings" (2016, 2), and he adds that "each experience we have includes not only itself but also all other experiences of all other sentient beings at all times, as viewed in all possible ways" (1). All three of the above-mentioned examples illustrate such an understanding of omnipresence, according to which a person or a phenomenon is omnipresent if it pervades all space and time, whether in a material or an immaterial way.

The second meaning of "omnipresence" is not literal. Before giving a definition of this second meaning, let us look at a concrete use of this term in relation to psychology: "An omnipresence of psychology in our contemporary life—represented by a very high saturation of ordinary language and institutional practices with psychological concepts and explanatory models—has become pervasive to such an extent that it is possible to speak of a psychological age. The signifier 'psychological' distinguishes our age from the previous one dominated by religious generative axes" (Jovanovic, 2003, 11). In a similar vein, Nikolas Rose (1998) comments on the phenomenon of the omnipresence of psychology in the contemporary life in the following way: "A psy-ontology has come to inhabit us, an inescapable interiority that hollows out, in the depths of the human, a psychic universe with a topography that has its own characteristics" (190). These examples of talking about omnipresence in the non-literal sense demonstrate that this term can be used in reference to an immaterial phenomenon, like psychology.

However, the term "omnipresence" in the non-literal sense can also be used to refer to material objects. A good example is provided in a paper entitled *An Ontology of Omnipresent and Omniscient Cameras: Changes to Telejournalism and the Ubiquity of Devices for Recording Reality* by Maura Oliveira Martins. When

Martins talks about the contemporary omnipresence of cameras—in the form of professional cameras, but also amateur cameras, such as digital cameras, cameras in cell phones, cameras in tablets, webcams, GoPro cameras (2016, 105–108)—she does not mean that cameras are literally everywhere.

It is also conceivable that the term "omnipresence" could refer to a kind of a person: for instance, one could potentially talk about the omnipresence of Internet trolls, as a type of a person, within the virtual reality of Internet. In fact, scholars from Stanford and Cornell Universities present research suggesting that, under the right circumstances, any one of us can become a troll: they say that "while prior work suggests that trolling behavior is confined to a vocal and antisocial minority, we demonstrate that ordinary people can engage in such behavior as well (…) under the right circumstances" (Cheng et al., 2017, 1217).

In the quotation about the omnipresence of psychology, the expression "high saturation of ordinary language" is used to explain the phenomenon in question. However, note that the word "language" (understood as the Saussurian *langue*) denotes a *potentiality* which is realizable in utterances (see, for instance, Grzegorczykowa, 2007, 13). Therefore, talking about a high saturation of ordinary language should not be understood to entail a high saturation of the entire contemporary reality with psychologically-laden utterances. Rather, it seems more accurate to say that the term "omnipresence of psychology" entails a high potentiality that at any time, at any moment, any person could use psychological concepts and explanatory models in an utterance. While some concrete domains of reality could be identified as highly saturated with psychologically-laden utterances, it would be excessive to say that the entire contemporary reality is highly saturated in this way.

In a like vein, it appears correct to interpret the omnipresence of cameras in Martins' paper as implying—first and foremost—a high potentiality for some kind of a camera to be used, at any time, at any moment, by any person. Again, some concrete domains of reality could be identified as being highly saturated with cameras being used to film at the same time, but it seems excessive to say that the entire reality is saturated in this way. It is not the case that all people who own cameras use them to film all the time, in all possible places. But they *can*.

Similarly, the omnipresence of Internet trolls—within the virtual reality of Internet—would be best understood as a high potentiality of an Internet troll to manifest at any time, at any moment, and in any person.

To sum up, omnipresence can be understood either as presence which literally pervades all space and time, or in a more modest and limited, non-literal sense as a high potentiality for a type of a phenomenon, object, or person to appear everywhere and anytime in reality (this can sometimes manifest as high saturation of certain domains of reality with the presence of a type of phenomenon, object, or person). The first meaning of omnipresence is typically used to make an ontological statement about how reality has always been and will always be constructed; in other words, it is used to refer to an *a priori* mechanics of the world, which human beings are subjected to, but which they did not bring about. In the second meaning, the omnipresence of a type of phenomenon, object, or person is temporary—it has not always been the case, and it is likely to pass at some point, as the history of the human kind evolves. Also, the term "omnipresence" in the non-literal sense often refers to the kind of pervasiveness which has been caused by human beings and which can be counteracted by human beings as well.

1.3. Everyday Manifestations of the Omnipresence of Advertising[4]

Many authors (i.e., some academics, activists, and a lot of journalists) writing about the presence of advertising in space use the adjective "ad-free"—meaning "not containing any advertising" (Cambridge Dictionary)—to refer to space within which advertising does not (and/or should not) appear because its presence would be unusual, unwanted, inappropriate (see, for example: Karpatkin, Holmes, 1995, sec. *Have It Your Way*; Alexander, Crompton, Shrubsole, 2011, 44; Vedrashko, 2006, 28; Mahdawi, 12 Aug 2015; Wall, 11 May 2018). Therefore, there seems to exist a theoretical division into space where advertising can be present and space which is (and should be) ad-free. And yet, despite the existence of this theoretical division, it is more and more difficult to find such *types* of space within the contemporary reality that would still be ad-free. Even though one can surely find particular *tokens* of space which are free from advertising, ad-free *types* of space seem to be on the verge of extinction. Below the reader will find a list of examples of types of space that used to be ad-free, but have already

4 It should be stressed that the empirical material provided in this chapter is not meant to be exhaustive, but rather illustrative, i.e., only selected examples of the omnipresence of advertising have been discussed. For instance, I have not discussed the ways in which advertising pervades people's telephone communication, their digital email accounts, social media profiles, or the majority of Internet sites people use every day. These and other examples have been left out on purpose because a truly comprehensive presentation of all the ways in which the omnipresence of advertising manifests itself in the contemporary reality would take up an enormous amount of space without adding much more illustrative quality.

been appropriated as advertising spaces: these examples illustrate how the omnipresence of advertising manifests in the everyday reality of many people around the world. Several examples are taken from the United States, because this is the country that often pioneers in transforming certain ad-free spaces into advertising spaces. However, I have also provided examples from many different countries.

1.3.1. Jails

Since 1999, a California-based corporation, Jail Advertising Network, formerly known as Partners for a Safer America, has been providing U.S. jails with an opportunity to alleviate their financial problems by offering funding in exchange for in-jail advertising (Jail Advertising Network). Jail Advertising Network makes it possible for bail agents and attorneys to advertise themselves to the arrestees and for the jails to receive a part of the revenue generated in this way. A company with a similar *modus operandi*, Metrodata Services, has been described by Sandel (2013, 196). Sandel gives an example of the Erie County Holding Center in Buffalo, New York, which has been profiting from the cooperation with Metrodata Services since 2011. The defendants of Erie County Holding Center see ads running on a high-definition television screen just a few moments after they arrive at the jail. Another screen is present in the lobby where families and friends wait to visit the detainees. A commercial is sold for 40 USD per week with a one-year commitment from the advertiser. In an interview for Buffalo News, Anthony N. Diina, president and owner of Metrodata Services, observed: "You want to advertise to someone exactly when they want to make their decision. That is the case here (…) This is the ultimate captive audience" (Sandel, 2013, 196; Spina, 27.03.2011). Although the idea has proved to be a financial success for many different jails from across the country, some doubts about the project have been expressed as well. For instance, a criminal defense attorney, James Auricchio, commented on in-jail advertising: "I wouldn't [buy this kind of advertising] even if I was subsisting on Ramen noodles (…) It's just poor taste in my mind. It strikes me as inserting a commercial aspect into something when I don't feel there is any place for it" (Watson, Feb 2013, 41). Also, on an online blog devoted to branding strategies, Alexander Villeneuve, has likened in-jail advertising to "ambulance chasing," an unethical practice of lawyers soliciting clients at a site of a disaster[5]: "The strategic pitfall to captive ads is summed up by the pop[u]lar

---

5 The ethical guidelines of the American Bar Association prohibit this practice. See: American Bar Association, Center for Professional Responsibility, "Rule 7.3, Direct

aphorism coined by the late Marshall McLuhan: the medium is the message. That medium, designed to capitalize on the attention of people in a vulnerable state, clearly sends the message of being the criminal-defense equivalent to ambulance chasing. It's a medium that poorly reflects the truly valuable service an attorney is *sworn* to provide for their clients" (Villeneuve, 2011).

1.3.2. Police Service

The idea to use police cars as advertising space came to the U.S. from Great Britain. It all started in the 1990s, when a new regulation was issued by the Home Office, which allowed the British police departments to compliment their annual budgets with money raised from sponsorships, on condition that the amount raised in this way could not exceed 1 percent of the annual budget (Nowicka, 8 Sep 1996; Tendler, 6 Jan 1997; Sandel, 2013, 195). One of the first examples was a London police patrol car with an inscription "This car is sponsored by Harrods" (Nowicka, 8 Sep 1996; Sandel, 2013, 195). Other companies mentioned among the first sponsors were Thresher, a producer of wine and spirits, the Body Shop, a cosmetics manufacturer, and Ford, a car dealer (Nowicka, 8 Sep 1996). Sandel quotes a police officer's comment concerning advertising on police cars: "It's been forbidden territory until recently. Now everything is up for grabs" (Sandel, 2013, 195). The British did not stop at the corporate sponsorship of police cars: 1990s also saw money from corporate sources being used to help build a new police station, furnish suites for victims of sex assaults, acquire mobile phones and pagers for the police (Nowicka, 8 Sep 1996). A sponsorship and marketing officer from the North Yorkshire police force expressed an opinion that "in some respects, sponsoring us [the police force] is no different from sponsoring a sports event" (Nowicka, 8 Sep 1996). However, not all sponsorship projects were accepted. For example, "an eye-catching Thresher's logo on a van donated to Avon and Somerset was scaled down after complaints" (Nowicka, 8 Sep 1996). Similarly, the Hampshire police never went through with a commercial campaign idea, according to which the police should stop motorists, ask them to read a number plate, and provide them with vouchers for a free sight test if the motorist could not read the plate: the project was vetoed and officially rejected (Nowicka, 8 Sep 1996). In the 21st century, new ways of acquiring sponsorship money by the police were reported: the corporate sponsors begun paying police to carry out

Contact with Prospective Clients," [in:] *Model Rules of Professional Conduct.*

criminal inquiries, as well as giving money for awareness campaigns and local crime reduction projects (Duffin, 2 May 2013).

In the U.S., the first attempt to use police cars as advertising space in the early 2000s was unsuccessful (Sandel, 2013, 193–195). The offer to equip the police with brand new patrol cars for 1 USD per year came from a company in North Carolina: in exchange, the cars would have to be embellished with advertisements and commercial logos (193). Among the voices defending the idea was a city councilman from Omaha who said: "Our stadium has ads on the fences and corridors, as does our civic auditorium. As long as it's done tastefully, advertising on police cars is no different" (Wood, 3 Oct 2002; Sandel, 2013, 194). Others said that since city buses and dog-catcher trucks are already emblazoned with advertising, then it is only logical that advertisements on police cars should be the next step (Wood, 3 Oct 2002). But the project raised too much controversy and protest, and was not realized: some arguments against it included the fear of police's preferential treatment of its commercial sponsors, as well as the worry about demeaning the dignity and authority of law enforcement (Sandel, 2013, 194; 29 Nov 2002, Charleston Post and Courier; 28 Jan 2003, Hartford Courant; 29 Nov 2002, Roanoke Times & World News; 6 Nov 2002, Toledo Blade). Edward D. Flaherty, police chief in Waterbury, Connecticut, and president of the Connecticut Police Chiefs Association, said: "We supply a public service. We're not there to be a representative of a private industry, and we shouldn't be"; he also referred to the idea as "demeaning" (Holz, 9 Feb 2003). In a like vein, councilman Gerard J. Couture, a former Bristol police officer, said that "police are sworn to protect and serve, not to try to explain why a Bayer aspirin or a McDonald's sticker is on the side of their vehicle" (Holz, 9 Feb 2003). Moreover, some people were worried that the advertising project might negatively affect the public's motivation to provide funding for the police and other essential public services, and that this might have bad consequences for the functioning of the society in general (Sandel, 2013, 194). Sandel quotes the columnist Leonard Pitts, Jr., who—in an article entitled *Don't Let Cop Cars Become Billboards* (10 Nov 2002)—said: "Some things are so fundamental to the orderly operation of a society, so intrinsic to its dignity, that they have traditionally been entrusted only to people hired and equipped by all of us, collectively, in the interest of the common good. Law enforcement is one of those functions. Or at least, it used to be" (quoted in Sandel, 2013, 194). Furthermore, Michael Maynard, Professor of journalism, advertising, and PR at Temple University offered his critical comment: "American society has really gone beyond the pale in turning every part of the environment into ad space. There should be some things that are off limits" (Wood, 3 Oct 2002).

However, despite the failure of this initial project, the second attempt at turning police vehicles into advertising space was successful: the first U.S. police patrol car carrying advertising was introduced in Littleton, Massachusets, in 2006 (Burge, 14 Feb 2006; Dobbin, 26 Dec 2011; Sandel, 2013, 195). The three advertisements displayed on the patrol car were more subtle than what had originally been proposed in the early 2000s, but—nevertheless—another limit has been crossed (Sandel, 2013, 195).

1.3.3. Fire and Rescue Service

By the same token, a boundary is being crossed with advertising on fire department equipment. In his book, Sandel described a deal that Kentucky Fried Chicken made in 2010 with some fire departments in the state of Indiana in order to promote a new product: "fiery" grilled chicken wings (2013, 195; Schoettle, 9 Jan 2010). The promotion included putting logos on fire hydrants, as well as on fire extinguishers at city recreation centers, and a photo shoot with the firemen from the Indianapolis fire department (Sandel, 2013, 195). In 2013, it was still safe for Sandel to write that "no one has tried to sell advertising space on fire trucks" (195), but things have progressed since then, and from the November 2017 issue of a specialist fire rescue magazine we learn that the fire department from Arizona is the first large-scale fire department in the U.S. to display advertising on the sides of fire trucks (FireRescue1 Staff, 30 Nov 2017).[6] The magazine that published the information has encouraged its readers to voice their opinions on the propriety of fire-truck advertising. Some people were in favor, saying that as long as the work of the firemen is not impeded by the presence of advertising, the fire department should go ahead with the project, or that in the light of advertising on ambulance trucks, advertising on fire trucks is also ok. The majority of the readers, however, deemed this type of advertising inappropriate. One fireman commented that if corporations want to support fire departments, then instead of striking an advertising deal, they ought to donate; he added, "we're not race car drivers that need sponsors and decals on fire trucks" (FireRescue1 Staff, 30 Nov 2017). Other people protested by saying that fire trucks are not mobile billboards, "they are a piece of equipment to help save lives and people's houses, full of special equipment and gear to do that with"; the resentful readers further

6 The first advertising project of this sort involving a small-scale fire department seems to be a 2014 initiative of the Palatine Rural Fire Protection District from Illinois (Graham, 24 Mar 2014). However, it is not clear whether the department went through with the project.

commented that advertising on fire trucks will make "the community forget what the apparatus are really for" (FireRescue1 Staff, 30 Nov 2017). Another person added that the exterior of the fire trucks is designed in a way to prevent the other drivers from hitting the fire vehicles and that advertising will interfere with the other drivers' perception of fire trucks, thus endangering everybody's safety on the road (FireRescue1 Staff, 30 Nov 2017). Yet another individual warned that the whole idea was a slippery slope and predicted that this type of advertising might lead fire departments into unnecessary law suits and other similar "problems which are not needed in this profession" and which will only distract firemen from doing their jobs (FireRescue1 Staff, 30 Nov 2017).

1.3.4. Medical Service

Hospital ambulances have already served as advertising space for noncommercial type of advertising for quite a while. For example, selected ambulances in California carry advertising for non-profit organizations; importantly, this type of advertising is done for free, and these ambulances are not the ones that respond to emergencies (Pinion-Whitt, 4 Aug 2010; Duck, 10 Aug 2010). In an online article, an Emergency Medical Service provider, Arthur Hsieh, reports that an ambulance service near where he lives displays logos of local high schools on the side of their standby ambulance vehicles during football games (Hsieh, 5 Aug 2010). Hsieh also gives the example of London Ambulance Service emergency ambulances which carry advertisements that warn people not to overuse the 999 emergency number (Hsieh, 5 Aug 2010). The purpose of Hsieh's article was to discuss the advantages and disadvantages of using ambulances in the ways described above. On the one hand, he says, this type of advertising "can help promote a closer sense of community and greater awareness of matters related to public safety or public health" (Hsieh, 5 Aug 2010). On the other hand, this could create a slippery slope: for example, it is not inconceivable that a manufacturer of emergency equipment could make a convincing argument for having the equipment advertised on the side of an ambulance in exchange for covering some part of the operational costs of the vehicle (Hsieh, 5 Aug 2010). Hsieh says that "through small degrees of rationalization" the medical service "could eventually get there," and he points out that the fire and rescue service in the U.S. has already gone in that direction (Hsieh, 5 Aug 2010; see Section 1.3.3).

Another Emergency Medical Service provider, Christopher Ferbrache, comments that the "idea of advertisements on ambulances is a rather new concept in the United States, but it is only a matter of time until it's more common" (Ferbrache, 28 Oct 2015). He realizes that the project raises controversy since many people are idealistic and "consider EMS [Emergency Medical Service] as somehow being above selling advertising space," but he believes that the professionalism of the medical personnel working inside emergency vehicles that carry advertisements shall remain unaffected by the presence of advertising (Ferbrache, 28 Oct 2015). Furthermore, he hopes that, eventually, people will start thinking pragmatically: "Once the public is aware of the financial pressures ambulance services face, it will see greater value in such a proposal. Then the human impact of such a decision can be compared with alternative funding options, or lack thereof" (Ferbrache, 28 Oct 2015).

The human impact that Ferbrache talks about can already be observed outside of the U.S. In Mumbai, India, around 40% of the 1298 Ambulance Service revenue is generated through commercial advertising on the sides of emergency vehicles (Ferbrache, 28 Oct 2015; Jain). The 1298 Ambulance Service is a fruit of a genuinely revolutionary initiative called Ambulance Access for All (AAA), developed in the early 2000s in a partnership with London Ambulance Service, New York Presbyterian, and Harvard Humanitarian Initiative, and it is meant to provide emergency medical service to all the inhabitants of Mumbai, no matter how poor (Jain). In a nutshell, the 1298 Ambulance Service is the first emergency medical service available to everyone in the region (Jain).

India is not the only country, however, where emergency vehicles carry commercial advertisements. In Great Britain, London's Air Ambulance (LAA)—an emergency medical service provided by helicopter to all Londoners since 1989—has been open to displaying commercial advertising on the sides of its vehicles for a long time already (Ferbrache, 28 Oct 2015). To give a concrete example, LAA had been carrying the logo of the Virgin Records for as long as fifteen years, from 1997 to 2012 (Branson, 25 Jan 2017).

But advertisements on the sides of emergency vehicles are not the only way in which advertising can be intertwined with the space devoted to providing medical service. Another good example is the doctor's waiting room. Probably the cheapest way to introduce advertising into this space is *via* reading materials that the patients can scan through: this can either be branded magazines (Brueggeman, 4 Jan 2015) or non-branded magazines, which are wrapped in special covers that display advertising which the patients look at before opening the magazine (Matrix Media Outdoor Advertising Experts, 7 Jan 2013). A different way for corporations to be present in the doctor's waiting room is by providing branded tissue boxes (Matrix Media Outdoor Advertising Experts, 7 Jan 2013) or branded charging stations, i.e., stations with the company's logo for the patients to charge their electronic devices (Brueggeman, 4 Jan 2015). Finally, there is the option of installing digital monitors which display video advertisements (PlayMyAd; Matrix Media Outdoor Advertising Experts, 7 Jan 2013).

When talking about the benefits for corporations of connecting the advertising of their brand with medical service, advertising agencies typically stress that people are more likely to trust a company that makes such a connection: the credibility of doctors seems to enhance the credibility of the advertised company (Brueggeman, 4 Jan 2015; PlayMyAd). Moreover, the doctor's waiting room constitutes "a distraction-free environment," in which the audience can be more receptive to advertising; in fact, it seems that patients "actively seek ways to pass their time" in such places (Brueggeman, 4 Jan 2015). However, even if this is true about patients waiting for a doctor's appointment, it does not mean that occupying their attention with advertising is beneficial (or most beneficial) for them. Provided that they have a need to be occupied in some way in the waiting room (which not every patient needs to have), alternative ways to meet that need could be imagined: to give some examples, one pediatric clinic decided to furnish their waiting room with digital monitors which provide live webcam broadcasts from the local zoo, while a dentist's practice installed a waiting room massage chair (PatientPop, 23 May 2017).

Finally, advertising has already entered the space of hospitals as well. In Poland, for example, maternity wards in many public hospitals provide their patients with a lactation manual sponsored by Femaltiker, a supplement meant to stimulate lactation: the booklet has the supplement's logo on the front page, as well as additional advertisements inside the booklet, and samples of the product are attached to the booklet. Furthermore, when leaving the public hospital with a newborn baby, a mother often receives sampling packages (sometimes more than one). One example of such a package is the "Blue Box 'A Child's Treasure'" ("Niebieskie Pudełko 'Skarb Malucha'"): apart from a brief parents' manual, in which the content written by a pediatrician is interspersed with advertisements, the Blue Box is packed with advertising leaflets, branded samples of products, and discount coupons. The Blue Box is a direct marketing initiative of an advertising agency called Pelargos Family Service. The agency specializes in sampling packages, as well as advertising content placed within parenting manuals. As mentioned in the previous paragraph, the agency stresses to its potential clients that the packages and manuals are given to parents by highly trusted medical professionals, thus suggesting that the credibility of pediatricians, gynecologists, and midwives is likely to enhance the credibility of the advertised products (Pelargos Family Service). Another advertising agency, Present Service Marketing Communication, produces a similar sampling package—"Baby" ("Dzidziuś")—distributed in public hospitals to parents of a newborn.[7] Apart from samples and advertising leaflets, the package also includes a brief parents' manual, in which the content written by doctors and psychologists is interspersed with advertisements and sponsored articles (Present Service Marketing Communication). As the evidence on mothers' discussion forums suggests, the sampling packages have been present in Polish hospitals at least since 2005 (adi771, 10 August 2005).

South Africa is yet another example of a country in which hospitals are no longer ad-free. As explained on the website of Medical Practice Consulting, a private South African company that offers in-hospital advertising, large digital screens can be installed "in the main waiting areas and high traffic areas of the hospitals, clinics and medical facilities" in order to display advertising in the form of videos with subtitles, scrolling text, animation videos, and HD images; as advertised on the website, an in-hospital advertising campaign constitutes a particularly "effective call to action campaign for pharmaceutical industry, whilst the consumer is waiting at the hospital reception" because a hospital is a place where "the consumer" is focused on enhancing their personal health (Medical Practice Consulting).

1.3.5. Schools

Since 1990, millions of young people in elementary schools, middle schools, and high schools all over the United States are required to watch Channel One News, the commercial-sponsored twelve-minute in-school television news program (Sandel, 2013, 196). Chris Whittle, the entrepreneur who launched Channel One News in 1989 made the following deal with the schools: the schools would get free television sets, video equipment, a satellite link, and some free educational materials, and in exchange they would make the children watch the program as an obligatory part of everyday school routine, including two minutes of commercial advertising. The enterprise proved to be a big financial success, running advertisements of some of the most famous brands (e.g. Pepsi, Snickers, Reebok). At a youth marketing conference in 1994, a Channel One executive said: "The biggest selling point to advertisers [is that] we are forcing kids to watch two minutes of commercials. The advertiser gets a group of kids who cannot go to the bathroom, who cannot change the station (…), who cannot be playing Nintendo, who cannot have their headsets on" (Baker, Smith, 12 Feb 2001, quoted in Sandel,

7 The other sampling packages offered by the company are distributed outside of hospitals, at birth courses and in kindergartens: "9 months" ("9 miesięcy"), "Toddler" ("Szkrab"), "A Preschooler's Package" ("Paka Przedszkolaka").

2013, 197). By 2000 the audience of Channel One reached eight million students (over 40 percent of the American children) in twelve thousand schools, with most states embracing the program, and only New York State banning it from the schools. Nowadays, Channel One is no longer that powerful (it now has about a third of the schools it used to have), but it has most certainly "succeeded in shattering a taboo against commercials in the classroom," paving the way to the current abundance of forms of advertising at the US schools (Sandel, 2013, 197).

The first documented instance of the presence of commercialism in the American classrooms that Sandel mentions is Ivory Soap donating the company's soap bars to schools for soap-carving competitions in the 1920s; also, the 20th century in the U.S. saw companies placing their logos on scoreboards and paying for ads in high school yearbooks (197). But it was only at the end of the century—in the 1990s—when the corporate involvement in schools intensified dramatically. In particular, many companies started to manufacture the so-called "sponsored educational materials" for the schools in order to make children remember the names of brands, i.e., free videos, posters, "learning kits" (197). Sandel provides many good historical examples of sponsored educational materials, such as Procter & Gamble's environmental course materials that showed the children why disposable diapers were good for the earth, Hershey's or McDonald's educational materials on the topic of nutrition, and Cambell Soup Company's free science kit, in which the students learned how to prove that Campbell's Prego spaghetti sauce was thicker than that of the rival brand, Ragú (198).

But the corporate presence in the classroom is not confined to the educational materials; as observed by Sandel, advertising has begun to pervade "every conceivable space" in the classrooms (199). One such space that one would expect to remain ad-free within the classroom are report cards, i.e., cards which report the students' progress at school. However, in 2011, a school district in Colorado sold the space on their report cards as advertising space. Not long after that, a Florida school followed with a similar initiative: the school's report cards were issued in special colorful jackets with the McDonald's logo and a cartoon of Ronald McDonald. In addition, the children who scored only A's and B's, or which had fewer than three absences, could go to McDonald's with their report card and get a free Happy Meal. The promotion was finally cancelled due to local opposition of the initiative (199).

But the U.S. trend to sell advertising space on the school paperwork did not begin in 2011. In a 2009 online article for the website dedicated to the *Campaign for a Commercial-Free Childhood*, Jessie L. Bonner described a resourceful Idaho teacher of history and economics in Pocatello High School, Jeb Harrison, who had signed a sponsorship deal with a local pizza shop, Molto Caldo Pizza

(Bonner, 25 Mar 2009). Since the school was lacking in such basic resources as paper, the pizza shop agreed to provide the five classes conducted by Harrison with a supply of 10,000 sheets of paper in exchange for placing the company's advertisement "in bright red, inch-high letters" at the bottom of every test, handout, and worksheet passed out by the teacher to his students (Bonner, 25 Mar 2009). The teacher expressed his opinion that he did not think that "this small amount of advertising" would change his classroom, especially that the school had already been selling advertising space in the yearbook and the school newspaper (Bonner, 25 Mar 2009). The principal of Pocatello High was not thrilled, but did not put a stop to the initiative either. He said: "we've let this happen because it makes a point about what economic hard times can force people to do" (Bonner, 25 Mar 2009). Susan Linn, a psychologist from Harvard, who is also the director of the *Campaign for a Commercial-Free Childhood*, issued a critical comment on the matter: "It crosses a line (…) When teachers start becoming pitchmen for products, children suffer and their education suffers as well" (Bonner, 25 Mar 2009).

Another way to earn some extra cash for the schools' needs is to sell advertising space on school buses (Sandel, 2013, 199–200). The trend began in the 1990s in Colorado, and then the states of Texas, Arizona, Tennessee, Massachusetts, Utah, and New Jersey followed (Rampell, 15 Apr 2011). Standing out of the crowd, Idaho's legislature prohibits such initiatives. However, in 2011, *New York Times* reported that other states had been considering legislation that would allow advertising on school buses (Rampell, 15 Apr 2011). The article quotes Valery Lynch, a teacher from Texas, commenting on the financial difficulties which push the schools to endorse school bus advertising: "If the alternative is huge classroom sizes and losing teachers and losing qualified personnel, yes, this seems like something we should consider (…) But I know that it's a bag of worms, and people are going to ask 'What's next? An ad on the classroom clock?'" (Rampell, 15 Apr 2011).

Indeed, advertising in schools is now present indoors as well: in the previous sections we have already seen examples of classroom materials being adorned with a commercial logo. But indoor advertising also means using the school walls and furniture as advertising space. Sandel reports that Colorado was among the first states to accept advertising in the school hallways (2013, 200). First, this type of advertising simply meant posters hanging on the walls. More recently, however, these advertisements have evolved into "massive 'supergraphic' ads on walls and floors, shrink-wrapped over lockers, locker room benches, and cafeteria tables" (2013, 200; see also Hoag, 19 Sep 2010; Hardy, 16 Oct 2011). Megan Keller, a concerned parent from Utah, commented on her son Colin's daily exposure to advertisements of sugary cereals in the school's cafeteria: "I have a 5-year-old who doesn't understand what ads are (…) I don't like that he thinks, 'Oh, this is good because it comes from my school,' and I'm having to explain to him why that's not true" (Rampell, 15 Apr 2011).[8] The next step after the "supergraphic" ads was digital advertising: in 2015 two Arizona districts allowed the hallways of its schools to be adorned with "digital billboards that resemble large touch-screen tablets" (DeNisco, 16 Mar 2015).

Advertising has also found its way into naming rights connected with schools. The Brooklawn elementary school in New Jersey was the first U.S. school to sell naming rights to a corporate sponsor: in 2001, for the sum of 100,000 USD the local supermarket bought the right to rename the school's gym *the ShopRite of Brooklawn Center* (Sandel, 2013, 199). The president of the Brooklawn school board, Bruce Darrow, commented: "It's the wave of the future (…) I'm looking into selling advertising on the children's basketball uniforms" (Pennington, 18 Oct 2004). Dr. John Kellmayer, the school district superintendent, added: "Twenty-five years from now, when this is widespread and accepted, people will say it all started here (…) I'm fine with that. I wish we had started earlier and done more of it" (Pennington, 18 Oct 2004). After this precedent, other schools followed, making the best money out of selling naming rights to their football fields: the price ranging from 100,000 USD to over 1 million USD (Sandel, 2013, 199; Pennington, 18 Oct 2004). While some schools chose a more minimalist strategy, others tried to make a profit from selling as many naming rights as possible. The *New York Times* gives an example of a newly-opened public high school in Philadelphia, which in 2006 gave its potential corporate sponsors a whole list of naming rights to buy: i.a. "$1 million for the performing arts pavilion, $750,000 for the gyms or the main administrative suite (including the principal's office), $500,000 for the food court/cybercafe, $50,000 for the science laboratories, $25,000 for each of the classrooms"; finally, for 5 million USD a generous sponsor could buy the right to name the school itself (Lewin, 26 Jan 2006). Paul Vallas, chief executive of the school, said: "There are tremendous needs in this system where 85 percent of the kids are below poverty level. I'm not uncomfortable with corporations giving us money and getting their names on things. As long as it's not inappropriate, I don't see any downside" (Lewin, 26 Jan 2006). Despite the growing trend, some public schools still reject the idea of selling their naming rights to corporate sponsors. In Seminole County, Florida, Dede

8 In protest, Keller has finally transferred her son to a nearby charter school which implements a no-advertising policy (Rampell, 15 Apr 2011).

Schaffner, one of the five school board members of the local school, expressed her thoughts after the board's vote against the initiative to sell the school's naming rights: "If we get to the point where you can put your name on a school just because you have a fat wallet, that's not right. Sure we could use more money, but I just wasn't ready to sell our soul, and I felt that's what we were being asked to do" (Lewin, 26 Jan 2006).

The topic of the naming rights introduces another subject: the presence of advertising in the realm of school sports. But the commercialization of the school sports does not end at naming rights—advertising is now present on the tickets for the school sports events, scoreboards, billboards in end zones, gym walls, etc. (Pennington, 18 Oct 2004). In making these choices, the schools are simply mimicking the world of professional sports, "because the apparent model for the future—the typical professional stadium awash in ads and slogans—is so omnipresent" (Pennington, 18 Oct 2004). Gary Ruskin, executive director of Commercial Alert, a watchdog organization from Portland, Oregon, which aims to put some limits on commercialism, commented: "But high schools are not pro stadiums, so it's pathetic to have a Rust-Oleum Field at a public, taxpayer-funded institution [at Vernon Hills High School, north of Chicago]. Schools exist to teach children to read, write, add and think, not to shop. So what are we teaching them with big corporate ads on civic institutions?" (Pennington, 18 Oct 2004). Alex Molnar, a professor of education policy and the director of the Commercialism in Education Research Unit at Arizona State University, expressed a similar opinion, saying that it is the duty of schools to protect the unprepared and impressionable minds of school-age children from commercialism; according to him, endorsing the marriage of advertising and public education is "a violation of public trust" (Pennington, 18 Oct 2004). He also said: "We're losing our public education system in this country. It is being eroded, inch by inch, by an ongoing blurring of the distinction between public interest and private good" (Lewin, 26 Jan 2006).

Apart from the examples presented in this section, new ways of bringing commercialism to schools are being invented: from corporate sponsorship of a prom (A Night To Remember) to the idea of using the school roof as advertising space (Lewin, 26 Jan 2006). Therefore, the list of examples of in-school advertising provided here is not exhaustive, but rather illustrative.

1.3.6. Sports Facilities and Broadcasts

It is a truism to say that professional sports are now permeated with advertising. Apart from the possibility of corporate presence on stadiums in the form of billboards, which in the U.S. started in the early 20th century (Dudek, 24 Apr 2015), the most important way for a company to be present in sports nowadays is through naming rights. Taking baseball as an example, in 1994 only one baseball stadium in the U.S. had a name connected with a corporate sponsor, while in 2014, only nine out of thirty Major League Baseball Stadiums did not have a name inspired either by the name of the corporate sponsor or a commercial product (Moran, 06 Feb 2014). It was precisely in the 1990s that the attitudes towards naming rights changed significantly, and what used to be deemed inappropriate has become a norm. Some good examples of the sale of naming rights from that period are: (1) Riverfront Stadium (named for a geographical location), home of Cincinnati Reds, becoming Cinergy Field in 1996, named for an energy provider; (2) Jack Murphy Stadium (named for a sportswriter, Jack Murphy), home of the San Diego Padres, becoming Qualcomm Stadium in 1997, named for an IT company (in 2004, the San Diego Padres moved to another sports facility with a corporate name—Petco Park—named for a pet supply company); (3) the legendary Candlestick Park (named for a geographical location, Candlestick Point, which in turn was named for the local Candlestick birds), home of both San Francisco Giants and the NFL's 49ers, becoming 3Com Park in 1995, named for a digital electronics manufacturer—since then the Giants moved to their own stadium in 2000, and during the following six years their new stadium underwent three corporate name changes (Moran, 06 Feb 2014).

Sports facilities connected with other sports fall prey to the same trend. By 2004, "more than half of all the [U.S.] arenas and stadiums in professional baseball, football, basketball, and hockey" had naming right deals with corporate sponsors, and "by 2010, over one hundred companies had paid to name a big-league stadium or arena in the United States" (Sandel, 2013, 170).

Sandel emphasizes that nowadays corporate naming rights mean much more than just a sign on the stadium gate: very often they also imply that the broadcasters have to use the corporate name when describing the action on the field (170). For example, a naming rights deal required the Arizona Diamondbacks not only to name their stadium "Bank One Ballpark"; it also obligated the team's broadcasters to call each home run of the Diamondbacks a "Bank One blast" (170–171). A comparable practice is to sell naming rights to pitching changes, meaning that the name of a corporate sponsor has to be mentioned during the announcement about a new pitcher entering the game (171). Similarly, some contracts obligate a team to mention the corporate sponsor whenever a player slides into the home base: by 2014, ten major league baseball teams had signed such contracts with New York Life Insurance Company, and—as a result—when a player slides into a base, the corporate logo must appear on the screen, along with the spoken announcement: "Safe at home. New York Life" (171). The company's vice president and advertising director commented that "this message integrates naturally into the action of the ballgame" (171).

Yet another way for corporations to advertise themselves during a game is to mark their presence on player uniforms. First of all, many producers of sportswear are interested in long-term sponsorship of teams (for example, Nike signed such a sponsorship contract in 2016 with Chelsea F.C. for a whole decade; see M.F., 31 Aug 2016) or sometimes even of the whole leagues. Taking the example of basketball in the U.S., Adidas used to have a long-term sponsorship contract with the entire NBA: for years it would provide the players of all the NBA teams with apparel and uniforms. However, it is noteworthy that the uniforms which Adidas provided did not have the logo of the company (Lauletta, 17 Oct 2017). This has changed since Nike took over the sponsorship in 2017: now the uniforms of all thirty NBA teams bear the logo of Nike (Lauletta, 17 Oct 2017).

More importantly though, nowadays, the corporate presence on player uniforms does not end with the logo of the company that provides the uniforms. Many teams decide to lease advertising space on the uniforms to other companies willing to become sponsors: until quite recently, the typical way in which such an advertisement used to be displayed was in the form of a relatively small patch in the upper right corner of the uniform (Lauletta, 17 Oct 2017). This can be observed on the example of many NBA teams, such as Atlanta Hawks, Boston Celtics, Brooklyn Nets, Denver Nuggets, or Chicago Bulls. Recently, however, the sports uniform advertising has gone beyond the simple combination of the logo of the uniform provider and a small advertising patch in the upper right corner of the uniform: the latest trend is to use the very center of the uniform, i.e., the space that used to be reserved for displaying the name of the team.[9]

9 Although the growing popularity of this idea in the U.S. sports is a recent development, the roots of the trend lie in the European football of the last quarter of the 20th century. Until 1976, all football jerseys were completely ad-free, but in 1976 Southern League Kettering Town signed a contract with Kettering Tyres, obliging the team to place the sponsor's name on the team's shirts for a match against Bath City in January 1976 (Wolfson, 17 Feb 2015). The advertisement of Kettering Tyres occupied the very center of every player's shirt (Wolfson, 17 Feb 2015). The English Football Association (FA) reacted immediately, saying that displaying the sponsoring company's name on shirts is against the rules (Wolfson, 17 Feb 2015). In order to try to leave the advertisement on the team's jerseys, the chief executive of the team shortened "Kettering Tyres" to "Kettering T", claiming that the T represented "Town", not "Tyres" (Wolfson, 17 Feb 2015). The FA did not fall for this trick: the team was threatened with a 1,000 GBP

The idea to use the center of the player's shirt to display an advertising slogan has recently started spreading to other leagues, like Major League Soccer (MLS) and the Women's National Basketball Association (WNBA) in the U.S. In the article entitled *Is Advertising on Professional Sports Teams' Jerseys Going Too Far?*, a university newspaper sports journalist, Parker Reed, writes: "On the front of these leagues' jerseys lies a gigantic sponsor logo, and the name of the sports team has been reduced to a small patch in the upper right corner of the jersey or omitted entirely (like in the WNBA)" (Reed, 10 May 2017). Reed comments that although "sponsors are essential to the wellbeing of any sports franchise", this time "they may be crossing the line" (Reed, 10 May 2017). The journalist goes on: "This strikes me as foul for one very important reason: It turns these athletes into walking billboards" (Reed, 10 May 2017).

As observed in the article entitled *How Many Advertisements is Enough?*, in certain cases advertising on professional players' shirts is becoming much more extensive: some professional football clubs try to use as much advertising space on the uniform as possible (Wolfson, 17 Feb 2015). One good example is a Brazilian football club, Corinthians: during the 2009 season, the team's shirts displayed advertising slogans of as many as six different corporate sponsors, placed all over the shirt (Wolfson, 17 Feb 2015).

Finally, corporations can also advertise themselves by making the name of their company an integral part of the name of the sports team. The company that uses this technique extensively is Red Bull, the producer of energy drinks. Five football clubs in the world are currently named after this sponsor: (1) New York Red Bulls, from the U.S.; (2) FC Red Bull Salzburg, from Austria; (3) RB Leipzig, nicknamed The Red Bulls, from Germany; (4) Red Bull Brasil; and (5) Red Bull Bragantino, another Brazilian football club (Wikipedia).

Some forms of advertising connected with sports raise little controversy: when NBA introduced the advertising patches on player jerseys in 2017, only a minimal number of fans were reported to protest (Jarvis, 14 Jul 2017). However, when Major League Baseball wanted to place advertisements of *Spider-Man 2* on bases in 2004, the uproar caused by angry fans was big-scale. In a letter of

---

fine until the slogan was removed (Wolfson, 17 Feb 2015). But this ban on advertising on shirts was lifted in 1977 because many clubs had been pressing the FA in this direction (Wolfson, 17 Feb 2015). Since then, more and more football clubs have begun selling advertising space on players' shirts, including the space previously reserved for displaying the name of the football team. Nowadays, watching a professional football match in which the clubs would not use this type of advertising is nearly impossible.

protest, Congressman George Nethercutt wrote that the plan to place ads on bases "undermines the character of America's pastime at every level" (Penner, 7 May 2004). The executive director of the consumer watchdog group called Commercial Alert, Gary Ruskin, urged the fans to take action: "It's time for baseball fans to stand up to the greedy corporations that are insulting us and our national pastime (…) How low will baseball sink? Next year, will they replace the bats with long Coke bottles, and the bases with big hamburger buns?" (Penner, 7 May 2004). And indeed, the fans' protests, which included boycotting the advertised film, were so intense that the advertisements were eventually pulled and the bases remained ad-free (Penner, 7 May 2004).

1.3.7. Means of Entertainment: Videogames, Films, Books, Songs

Sports are one of the many possible sources of entertainment which have come to be intertwined with advertising. Others include videogames, films (or television programs, or series), books, music.

Videogame advertising begun in the 1970s and 1980s (De la Hera, 2019, 48–52; Bogost, 2007, 200), manifesting as advergaming, in-game advertising (product placement, real-world analogs), or advertising around the game itself (pre-game, inter-level, post-game advertising).[10] The term in-game advertising often refers to product placement in videogames, meaning that the product is advertised through its integration into the game (Schulze, Jöckel, Will, 2007; Mráček, Mucha, 2011). A good example would be the integration of Procter & Gamble's Flash detergent into the game *London Taxi* (2005); as a part of the gameplay, the player had to use the detergent to clean the taxi by clicking on an

10 The typology presented here is a hybrid of (a) the older division into two categories of advergaming and in-game advertising discussed, for example, in Schulze, Jöckel, Will (2007), Mráček, Mucha (2011), and (b) the addition of the third category of advertising around the game itself (plus its subdivision into pre-game, inter-level, post-game advertising) discussed by Steiner (2008) (which he adopts from the 2007 *Game Advertising Platform Report* by The Interactive Advertising Bureau), and (c) the two types of advertising that I interpret to be subcategories of in-game advertising—product placement, real-world analogs—discussed by Vedrashko (2006). The division into three categories—advergames, around-game advertising, and in-game advertising—has already been discussed as recommended by Smith, Sun, Sutherland, Mackie (2014, 97); the authors refer to the recommendation issued in the 2010 update to the 2007 *Game Advertising Platform Report* by The Interactive Advertising Bureau.

interactive icon with the product's logo—thus, "the game naturally turned into a medium for the demonstration of the product's advantages" (Lehu, 2007, 183).

Similarly, on the sides of the virtual roads in a car driving game called *L.A. Rush* (2005) there were advertising banners for 40 different brands. Although this type of advertising is also classified as in-game advertising, rather than calling it "product placement" we would say that it imitates the non-virtual environment, in which the real-world road sides are often full of advertising banners. A similar example of virtual reality in videogames mimicking the kind of advertising that takes place in non-virtual reality can be found in videogames connected with football: the game *Football Manager* (2005–) would be considered less realistic without the advertising banners on the sides of its virtual stadiums and without the logos of sponsors on virtual players' uniforms (Lehu, 2007, 183). Tokens of this type of in-game advertising are adequately described as "real-world analogs" (Vedrashko, 2006, 45).

In contrast with in-game advertising, the technique of advergaming consists in constructing an entire game as a tool to promote one particular brand or product (De la Hera, 2019; Schulze, Jöckel, Will, 2007; Mráček, Mucha, 2011). A good example of an advergame is *Darkened Skye* (2002), promoting the Skittles brand: the Skittles candies are incorporated into the in-game dialogues, as well as into the gameplay: i.a. the main source of magic in the world of the game are the Skittles candies. One of the earliest examples of an advergame is *The Ford Simulator* (1987), a DOS game promoting the Ford brand (Vedrashko, 2006, 46).

Finally, there is advertising that is not ingrained in the game itself, but rather takes place *around* the gameplay (Steiner, 2008, 9; Smith, Sun, Sutherland, Mackie, 2014, 97). This can take the form of pre-game advertising, i.e., "the presentation of digital video or display advertisements before the game is played, as the game is loading", or inter-level advertising, i.e., advertising messages displayed between two levels of a game, or post-game advertising, i.e., advertising messages shown after the game is completed (Steiner, 2008, 9). These kinds of advertising are typical for online videogames.

Some similarity can be found between the ways that advertising manifests within and around videogames and the ways it appears within and around films. Nowadays, product placement can appear not only inside films,[11] but also

11 Interestingly, some form of product placement started already "with the first appearances of brands in Lumière films" (Newel, Salmon, Chang, 2006, 590): in the film entitled *Laveuses* (1896), two women were hand-washing the laundry in tubs, and "in front of the tubs were two cases of Lever Brothers soap, one with the French branding

within a movie poster or trailer, used as a medium to advertise both the film and the brands or products present in the film. For instance, in the poster for the film *Goal!* (2005) the actor Kuno Becker wears a tracksuit with the characteristic three stripes of the Adidas brand, which corresponds with Adidas being the most visible brand in the film (Lehu, 2007, 195). As for trailers, the one for Steven Spielberg's *The Terminal* (2004), for example, features as many as eight brands: Planter's, Nike, Baskin-Robbins, Dean & Deluca, United Airlines, Baja Fresh, Star Alliance, and La Perla.

In addition, just like advertising in videogames can take the form of an advergame, advertising in films can take the form of an adverfilm: a short film, with a brief but interesting plot and well-known actors, shot for the purpose of promoting a brand or a product. Good examples of adverfilms are: Martin Scorsese's *Street of Dreams* (2013), set in the streets of New York with Scarlett Johansson and Matthew McConaughey, produced to promote Dolce and Gabana's fragrance *The One*; or a short film promoting the Channel brand, entitled *Once Upon a Time* (2013), set in 1913 in Deauville, with Keira Knightley playing Coco Channel. A good example of a full-length feature film which is somewhere between product placement and adverfilming is *The Sisterhood of the Traveling Pants* (2005), set around a pair of jeans that four teenage friends share between them. Although in the book on which the film is based[12] the jeans have no brand, film producers made the jeans in the film carry the Levi's brand, thus making Levi's jeans the star of the film (Lehu, 2007, 194). A pair of Levi's, with the characteristic, small red label with the name of the brand, was also given the central role on the film's poster (195).

Finally, advertising can take place around the film: before and after (or sometimes in the middle, if the film is interspersed with advertising videos in the television or Internet). Advertising before the film typically appears in the form of short advertising videos that the television, Internet, or cinema play before the movie begins, or in the form of an insertion into the opening credits. A good example of the latter—which is less usual—can be found in the *Star Trek Generations* film (1994): during the opening credits, a champagne bottle of Moët et Chandon, Cuvée Dom Perignon, Vintage 2265 is floating in space, crossing the screen many times, and finally smashing against the hull of a spaceship (Lehu, 2007, 193). As stressed by Lehu, "the main motivation for an appearance in the

---

'Sunlight Savon,' the other with the German 'Sunlight Seife'" (Newel, Salmon, Chang, 2006, 579–580).

12 Brashares, A. (2001), *The Sisterhood of the Traveling Pants*, Delacorte, New York.

opening credits of a film (…) [when the film is screened in the cinema] is to address an audience that is already captive, since they are within the cinema auditorium, before they are absorbed by the story or the action of the film" (194).

By the same token, advertising after the film can take the form of short advertising videos, or it can appear in the end credits. An example of the latter can be found in the film *Cellular* (2004): the end credits seem to be rolling within the screen of a Nokia mobile phone (Lehu, 2007, 194).[13]

Quite similar advertising categories apply to books. As for product placement, in his famous novel *The Da Vinci Code* (2003), Dan Brown has mentioned, among others, the brands Citroën ZX, Mercedes, BMW, Audi, Rolls-Royce, Aston Martin, Porsche, Ferrari, Heckler and Koch, Smirnoff, and the Ritz Hotel (Lehu, 2007, 166). Another well-known writer, Tom Clancy, managed to place well over eighty brands within the novel *The Teeth of the Tiger* (2003).[14]

By analogy to advergames and adverfilms, there are books that we could call "adverbooks," i.e., works of fiction written for the purpose of advertising a particular brand or product.[15] The most famous example is *The Bulgari Connection* (2001), a novel by Fay Weldon (Brownrigg, 4 Nov 2001; Spence, Van Heekeren, 2005, 85; Lehu, 2007, 168; Sandel, 2013, 181). According to the contract with the Italian jeweller, the author was obliged to mention the name of the brand in the novel at least a dozen times (Lehu, 2007, 168; Sandel, 2013, 181). In the end, she managed to mention the name thirty-four times and include it in the title (Sandel, 2013, 181); furthermore, the whole plot revolves around the Bulgari jewelry and the Bulgari store in London (Spence, Van Heekeren, 2005, 85).

---

13 What has been described for films is true for television programs or series: for instance, in over two hundred and sixty-one episodes of the television series *NYPD Blue* (1993–2005) the credits include the placement of an advertising board for Coca-Cola (Lehu, 2007, 193).

14 A historical example of product placement in a novel is Charles Dickens's *The Pickwick Papers*: Pickwick was, in fact, a name of a London-to-Bath carriage line from Dickens' time (Fitzgerald, 1891; Newel, Salmon, Chang, 2006, 579). "The carriage line makes a cameo appearance in the story, and the coincidence of the title character riding in a carriage with his name painted on the outside is the center of one of the stories" (Newel, Salmon, Chang, 2006, 579).

15 There is a more general term, encompassing both product placement in books and advertising in the form that might be referred to as an "adverbook": this term is "fictomercial" (Brownrigg, 4 Nov 2001; Spence, Van Heekeren, 2005, 85), indicative of a mixture of literary fiction and commercials (Bauer, Lieber, Plag, 2015, 484).

Lastly, advertising in books can take place around the book itself: before, after, or in the middle of a book. In the case of printed books, this can take the form of advertising other books on the front page or the last pages of the book. A good example is the book *Advertising Ethics* by Spence and Van Heekeren (2005), the front page of which presents other books from the same series: this, too, is a form of advertising, however subtle. Similarly, several examples might be quoted for advertising on the last pages of a book: for instance, at the back pages of the J.R.R. Tolkien books by Ballentine (1976) the reader can find information about ordering other books by the same author, as well as Lord of the Ring Maps and posters (Johnson, 11 May 2012). Other publishing houses to have used the same advertising strategy include: Vintage Random House, Avon/Harper Collins, Apple Scholastic, Dell, Bantam, Penguin, Signet (Johnson, 11 May 2012).

A new practice that sparked some discussion and controversy is using a book's back cover as advertising space for products (and services) different than books. The first book to bear this kind of advertising was published in China in 2012: it is a book by John Rallo and Marina Ma, entitled *My Son, Yo-Yo*, telling the life story of the world-renowned cellist Yo-Yo Ma (Chen, 2 May 2012; Lea, 3 May 2012; Johnson, 11 May 2012). On the back cover of the book, a small logo of a Chinese textile manufacturer could be found—this was the first instance of the realization of the contract signed by the Publishers' Association of China with Jinghua Aobo, a Beijing-based advertising agency (Chen, 2 May 2012).

In contrast with videogames and films, traditional printed books do not yet have any advertising in the middle of the book. However, this kind of advertising is already the case when one reads an electronic version of a novel on a discount version of a Kindle device. The screensavers on this device are made of advertisements for Amazon products, usually books or products related with the Kindle device. Additionally, the home screen of Kindle, on which one can consult one's own library of books, always has a small advertisement at the bottom. In order to get rid of the advertisements, one has to buy the more expensive version of the Kindle device "Without Special Offers."

The last type of entertainment to be mentioned is music. As far as product placement goes, a brand or a product can be mentioned in the song lyrics, or it can appear in the music video, on the cover of a music album, or the artist may use the product during the concert. A good example of the latter is the group Run-DMC wearing their Adidas trainers to the concert that included the performance of a song entitled *My Adidas* (1986): during the concert, each member of the band took off one shoe and waved it at the ceiling; they also encouraged the audience to do the same (Lehu, 2007, 172). Soon after, a contract with Adidas followed (172). As far as commercial products appearing on an album cover are concerned, one of Cadillac's cars, for instance, appeared on the cover of a 1992 album entitled *It's My Cadillac* (with a hit single by the same name).

Mentioning products or brands in the song lyrics has a long history. Lehu gives some early examples of brands or products being mentioned in French songs in the 1930s, 1940s, and 1950s: the medication called Charbon de Belloc in *Le tango stupéfiant* (*The narcotic tango*) performed by Marie Dubas in 1936, Jeep in *Le bougie* (*The boogie*) performed by Bourvil in 1947, or Reader's Digest in Serge Gainsbourg's *Le poinçonneur des lilas* (*The ticket-stamper of the lilacs*) from 1958 (173).[16] Lehu also discusses some well-known American hits like Dire Straits' *Money for Nothing* (1985) that mentions the name of the music channel, MTV (Lehu, 2007, 172). Because the song by Dire Straits acts as an advertisement for the channel, *Money for Nothing* is still one of the most aired songs on MTV; the artists, too, have benefited from the popularity of their song caused by the product placement—"the album *Brothers in Arms* became number one in most of the countries where it was released, mainly thanks to 'Money for nothing'" (172).

Just like in the case of *Money for Nothing*, it is still very common for the contemporary artists to mention brands without signing any product placement contract and to draw benefits from promoting the brand only after the song is released. In a 2002 song *Pass the Courvoisier*, rappers Busta Rhymes and Sean (P Diddy) Combs mentioned the Courvoisier brand multiple times and placed the bottle of Courvoisier in many scenes of the video clip (175). Due to the fact that the song made the sales increase by 18.9 % the following year, Courvoisier then offered to sponsor events with P Diddy and other rap artists (175). In contrast, pre-ordering the lyrics to include a particular brand name is rather rare: music artists seem reluctant to let corporate sponsors interfere with song lyrics because this would place their "creative freedom under surveillance" and consequently they might be "criticized by their audience for having 'sold out' to marketing" (178).

However, this reluctance is limited to corporate interference with song lyrics. Pre-ordering a product being visually placed in a video clip that accompanies a music artist's song is much more acceptable. A good example is Sting's song entitled *Desert Rose* (Taylor, 2012, 219–220; Spence, Van Heekeren, 2005, 86). The song lyrics are completely independent of any corporate influence; the video clip, however, is a result of a product placement contract, and therefore features Sting travelling through a barren landscape in Jaguar S-type (Spence, Van Heekeren,

16 Translations by J-M. Lehu (2007).

2005, 86). In a similar fashion, the music artist Sia licensed her song *Fire and Gasoline* (2015) to the entrepreneur (former fashion model) Heidi Klum to produce a commercial video that promotes lingerie products from the Heidi Klum Intimates collection (Villa, 24 Apr 2015).

Next, there is a type of music that might be classified as advermusic. A good example is given by Spence and Van Heekeren (2005, 32): in Australia, when the confectionery Mars Incorporated wanted to promote their product Starburst, they did it by producing a jingle for the product and releasing it as a pop tune. The tune was given so much airtime on the radio that it became a hit single (32).

Finally, it is possible to talk about advertising around the song. The way the music videos are broadcast on YouTube is the best illustration of this kind of advertising. When clicking to play a music video on YouTube, a viewer knows that the song might be accompanied by a short advertising video at the beginning, the end, or even in the middle of the music video. Additionally, during the song broadcast, written advertisements typically pop up at the bottom of the music video screen, as well as to the right of the screen, where other recommended music videos are displayed.

1.3.8. Means of Transport

Nowadays, it is challenging to find any type of means of transport that would be ad-free.

As far as urban transport is concerned, advertising can appear inside the buses in the form of messages displayed on an LCD screen hanging from the ceiling or installed into the ticket vending machine. It can also appear on a small poster placed on the wall, ceiling, back of the seat, or inside a handle that the passenger holds on to. On the outside, advertising can be placed on the sides or the back of the buses in the form of posters that take a moderate amount of the bus exterior, or in the form of a giant poster wrapped around the majority of the bus exterior, sometimes even including the windows. Łódź is a good example of a European city, in which all these forms of bus advertising take place (Miejskie Przedsiębiorstwo Komunikacyjne Łódź Sp. z o.o.). Similar forms of advertising can take place in trams as well, and the tram and bus stops can also be emblazoned with advertising, typically in the form of posters.

Subway is yet another urban means of transport which is very popular with advertisers. Apart from regular billboards and screens on walls and floors of the subway stations, advertising messages can be placed on subway stairway steps, as well as inside the subway vehicles on floors, walls, windows, ceilings, handles, and seats; furthermore, posters can also be placed at the turnstile gates (at the moving arms or on the bigger metal parts of the machinery). One company has even figured out how to place ads in subway tunnels—the ads come to life with the movement of the train thanks to a technology based on the 19th century zoetrope system (Johnson, 17 Sep 2006). The New York City subway is a place where all of the above-mentioned ways of subway advertising have been realized. In Europe, the subway in Warsaw, Poland, has been subjected to all of these types of subway advertising, except the zoetrope-based advertising.

Taxi-cabs have also become popular as carriers of commercial messages (Spence, Van Heekeren, 2005, 85). Blue Line Media, for example, is an advertising company that operates in over 50 cities across the United States and offers all sorts of taxi-cab advertising: from a poster on the trunk or on the top of the taxi, to the "taxi full wrap," as well as advertising inside the taxi in the form of videos displayed on LED screens attached to the back of the seat in front of the passenger (Blue Line Media). In Europe, advertising in taxi-cabs is popular in such countries as Greece, Italy, Portugal, Spain, England, France, Switzerland, Austria, Denmark, Germany, or the Netherlands (see, for example, the company called Cabvertising, which provides taxi advertising in all of these cities). Sometimes, taxi advertising uses artificial intelligence to personalize the advertising message: for instance, a Polish advertising agency called IQ.screen offers intelligent advertising screens that analyze the age and gender of the travelling passenger and modify the advertising messages accordingly.

Interestingly, more and more advertisers are now using bikes as eco-friendly advertising media. Apart from the possibility to engage cyclists as full-time "brand ambassadors" with big billboards attached to the back of a bike (see, for example, the company called Alt Terrain), many companies now decide to advertise on bikes offered to regular city dwellers as free or minimum-cost means of transport. A good example is a London initiative, where an advertising agency called Buzzbike offers Londoners free use of bicycles "in exchange for the right to use said bike as a rolling advertising platform" (Gibson, 24 June 2016). To sign in, a cyclist has to sign a one-year or two-year agreement and put down a deposit of 100 GBP, refundable at the end of the agreement, if the bike is returned in a good state (Gibson, 24 June 2016). As a part of the contract, a cyclist agrees "to ride the bike to work at least 12 days each month" and preferably park on the street, if the weather allows it (Gibson, 24 June 2016). Similarly, in many cities with the municipal bicycle-sharing system, the city bikes are often used as advertising space.

One more type of urban means of transport worth mentioning here is elevators. Advertising inside an elevator might take the form of several small advertisements grouped together in a panel that also incorporates a mirror; this solution is offered, for example, by a Canadian advertising agency, Publicité

Ascension, which uses Montreal elevators as advertising space (Publicité Ascension). But elevator advertising can also take the form of medium or big posters that might even occupy one entire wall. Very often these bigger posters on the back wall are coupled with advertising on the outside of the elevator door to create one coherent visual effect, for instance, of a lobster being cut in half with a knife, or a married couple splitting and thus needing a divorce lawyer (Funtic, 15 Jun 2011).

Lastly, there are types of means of transport that take people from city to city, from country to country, from one continent to another. Nowadays, such means of transport often display advertising both on the outside and the inside of a vehicle. A good example is a plane. What used to be the norm is that the outside of the plane would only bear the logo of the air company it flies for. These days, however, it has become possible for commercial sponsors to use the outside of the plane as advertising space. EAM, a Los-Angeles-based advertising company that has done campaigns in over 65 airports worldwide, offers to wrap an entire plane in a giant advertising poster, and these "wraps can be purchased on a per-plane or per-fleet basis" (EAM 1). As far as exposure to advertising inside a plane is concerned, it often starts the moment one wants to put luggage in the overhead compartment, as it is now possible for the advertisers to place commercial banners on the compartment flaps. Then, as soon as the passenger is seated, right in front of their face they can usually see an advertisement on the back of the folded table tray; since during a part of the flight it is obligatory for the trays to be folded, it is almost impossible to avoid looking at these banners (one would have to continually have one's head in a position which is uncomfortable to maintain for a longer period of time). Very often, a complementary advertisement can be found on the other side of the table tray, which one sees when the tray is unfolded for a meal. A similar idea of treating passengers as a captive audience lies behind installing seatback screens or overhead screens: as stressed by EAM, an advertising spot played during take-off, when the passengers cannot use their own electronic devices, "has a fully captive audience and the ability to inform everyone on board about your brand" (EAM 1). Apart from that, commercial messages are often present when one reaches inside the seatback pocket: either in the form of advertising leaflets, or an in-flight magazine, dedicated almost entirely to shopping, with advertisements on every page. Additionally, a stewardess will usually make an announcement, listing products that are available for sale during the flight, like fragrances or toys, or she may even come to each passenger and offer product samples. Moreover, it is possible for a brand to sponsor "free" WiFi for passengers "in exchange for some customer information, or in exchange for their time spent watching a short video" (EAM 1).

Finally, the airport itself usually acts as one big advertising space that can be rented: most big airports display commercial messages on banners and dioramas, wall wraps, column wraps, as well as through a network of digital screens of various sizes. Many airports have also introduced small-scale posters that fit at the bottom of security tray bins. Finally, the "free" WiFi at the airport comes at a cost: in exchange for the Internet connection, the passenger has to endure exposure to a battery of advertisements in many different formats. Thus, the passenger is exposed to advertising in the concourse, at the check-in, during the security check, in the business lounge area, in the terminal connectors, as well as in the terminal itself while waiting to be boarded.

Just like planes, train vehicles are equally exploited as advertising space: on the exterior, a train wagon can carry the so called "racing stripes," i.e., narrow posters of the length of an entire wagon, typically with a slogan written on it; alternatively, the train wagon can carry the so-called "bulletin pairs," i.e., two posters per each side of a train, which have the height of an entire wagon, but are relatively short; finally, the advertiser can opt for a "full wrap" of a wagon, meaning that the entire wagon is covered in the advertising poster (Van Wagner, leaflet 1). To give an example, a California train company, Caltrain, is open to all three ways of using the exterior of their train vehicles as advertising space (Van Wagner, leaflet 1).

Another option is advertising within the building of a train station. Train station advertising possibilities range from a banner on the wall next to a ticket window, or a banner on the waiting room wall, column wraps, or hanging pennants, to floor graphics, or "double sided train track entrance banners", which greet passengers on both sides of the entrance to the train track (Van Wagner, leaflet 2). In some train stations, banners may also be placed on the walls of a platform.

As far as a train wagon's interior is concerned, the possible types of advertising are somewhat similar to those on board of a plane: from overhead screens displaying commercial spots and seatback advertisements (on stickers, posters, etc.) placed in front of a passenger's face, to advertisements on the luggage shelves. Also, the conductor of the train will typically advertise the services of the train bar. Samples may be given away, although due to the size of the train and the resulting number of passengers, it might be more convenient to offer samples at the train station as the travelers pass by—a solution chosen by Sydney Trains, for example. Since a train offers more space on board than a plane, this typically implies more advertising possibilities: thus, commercial banners can also be placed on walls, or on the wagon doors (Sydney Trains).

1.3.9. Private Cars and Houses

Private cars can also be turned into billboards-on-wheels. In the US, "ad agencies will pay up to $900 a month to let them wrap your car in a vinyl material bearing logos and product pitches" (Sandel, 2013, 182). According to the estimates of advertisers, around 70 000 people a day will be exposed to the commercial message a private vehicle carries when driving in the city traffic (182; Newman, 27 Aug 2007). An example of a company that acts as an intermediary between private car owners and advertisers is My Free Car (My Free Car). If one does not own a car, another option is to get a "free car" in exchange for the car being wrapped in advertising (Newman, 27 Aug 2007). Entering into a deal with an advertiser, typically means that the motorist—a "brand ambassador"—agrees to abide by certain rules of conduct (Newman, 27 Aug 2007). For example, that person should not litter, swear, drink, or smoke in or around their vehicle (Newman, 27 Aug 2007).

By the same token, one can also turn one's house into advertising space. Sandel describes a small advertising company from California, Godialing (formerly Adzookie), that started offering homeowners with financial difficulties advertising deals that could help them reduce their problems (2013, 182–183). In exchange for painting the entire facade of the house, excluding the roof, with brightly colored commercial slogans, Godialing is willing to pay the house owner's mortgage every month for as long as the advertising stays on the facade (182–183; Anonymous Reporter, 8 Apr 2011). The company stated: "We're looking for houses to paint. In fact, paint is an understatement. We're looking for homes to turn into billboards" (Hamati, Apr 2012). Originally, Godialing was hoping to strike 10 deals with homeowners, but by the end of the first day of their offer they already had 1000 interested subjects, and by April 2012 33,000 applications were filed (Hamati, Apr 2012).

1.3.10. Church Buildings and Church Grounds

The church building seems to remain among one of the few spaces that are still ad-free. The question is for how long. In the story of the advertising company Godialing, which offers financial assistance to house owners, one of the applications came from a church (Hamati, Apr 2012). None of the reports specify whether the deal between Godialing and the church was finalized, but the mere fact that a church has decided to apply for financial assistance in exchange for turning the church building into a billboard shows a certain mentality shift: using the church building as advertising space—for commercial advertising—has already become thinkable, even if the idea might have not been realized.

An idea that has already been realized is erecting a billboard right by the church building in order to advertise the church itself. A good example is St Matthew-in-the-city, an Anglican church from Auckland, New Zealand. The church is notorious for advertising itself with provocative posters—like the one with St Mary looking anxiously at a positive pregnancy test—displayed on the billboard placed in front of the church building (Chapman, 15 Dec 2011; Giantasio, 16 Dec 2011). The church uses its own billboard regularly and therefore keeps an archive of all the previous posters on the church's website (St Matthew-in-the-City).

It is worth emphasizing that whether it is appropriate for a church to advertise itself is not relevant to the subject matter of this book, and therefore I shall not give examples of a church advertising itself outside of the church grounds, i.e., in buses, on the highways, etc. What is relevant to the work herein is the appropriateness of the possibility of using the church building and the church grounds as advertising spaces.

1.3.11. More Municipal Advertising: Green Areas, Pouring Rights

Among the important facilities provided by the city are the city's green areas, i.e., city's shrubs, trees, gardens, parks, beaches. Nowadays, the municipal green areas no longer constitute a type of space which can be classified as ad-free.

In India, for instance, it is popular to place advertisements on tree guards, i.e., devices that protect the tree trunk from animals or mechanical injuries. The tree guards with advertisements typically appear in groups at the roadside, in gardens or parks (TDI India).

In Europe, United Kingdom is an example of a country where advertising within the city's green areas is no longer taboo. Supposedly motivated by care for an uncertain financial future of many UK parks, an organization called Prosperous Parks provides park managers and local authorities with "ideas and information about sustainable commercial income for parks" (Prosperous Parks). One such idea is for a park to get a commercial sponsor who subsidizes the whole park or a particular part of the park. If the sponsor requires that the company name or logo be displayed within the park's area in exchange for the subsidy, then the sponsorship *de facto* turns into advertising. Thus, a commercial logo can be placed, for example, on park benches and other furniture, sports facilities, playgrounds, buildings, flower beds and borders. Apart from getting sponsorship deals, UK parks sell advertising space within the park's area. As suggested by Prosperous Parks, advertising can be placed in park leaflets and park newsletters, on parking tickets, signage boards, park websites, as well as in the park toilets. It can also be present in the form of hoardings, i.e., big-scale billboards, or as hard surface stencilling, known as "clean advertising"—the name comes from the fact that the advertising message is displayed on a hard surface which is dirty, such as a park pavement, by means of cleaning a part of the surface within the stencil. As explained by one marketing agency, "while the dirt is all removed within the stencil, it stays around it leaving your advert or logo 'cleaned' onto the ground" (William, 1 Oct 2017).

However, United Kingdom is also a good example of a country in which civic protests against advertising in public parks made the authorities of some cities partially restrict the advertisers' access to the municipal green areas. In a 2018 online issue of the *South Bristol Voice*, we can read that "THE COUNCIL has announced it will not allow large advertisements in parks after being confronted with a wave of opposition to the idea"—more than 4000 signatures of Bristol's citizens were gathered on a petition (Anonymous Reporter, 23 Mar 2018). Nonetheless, the author of the article stresses that the decision of the city council "did not rule out some unspecified smaller adverts being paid for by companies in Bristol's parks and open spaces" (Anonymous Reporter, 23 Mar 2018).

As the opposing voices emphasize, allowing advertisements into a city's public parks is in fact a way of commercializing and thus privatizing a space which is public (Anonymous Reporter, 23 Mar 2018). Moreover, "parks are retreats from our urban milieu and the relentless drumbeat of commerce. They are also a core city service and do not exist to generate revenue"; consequently, people who use public parks "should not be offered up as marketing targets" (Butler, 23 Aug 2011). Furthermore, if a corporate sponsor really cares about the fate of a public park, they can make a donation without expecting advertising in return. As stressed by Bernadette Soter, a founding board member of Friends of Griffith Park in Los Angeles, a city where a battle over advertising in city parks has been fierce since (at least) 2010, "It is a shame to see the vocabulary of philanthropy employed to mask self-interest and for-profit intent. What are being called 'donations,' are really transactions. Real donations don't require payback. Throughout Los Angeles, corporate benefactors are duly thanked and acknowledged on institutional donor walls bearing no logos or references to the companies' products or services" (Butler, 23 Aug 2011). As to the poor financial condition of public parks, the example of Los Angeles shows that while the local authorities are often ready to say that commercialization is the only way to keep the public parks going, they also manage to find the money to subsidize such institutions as the local luxury hotels; in the case of Los Angeles, it is therefore a matter of the authorities' arbitrary decision not to allocate the money which they do have to public parks (Butler, 23 Aug 2011).

As far as the municipal beaches are concerned, Sandel (2013, 189–190) gives examples of public beaches in the United States. First, he describes the advertising campaign of the summer of 1998 at the public beach in Seaside Heights, New Jersey; people arriving at the beach that summer discovered that on the sand across the whole beach there were five thousand imprints of Skippy Peanut Butter jars. This was a moment when a new device had just been invented which could stamp commercial messages into the sand—Skippy was one of the first companies to take advantage of the invention by paying the town a fee to place their advertisements on the municipal beach (190).

A good contemporary example of an agency that specializes in the so-called sand and sea advertising is Massive Media Experiential Agency. Apart from sand stamping, the agency also offers corporate sand sculptures, advertising messages in bottles, sailing billboards, boat billboards, and more (Massive Media Experiential Agency).

Yet another way to introduce advertising onto public beaches is to become a sponsor of beach rescues. For example, General Motors signed a 2.5 million USD sponsorship deal with Orange County, California, in order to promote its Chevrolet brand. The company provided county lifeguards with forty-two pickup trucks and Chevy Blazers emblazoned with advertisements saying that Chevrolet is the "Official Marine Safety Vehicle of Orange Coast Beaches" (Sandel, 2013, 190). The deal also included a free access to the beaches for commercial photo shoots (190).

Finally, a way to establish corporate presence at a beach or another place owned by a city is to buy pouring rights. For instance, in 1999, as a result of a 6 million USD deal, Coca-Cola became "the official soft-drink of Huntington Beach, California" (190). The exclusive pouring rights meant that Coca-Cola's soft-drinks, juices, and bottled water were the only drinks that could be sold at city beaches, parks, and city-owned buildings. In addition, Coca-Cola could use Huntington's Beach Surf City logo as a part of its advertising campaign (190). Several such pouring rights deals followed in other cities (IEG Sponsorship Report 2014, 30 Jan 2014 I).

1.3.12. Municipal Marketing in Public Toilets

Public toilets—in public parks, at public beaches, or anywhere else in the public space of a city—are another instance of municipal marketing. The idea of placing advertising in public bathrooms seems to have originated in the US, around the early 2000s, with the advertising agency called Wizmark (Johnson, 17 Sep 2006). Since then, the idea has gained popularity in many other countries of the world: advertisements are now being placed on the bathroom door, wall, or floor, as well as in the sink, on the mirror, inside the urinal or right above it. These advertisements can appear in the form of a poster, a wrap, an audio or audio-visual device: the audio or audio-visual messages may be triggered when a person starts to use the urinal, for example. Sometimes, even a soap dispenser or a toilet paper holder might serve as advertising space (Design Swan, 20 Jan 2010).

1.3.13. Branded Nature Outside the City

In *One-Dimensional Man*, a book written in 1964, Herbert Marcuse describes a walk in a national park; the space around the park is pervaded with billboards, but the park itself is free from advertising and the stroller is thankful for that (1964/2007, 231). Nowadays, the reality described by Marcuse is no longer the case, and the physical boundaries of national parks have ceased to be impenetrable to advertising. To give an example, public parks in Virginia and Maryland have had their trail markers branded with the logo of North Face, an outdoor apparel producer (Sandel, 2013, 192). Coca-Cola, on the other hand, has struck a deal with a California state park: in exchange for the sponsorship of a reforestation project, Coca-Cola has been given permission to display its logo in the park's area (192). By the same token, Odwalla, a juice producer, has become a sponsor of a tree-planting program and gets "brand recognition at state parks across the country" in return (192). A similar deal binds several New York state parks and Nestlé's Juicy Juice brand: in exchange for sponsoring playgrounds, Nestlé's product is being advertised on the parks' signs (192). But this phenomenon is by no means restricted to the US nature reserves. To give a European example, advertising is present on some Polish nature trails. For instance, in the summer of 2018, at both entrances to the nature trail in the Chłapowska Valley (Dolina Chłapowska) at the Polish seaside there was an advertisement of a mobile phone company (Plus) as the sponsor of an emergency hotline for the tourists; in addition, the information sign about the valley itself had several logos of sponsors, including corporate sponsors. As stressed by two Polish geographers, "areas of high natural value are perceived by outdoor advertising agencies and individual entrepreneurs as areas which ensure that the advertising message is conveyed successfully to a large audience" (Listwan-Franczak, Franczak, 2015, translation mine). Shari Boyer, the CEO of a company that mediates deals between corporate sponsors and state parks in the US, says that the park setting is "a great place to reach people" because it is "a very quiet marketing environment," in which potential consumers are "in the right state of mind" due to the lack of distractions (Sandel, 2013,193).

Similarly, people are "in the right state of mind" when they are looking up, admiring the sky. Thus, nowadays, the sky is no longer an ad-free space: advertisements can be displayed in the sky using "skywriting" (Spence, Van Heekeren, 2005, 85, 91), a technique that consists in a small type of aircraft emitting special smoke that forms readable patterns in the sky that can be deciphered by viewers on the ground. AirSign, which has existed since 1996, is a good example of a company that specializes in this type of advertising. On the company's website, we read that "Now more than ever, people's attention spans are shortening and it is difficult for companies to stand out in the sea of noise and distractions. But there is a method that rises above the noise, can't be turned off and actually attracts favorable attention instead of prompting people to change the channel" (AirSign). The brands that have used the services of AirSign include Ford, Google, Virgin, and Uber.

For now, a space that seems to remain ad-free are body parts of non-human living organisms. However, in 2006 a team of researchers at the University of Buffalo announced the creation of the world's first genetically modified butterfly, implanted with special fluorescent genes that the scientists could activate (using laser) to create fluorescent markings (Ramos, Kamal, Wimmer, Cartwright, Monteiro, 2006). Since then, speculations have arisen about the possibility of using this technology to emblazon butterfly wings with commercial logos and slogans. One of the first to react with concern about the possible commercial uses of this technology was a journalist of the Daily Telegraph, saying that the accomplishment of the University of Buffalo team "could herald the day that the insects are adorned with adverts and slogans" (Highfield, 21 Nov 2006). Later on, Koert van Mensvoort, a Dutch artist and philosopher interested in the intertwinement of nature and technology, generated an image of a butterfly he called *Papilio Nike Ulysses*, a genetically modified version of the butterfly *Papilio Ulysses*, with the Nike brand on one of its wings; van Mensvoort said that he created "this speculative *designer organism* to explore the limits of corporate branding" (Van Mensvoort, 17 Dec 2006; Van Mensvoort, 2007). However, till now such uses of the new technology remain purely speculative, and body parts of non-human living organisms seem to remain ad-free. At least in the sense that there are no big-scale advertising campaigns that use animal bodies as advertising space. As far as small-scale advertising campaigns are concerned, in 2012, on a public forum called Reddit.com, a user has published a photo of a real-life cow dyed purple in order to advertise a local delicatessen in Kentucky (u/Zippo16, 4 Jul 2012).

1.3.14. Human Body

The origin of the idea to use human body as advertising space can be traced to a local advertising initiative in San Francisco, where in 1998 the owners of a small Mexican restaurant offered a free lunch for life to people willing to tattoo the restaurant's logo onto their body; as a result, within a few months forty people took the restaurant up on the offer and got permanent tattoos with the restaurant's logo (Sandel, 2013, 183). A few years later, a professional advertising agency from London followed up on this idea by recruiting university students willing to lease advertising space on their foreheads: the students were expected to embellish their foreheads with temporary tattoos featuring company logos for 4.20 GBP per hour (183; Rubenstein, 14 Apr 1999).[17]

Another example is native to Japan, where young women can rent the billboard space on their thighs between overknee socks and a miniskirt: this particular space on a woman's body is called *zettai ryouiki*, meaning "absolute territory," and the women can rent this space for advertising via an agency called Absolute Territory PR, operating since 2012 (Masuda, 15 Nov 2012). In 2018, a new Japanese agency, The Wakino Ad Company, started operating around a similar idea of renting the bare skin of women's armpits as advertising space (Sanya, 26 Jul 2018).

Apart from such big campaigns organized by the professional advertising agencies, examples of private, small-scale initiatives can be found: for instance, in order to pay for her son's education, Karolyne Smith (now Karolyne Williams), a single mother from Utah, sold the space on her forehead to an online casino for 10,000 USD. As a result, the casino's website address—GoldenPalace.com—has been permanently tattooed on her forehead (Sandel, 2013, 184; Falk, 30 Jun 2005).

1.4. First Approximation at a Definition of the Omnipresence of Advertising

On the basis of the theoretical component of this chapter (Section 1.2) and the empirical data illustrating the everyday manifestations of the omnipresence of

17 Since then, different variations of the original idea have been developed. For example, in an advertising campaign for Air New Zealand thirty people were hired to serve as "cranial billboards" (Sandel, 2013, 184). On the back of a shaved head of each participant there was a temporary tattoo with the following slogan: "Need a Change? Head Down to New Zealand" (184; Newman, 18 Feb 2009).

advertising (Section 1.3), it is now possible to offer a first approximation at a definition of the phenomenon.

To begin, it can be observed that advertising is man-made and temporary: it has not been present from the very beginning of the world, and it is not—at least theoretically—impossible that it could disappear in the future. Second, advertising is not present literally everywhere in space. For these reasons, using the term "omnipresence" in the literal sense would be an obvious mistake. Nevertheless, we can talk about the omnipresence of advertising in the non-literal sense indicating a high potentiality for advertising to appear anywhere, anytime: as empirically illustrated in Section 1.3, any type of space (and any type of event) can serve as an "advertising carrier," even those types of space (and events) that used to be ad-free. Omnipresence of advertising understood in this way can sometimes manifest as high saturation of certain areas/domains of reality with advertising: the New York City subway or some American stadiums are good real-life examples of areas with high saturation of advertising (see Sections 1.3.8 and 1.3.6).

It is noteworthy that if the omnipresence of advertising is understood in the non-literal way, as having its spatiotemporal limits and being brought about by human beings, then—in principle—it can be counteracted by human beings as well. This is not to say that the attempts to regulate the omnipresence of advertising can bring instantaneous results. It is only to say that the definition entails that we are not helplessly subjected to this phenomenon (the way one might be considered helplessly subjected to the literal omnipresence of certain phenomena) and the possibility of creating regulations exists, even if tangible effects of such regulations could only be observed in the long term.

1.5. Conclusions

The first conclusion that I wish to draw from this chapter is that the phenomenon of the omnipresence of advertising may be divided into two subtypes: the omnipresence of advertising which is more local and the omnipresence of advertising which is global in character. The more local manifestation is limited to a certain area, like school premises, a stadium, or a metro station. If this limited area is highly saturated with advertising, we may say that advertising is omnipresent within this particular area. In contrast, the omnipresence of advertising manifesting on a global scale does *not* consist in the high saturation of the entire reality with advertising, but in the gradual disappearance of types of space (and types of events) which are ad-free. The fewer types of space (and events) there are in the world which are off-limits to advertising, the more we are dealing with the phenomenon of the omnipresence of advertising on a global scale, and—normatively speaking—the more prominent is the message that it is permissible for advertising to be everywhere.

A general observation that could be added is that apart from the purely spatial aspect of the omnipresence of advertising, there is also a temporal one. Focusing on the local manifestation, a person participating in a sports event, like a baseball match, experiences a presence of many advertisements not only in the *space* of the stadium, but also in time: the *time* during which the match takes place is also pervaded with advertising, and while some advertisements are present throughout the whole match (like the billboards around the stadium), others are to be seen or heard only during certain moments of the match (like the commercial messages announced when a new player enters the field or when a player slides into the home base). Similarly, the temporal aspect of the omnipresence of advertising is the key element of analyzing a person's exposure to advertising throughout the day, when a person commutes from one type of space (like home) through another type of space (like the streets of the city) to yet another type of space (like school or work), and so on. A good example of an analysis of this sort is a 2007 USA-based report, according to which an average American adult has potential daily exposure to 600–625 ads per day (15 Feb 2007, Media Matters).

The daily exposure analysis shows that there have been attempts to measure the saturation of fragments of contemporary reality with advertising. Other instances of these attempts include a 2014 report, which gives a lower number of 362 ads per day (Media Dynamics Inc. 2014; Johnson, 29 Sep 2014), and a Yankelovich Monitor poll from the nineties which gave a much higher number that has become famous and much debated ever since: 5000 ads per day (13 Nov 1995, ADWEEK-W.EDITION; Ayres, Funk, 2003, 95, ftn 71). To my best knowledge, no attempt has been made to measure the saturation of any fragments of contemporary reality in purely spatial terms, i.e., how many ads there are per kilometer/meter in a given location. However, notice that apart from the evident temporal dimension, the ads-per-day analysis has a spatial dimension: the daily exposure is measured in a certain geographical location.

If the saturation component of the omnipresence of advertising were key to understanding the nature of the phenomenon, such analyses would be of high importance to the topic of this book. However, from the combination of the theoretical (Section 1.2) and the empirical (Section 1.3) components of this chapter, I have concluded that the omnipresence of advertising signifies—first and foremost—a high potentiality for advertising to appear anywhere, anytime, in any type of space, during any type of event. Also, contrary to the intuitions of some scholars like Arrington (1982), Durham (1984), Wright (1997), Sneddon

(2013), or Villarán (2017) (see the Ethical Appendix and the Legal Appendix), the omnipresence of advertising does not imply high saturation of the *entire* contemporary reality with advertising, although there might exist *some areas/domains of reality* which are highly saturated with advertising. The understanding of the omnipresence of advertising presented herein seems to agree with the discourse of Sandel (2013), as well as Spence and Van Heekeren (2005), concerning the phenomenon in question (see the Ethical Appendix): the scholars do not express this explicitly, but their discussion does not appear to be focused on the amount of advertising, i.e., on the idea of high saturation of the entire contemporary reality with advertising.

In this book, the de-emphasis on the amount/saturation aspect of the omnipresence of advertising is deliberate and explicit. From this perspective, while saturation analyses may be of some interest to the topic of the omnipresence of advertising, they are not vital to it, both in terms of understanding the phenomenon, as well as in terms of comprehending the harm to human beings it may cause, and also in terms of finding solutions to the problems it brings along. This deliberate de-emphasis on the amount/saturation aspect of the omnipresence of advertising implies that we no longer have to try to consider a person's sensitivity to the number of stimuli received, which is difficult to measure and theorize in a way that would be relevant to advertising alone and to all human beings in their entirety. Instead, we can focus on studying the progressive elimination of ad-free types of space and events and on discussing the reasons why some of these types of space and events ought to be legally protected as entirely free from advertising.

The final two-part conclusion of this chapter would go as follows. First, the fact that we can describe some spaces or events as "ad-free" suggests that individuals who have access to such spaces and events can enjoy "ad-freedom." In this way an important dimension of freedom can be identified, which could be a key concept in an ethical analysis of the omnipresence of advertising. Second, the gradual loss of types of space and events which are ad-free—illustrated in the empirical part of this chapter—would signify the gradual loss of *ad-freedom*: the type of freedom enjoyed owing to the existence of and access to ad-free spaces and events. The questions that arise from this last conclusion are the following. How to formulate a good definition of *ad-freedom*? Could the discussion of the phenomenon of *ad-freedom* be important from the point of view of ethics? The third chapter shall address these queries.

2 Arguing Against the Omnipresence of Advertising Through the Lens of Relational Autonomy

> "Advertisers' common defense—if you don't like advertising, don't watch it or don't buy the products it promotes. But do we have a choice?"
> A. Cunningham, "Autonomous Consumption" (2003)

> "(...) the triviality (...) of commercials tends to no extent whatever to imply the triviality of being forced to listen to them."
> C. Black, "He Cannot Choose but Hear" (1953)

2.1. Introduction

As illustrated in the empirical part of the previous chapter, many people seem to intuitively feel that there is something inappropriate and harmful about omnipresence of advertising. But what is the harm exactly? The purpose of this chapter is to identify and elucidate different kinds of harm caused by this phenomenon, using the definition provided in the previous chapter as a foundation. Therefore, because the definition of omnipresence of advertising has emphasized the significance of high potentiality for advertising to appear anywhere, anytime, in any type of space and event (and de-emphasized the importance of the amount of advertising in the contemporary reality), almost entire argumentation in this chapter focuses on the consequences of the gradual elimination of ad-free types of space, events, and relationships (and only one half of the first argument is devoted to the consequences of the omnipresence manifesting through high saturation of a limited domain of reality).

This chapter is composed of two main parts: theoretical and argumentative. In the theoretical part (Section 2.2), I flesh out a theory of autonomy that I will apply in the argumentative part. Some readers may want to skip the theory and go straight to the original argumentation developed in the second part of this chapter (Section 2.3). Feel free to do so: the argumentative part is indeed the "juicy bit" of this chapter.

In the argumentative part (Section 2.3), I argue that the phenomenon I refer to as the omnipresence of advertising is detrimental to personal autonomy. In *the argument from a captive audience* (Section 4.3.1.1), I try to show that both the global and the local kind of omnipresence of advertising produce what the

American legal doctrine calls "captive audiences" (see the Legal Appendix), thus making it impossible for people, who become these captive audiences, to act on their choice not to be exposed to advertising. In *the argument from hindering critical reasoning* (Section 4.3.2.1), I argue that when types of space that should retain critical distance from advertising lose their status as ad-free as a result of the global manifestation of the omnipresence of advertising, this has a negative impact on the cultivation of people's critical reasoning skills. Finally, in *the argument from non-benign objectification and the erosion of trust* (Section 4.3.2.2), I attempt to show that the global manifestation of the omnipresence of advertising erodes relationships of trust necessary for developing, maintaining, and exercising autonomy competency.

2.2. The Theoretical Part: Autonomy

2.2.1. Personal Autonomy

To begin, I wish to clarify that in the analysis that follows I will not be concerned with moral autonomy. Instead, I will focus on personal autonomy, which is not restricted to the realm of moral obligations: in the words of John Christman, individuals can exhibit personal autonomy "relative to any aspect of their lives" (Christman, 2020; see also Meyers, 1989, 82; and Friedman, 1997/2018, par. 6).

To avoid repetition, I will henceforth use the term "autonomy" whenever I wish to refer to "personal autonomy."

2.2.2. Relational Autonomy

The view of autonomy applied in this chapter is relational (contextual) autonomy, inspired by and aligning with the feminist perspectives on autonomy that have bloomed out of Carol Gilligan's critique of Lawrence's Kohlberg account of moral psychological development (Gilligan, 1982). In line with the feminist relational autonomy theorists, I will claim that the self is essentially interdependent, dynamic, social/relational, embodied (see, for example, Meyers, 1987, 1989, 2005; Nedelsky, 1989; Held, 1993; Barclay, 2000; McLeod, Sherwin, 2000; McLeod, 2002; Donchin, 2001; Goldberg, 2003, 2008; Goering, 2008; Westlund, 2009; Kong, 2017; Brison, 1997/2018), and that a capacity for autonomy, like a capacity for language, needs to be developed, maintained, and exercised within a social/relational context (see, for example, Nedelsky, 1989, 8; Barclay 2000; Meyers, 1989, 135–136). Just like there is no "private language," there is also no "private autonomy": we develop, maintain, and exercise autonomy competency through ongoing practice that takes place during interactions with other people and the environment that surrounds us, not in isolation. The implication of perceiving autonomy relationally—or contextually—is that the context of autonomous agency matters in "determining the degree to which an individual is able to act autonomously," because the context influences the agent's opportunities to develop, maintain, and exercise the autonomy competency (McLeod, Sherwin, 2000, 259–260).

Although the work in this chapter is multi-influenced, the feminist relational autonomy theory most significant to the approach applied here is the one proposed by Diana Tietjens Meyers (see especially 1987, 1989, 2005). Following Meyers' reasoning, I will not consider autonomy a special case of free will (1989, part 2, secs. 1–2), thus shunning the ontologically-oriented discussion and conceptualization of autonomy. Instead, as mentioned in the previous paragraph, I will consider autonomy to be a competency (part 2, secs. 2 and 4), which is possible through the exercise of various self-reading and self-actualizing skills that are developed and kept in good shape within a social/relational context, and not by transcending and abstracting oneself from socialization (part 2, sec. 4). As Meyers rightfully points out, with no socialization to help a person develop, a human being would most probably be in the state of mind much too crude to be an autonomous agent: "As portrayals of children who have grown up without the benefit of socialization reveal (Francois Truffaut's *The Wild Child* is a well-know example), a great deal of nurturance is required for the most rudimentary self-understanding" (29). Also, the social and relational interactions constitute an important environment in which one can exercise autonomy skills, and without the exercise, these skills would go into atrophy (part 2, sec. 4). Therefore, although some forms of socialization may pose a threat to autonomy (44; see also part 3, secs. 2–3; Meyers, 1987, 623–624), overall, socialization is beneficial to the development, maintenance, and exercise of autonomy competency (Meyers, 1989, 135). Consequently, being an autonomous person is not about purging oneself of all social influences, but rather about exerting some sort of control over them (44).

Conceptualizing autonomy as based on social (and environmental) embeddedness seems particularly relevant to the discussion of the threats posed by the omnipresence of advertising. As observed by Barclay, "a commitment to protect the autonomous individual in social and political life requires scrutiny of the various social forces that affect the development of autonomy competency and a preparedness to alter them" (2000, 56). As will be shown later in this chapter, the omnipresence of advertising influences the social forces that affect the development, maintenance, and exercise of autonomy competency.

2.2.3. An Amalgam of Meyers and Sneddon, and an Additional Element

Despite being significantly influenced by Meyers, the theory of autonomy developed in this chapter will not simply mirror her theory of autonomy: rather, it will be a sort of an amalgam of her account and the account presented by Andrew Sneddon—an amalgam to which I will add some additional ingredients. Most importantly, I will add the element of self-trust which is not explicitly present in either of these accounts, and which I consider important as the link between the other components of the autonomy theory that I will propose.

I hope that this amalgam will be felicitous, as the two philosophers seem to agree in many important respects. (1) They both consider autonomy to be a competency, the development, maintenance, and exercise of which is shaped by the presence of other people (Meyers, 1989, part 2, secs. 2 and 4; Sneddon, 2013, chap. 2, pars. 3 and 22, and chap. 4). (2) They both agree that self-knowledge and self-discovery go hand-in-hand and that these are important elements of the autonomy competency (Sneddon, 2013, chap. 3, sec. *Autonomy of persons: Self-knowledge*; see, for instance, Meyers, 1989, 179–183; see Section 2.2.8 below for further discussion). (3) They both find self-shaping to be a crucial element of the autonomy competency (exercised with regard to the kind of person one wants to be): Sneddon uses the term "self-shaping" explicitly (Sneddon, 2013, chap. 3, sec. *Autonomy of persons: Self-shaping*), while Meyers prefers to use the term "self-definition" to denote a similar phenomenon (Meyers, 1989, 43–48), and she makes use of the term "shaping" one's self or one's life more sparingly.[18] (4) They both believe that autonomy should not be reduced to being purely rational (Meyers 2005, 28–29; Sneddon, 2013, chap. 3, sec. *Autonomy of persons: Self-knowledge*). (5) They both hold that a good theory of autonomy must allow for a retrospective exercise of autonomy competency, in addition to its anticipatory and introspective use (Meyers, 1989, 54–55; Meyers, 2005, 28; Sneddon, 2013, chap. 2, sec. *Autonomy of choice*, par. 3). (6) They both differentiate between an incidental use of autonomy competency to make a particular choice and long-term ongoing use of autonomy competency to express the kind of person one wants to be. Meyers uses the term "autonomous episodic self-direction" to refer to the incidental use of autonomy competency (Meyers, 1989, 48) and Sneddon calls it "shallow autonomy" in his earlier work (Sneddon, 2001b, 2001a, 2006;

---

18 For examples of Meyers' use of the term "shaping" one's self or one's life, see Meyers, 1989, 47, 61.

see the Ethical Appendix for more details) and "autonomy of choice" in his later work (Sneddon, 2013, chap. 2, sec. *Autonomy of Choice*). Conversely, the long-term ongoing use of autonomy competency expressive of the kind of life one wants to lead as a person is called "autonomous programmatic self-direction" in Meyers' parlance (Meyers, 1989, 48), "deep autonomy" in Sneddon's earlier work (Sneddon, 2001b, but also Sneddon, 2001a, and 2006) and "autonomy of persons" in his later work (Sneddon, 2013, chap. 3).[19]

2.2.4. Autonomy of Choice and Autonomy of Persons

For the purpose of the theory of autonomy developed in this chapter, I have decided to use Sneddon's terminology from his later work. The long-term ongoing use of autonomy competency is the expression of the kind of person one wants to be, and therefore calling it "autonomy of persons" seems to be the simplest way of rendering that meaning. Similarly, the incidental use of autonomy competency is about making a particular choice, and thus referring to it as "autonomy of choice" is very straightforward, intuitive, and logical.

Sneddon adroitly shows that, on the one hand, the two phenomena are independent of one another: (a) one can be an autonomous person, yet sometimes make non-autonomous choices, and (b) one may make an autonomous choice, and yet be a non-autonomous person (Sneddon, 2013, chap. 2, pars. 23–28). Also, an autonomous choice—to join a religious cult, for example—might go against the further development of one's autonomy as a person (chap. 3, sec. *Autonomy of persons: Self-knowledge*, par. 23). On the other hand, Sneddon explains how autonomy of choice and autonomy of persons are closely interconnected: exercising autonomy of choice with regard to a specific topic—oneself—is a necessary, though not sufficient, condition of autonomy of persons (chap. 3, par. 5).

2.2.5. Autonomy of Choice

To begin, for a choice to count as autonomous it has to be acted on (Meyers, 1989, 52; Meyers, 2000, 156; Sneddon, 2013, ch. 2, sec. *Autonomy of choice*, par. 7). Secondly, it is how people arrive at a decision that determines whether a

19 In his book from 2013, Sneddon proposes to renounce the earlier nomenclature, believing that the names "shallow autonomy" and "deep autonomy" seem to mistakenly suggest that deep autonomy is somehow better and should be favored (Sneddon, 2013, ch. 3, sec. *Reading Guide*).

certain decision is autonomous or heteronomous (Meyers, 1989, 52; Sneddon, 2013, chap. 2, sec. *Autonomy of choice*, par. 1).

Similarly to Sneddon and Meyers, I will uphold that "[c]hoices can become autonomous—that is, can come under control by oneself—in various ways" (Sneddon, 2013, chap. 2, sec. *Autonomy of choice*, par. 2; see also Meyers, 2005): as a result of explicit rational calculation connected with the prospect of making a particular choice, as a result of consulting one's own feelings about the choice, as a result of retrospective reasoning (or feelings) about the choice which has already been made (Sneddon, 2013, chap. 2, sec. *Autonomy of choice*, par. 2; see also Meyers, 1989, 54–55). What matters is that the mental state (thought/desire/feeling[20]) which serves as a basis for making the choice is endorsed by the agent on a meta-level—i.e., a level of mental states that are about other mental states (for example, a thought about a thought)—or it would be endorsed, if one were to consult oneself about it (Sneddon, 2013, chap. 2, sec. *Autonomy of choice*, par. 8). Meyers says that it is important that a theory of autonomy makes room for such "implicit" endorsement, because "people usually do not reflect on their desires unless those desires are somehow called into question" (Meyers, 1989, 38).

Importantly, for the endorsed choice to be classified as autonomous, the endorsement on a meta-level should be the result of a deliberation during which various options of possible behavior are critically analyzed, using a set of autonomy skills that make the agent autonomy-competent (Meyers, 1989, 48). This kind of endorsement contrasts with the endorsement that stems from being manipulated into uncritically internalizing an attitude of another person or group: in other words, how the endorsement is generated matters.[21]

In terms of terminology, the above-mentioned endorsement of what one wants, which involves employing a set of autonomy skills, can also be referred to as "what one *really* wants" (Sneddon, 2013, chap. 2, sec. *Autonomy of choice,* par. 3). Throughout her work, Meyers almost never uses the term "endorsement" and generally prefers to speak of the agent "*really* wanting something." I will use the expressions "endorsement of what one wants" and "really wanting something" interchangeably.

20 Sneddon upholds that autonomy seems to be "delivered by a plurality of mental states" (2013, ch. 2, sec. *Other theories of autonomy of choice*, par. 6).

21 For instance, the procedural account of Harry Frankfurt (1971) did not take into account the way that the endorsement on a meta-level is generated, and it was therefore vulnerable to the Problem of Manipulation criticism.

2.2.6. Self-Shaping, Autonomy Skills, and the Dynamic Self

Similarly to Meyers and Sneddon, I assume that the self is *dynamic* and, thus, that it can be *shaped* by a person exercising autonomy competency (Meyers, 1989, chap. 2, Section 3; Meyers, 2000, 163; Sneddon, 2013, chap. 3). As stated by Sneddon, "we both learn new things about and create new features for ourselves all through our life" (2013, chap. 3, sec. *Autonomy of persons: Self-shaping*, par. 18). Complementarily, Meyers says that "autonomous people can adjust their own characteristics along with their behavior to match their respective conceptions of what kind of people they should be and what kind of life is worthwhile" (1989, 80). Overall, shaping a self involves consciously choosing the values one holds dear, projecting a personal ideal of life and self on the basis of these values, and living by the standards implicit in this ideal (Meyers, 1989, 61; Sneddon, 2013, chap. 3, sec. *Autonomy of persons: Self-shaping*, pars. 6, 18).

But these values and standards are not created *ex nihilo*: a person's "individuality is parasitic on socialization and enculturation" (Meyers, 2005, 30). And here comes the tricky part: in order for the assimilation of social norms, values, and attitudes to result from autonomous choice (rather than from an imposition), a person needs to be enabled to possess and exercise a set of well-developed autonomy skills (29–30), such as critical thinking; sensitivity to one's felt self-referential responses, especially to inner discord; good memory of what one has experienced; an ability to communicate with other people concerning one's needs, desires, values, concerns; sensitivity to others' feedback; ability to self-correct; and "a capacity to devise and carry out conduct congruent with the self" (Meyers, 1989, 83–84, 87–88).

Understanding autonomy competency relationally means that the development and maintenance of the autonomy skills are possible due to the nurturing and supportive existence of other people.[22] Differently put, in order not to passively absorb social norms, values, and attitudes, but to shape one's self autonomously, one needs other people to support the development and maintenance of one's autonomy skills. As adroitly put by Camillia Kong,[23] a "nurturing

22 Taking into consideration the information from Section 2.2.7, it should be added that these need to be *trustworthy* others, and that their assistance is also needed in developing self-trust which constitutes a foundation of the autonomy competency.

23 Kong is a wholehearted proponent of Meyers' understanding of autonomy as a competency which is acquired and maintained in relationships with others: Kong terms Meyers' approach to autonomy 'procedural-relational.' See especially Kong, 2017, ch. 3, sec. IV.

interpersonal environment can do a great deal to ameliorate vulnerabilities and empower the *intrapersonal* conditions of autonomy" (2017, ch. 3, sec. II, par. 2, emphasis in original). In contrast, when the need for support and guidance is repressed, this can put the procedural skills of autonomy competency in peril (2017, ch. 3, sec. II, par. 2; see also Westlund, 2009). In fact—drawing inspiration from Carolyn Ells (2001)—Kong maintains that "the move to seek assistance and support through others can itself be an important indicator of autonomy skills" (2017, ch. 3, sec. II, par. 6). For one, it may show that a person has a high degree of self-understanding and, as a result, that a person is capable of realistically assessing their possibilities, as well as their limitations (2017, ch. 3, sec. II, par. 6): aware of their personal constraints and the potential of every human being to be fallible, a person can reach out to increase the possibility of exercising autonomy competency well.

Dialogue with others can bring our attention to those areas that we might be tempted to avoid and ignore, like internal inconsistencies, ulterior motives (Kong, 2017, ch. 3, sec. 4, par. 7), or mechanisms of irrationality that hinder a fuller self-understanding (Meyers, part III, sec. 4). Meyers stresses that the process of self-reading and self-interpretation often requires the support of others who can offer their own interpretations of a person's situation in order for that person "to notice self-referential responses or in order to find plausible explanations of these responses. When this is so, conversation becomes central to the self-reading process" and consequently plays an important role in developing a "self-portrait," as well as "life plans" (1989, 79–80; see also 89, 91). In a similar vein, Kong writes that "dialogue with others facilitates reflection of our personal thoughts, feelings, and values through the interpretative lens of others" (2017, ch. 3, sec. 4, par. 6).

Finally, the support of others allows to cultivate, maintain, or regain autonomy skills in various situations of heightened vulnerability that compromise the exercise of the autonomy competency: some examples of being in a position of heightened vulnerability that calls for the autonomy-promoting assistance of others include living with impairment (Kong, 2017), becoming a parent (Goering, 2008), or being a trauma survivor (Brison, 1997/2018).

2.2.7. Self-Trust (and Trust)

Similarly to such authors as Carolyn McLeod and Susan Sherwin (2000) or Trudy Govier (1993), I will see autonomy as closely interconnected with and strongly dependent on self-trust. According to Govier, remembering confidently, thinking accurately, deliberating reasonably, having goals and pursuing them, making sound decisions and implementing them, and generally maintaining a sense of self, all necessitate what she calls "core self-trust" (108, 114–115): "Without core self-trust, a person is so open to the manipulations of others as to lose any sense of a meaningful agency. Only with self-trust can one conduct one's own life so as to lead an authentic personal existence not open to domination by other people, social convention, or passing fads" (115). She says that whilst some self-distrust in a particular situation or regarding a particular capacity is normal and need not be a handicap, distrusting one's "ability to observe and interpret events, to remember and act generally, is a handicap so serious as to threaten one's status as an individual moral agent" (108). In a like vein, McLeod and Sherwin see it as non-problematic that an agent might display self-distrust that applies to particular situations (2000, 264; they call it "situational" self-distrust); in contrast, they consider it "essential in developing the capacity to be autonomous that the agent trusts her capacity to make appropriate choices, given her beliefs, desires, and values [the authors identify it as type I of self-trust]; that she trusts her ability to act on her decisions [type II of self-trust]; and also that she trusts the judgments she makes that underlie those decisions [type III of self-trust]. These include judgments about values and motivations that lie behind her decisions and about the efficacy of her own decision-making skills" (2000, 262–263). Corroborating the reasoning of McLeod, Sherwin, and Govier, Paul Benson argues that profound self-distrust results in an agent being disengaged from her decision-making process and alienated from her actions and reasons behind them: Benson concludes that these are signs of a lack of the decision-maker's autonomy (2005, 130). In short, without self-trust, the decision-maker is not autonomous.

McLeod and Sherwin develop a typology of self-trust—visible in the quotation above—thus, differentiating between three types of self-trust. It is important to stress that type III of self-trust includes trusting one's judgment regarding one's own values and motivations, but also regarding one's own trustworthiness. Supplementing the authors' vision, two sub-types of self-trust could be further emphasized under what they identify as type III of self-trust, namely: trusting one's judgment concerning other people, and trusting one's judgment concerning the physical environment in which the agent functions. As to the former, being self-trusting would mean seeing oneself as a trustworthy judge of other people's character and therefore of their trustworthiness (see Baier, 2009, 193). This subtype of self-trust can be autonomy-relevant, sometimes to a lesser and sometimes to a greater degree. As Marina Oshana points out, "autonomy demands trust of both the interpersonal and intrapersonal varieties" (2014, 445). In the medical context, for example, managing our affairs as an autonomous agent might involve "trusting others enough to grant them temporary jurisdiction over what happens to our bodies" (443): in such cases, trusting oneself about who to trust is highly relevant to a person's autonomy. But the relevance of intrapersonal and interpersonal trust is not restricted to the medical context, nor to these extreme situations when—for a time—one is entirely incapable of making decisions about oneself. Rather, the need to experience some sort of support for the development, maintenance, and exercise of one's autonomy competency is a fundamental part of a relationally-autonomous agent's everyday functioning. Thus, from a perspective informed by relational autonomy, trusting one's own judgment about the trustworthiness of people in a position of autonomy-promoting others is of paramount importance for a person's autonomy.

The second sub-type of self-trust is about the "trust in ourselves as [competent] sensors (…), interpreters, and makers of inferences about our environment" (Baier, 2009, 203). Imagine losing your sight, and—as a result—losing trust in your eyes and in what they seem to see (194): according to Sneddon and Meyers, this and other kinds of disabilities and illnesses that affect the way we function within the physical environment (which our bodies are embedded in) "threaten our capacities for running our lives" (Sneddon, 2013, chap. 3, sec. *Autonomy of persons: Self-knowledge,* par. 14), or—in other words—"put autonomy in jeopardy" (Meyers, 2005, 31). Just as changes in our bodily abilities can cause self-distrust and threaten our autonomy, so can the changes in the physical environment itself. Sneddon comments: "The inclusion of environmental factors serves to underline the general way in which cognition can depend on context. While this might hold for our minds in general, it is a particularly important point for the psychology of autonomy, since self-rule concerns, in part, running our lives in the circumstances in which we find ourselves. To some extent individual effort might compensate for environmental changes, but we cannot assume that this will always be possible, and certainly not that it will be easy" (2013, chap. 2, par. 10, see also par. 8). Differently put, autonomous individuals are not only interdependent on one another (social context), they are also—to some extent—dependent for their autonomy on the physical environment in which they function (environmental context).[24]

---

24 This could be viewed as (at least partly) indirect (inter)dependence on other people: urban planners, architects, local governments, etc. For interesting examples on how the way public space is planned can restrict some possibilities or—in contrast—make available some previously restricted possibilities for human choice and behavior, see Gehl (2011, 2010).

In conclusion, the connection between self-trust and autonomy is very close. Like Govier (1993), McLeod and Sherwin (2000), and Benson (2005), I maintain that self-trust is a condition of autonomy,[25] but I also agree with McLeod and Sherwin when they say that "the relation works the other way as well": the more autonomous a person becomes, the more reasons that person has to trust themselves (2000, 277, ftn. 12). In fact, autonomy and self-trust develop alongside one another—each contributing to the development of the other.

Let us observe the relevance of the development and exercise of some autonomy skills to the cultivation of self-trust at a very young age, when the agent has not yet had plenty of reasons to trust themselves and is not yet what we might call "a fully autonomous person." This is what a Montessori teacher and educator, Simone Davies, writes about helping a child develop self-trust regarding the amount of food which is optimal for their body. "We want our children to learn to listen to their bodies to understand when they are full": Davies encourages a parent to serve a small amount of food for a toddler and leave more food in child's sight in case they want to serve themselves some more (2019, 145). She continues, "leave the child in charge (…) They will take as much as they need if we remove our control around food and trust them to listen to their bodies" (145). The child is inspired to trust their own judgment regarding the amount of food which is good for them, and this involves listening to themselves (self-observation), trying to read the physical cues from their body (self-reading), interpreting these cues (self-interpretation), and trying to understand what the cues mean (self-understanding). As a result, the child gains a portion of self-knowledge that serves as the basis of their decision: to stop eating or to continue eating. Thus, the development of self-trust involves becoming better and better (through practice) at exercising such skills as self-observation, self-reading, self-interpreting, self-understanding, and at taking optimum decisions concerning oneself. After a number of decisions taken in this way—a process which involves some experimentation, trial, and error, and thus it also involves critical thinking and the ability to self-correct[26]—the young person begins to perceive themselves as more and more worthy of their own trust, and more and more competent in the field of self-related decision-making. It is imperative to stress the importance

25 For an opposite view that autonomy is the condition of self-trust, see Lehrer (1997, ch. 4, secs. *The Need for Autonomy* and *Autonomy Analysed*).

26 Relevantly, McLeod and Sherwin say that self-trust "develops, at least in part, through inductive reasoning about past successes and failures at using or attempting to use our various abilities" (2000, 265).

of the ability to think critically and the ability to self-correct to the process of developing of self-trust, as they allow to differentiate between self-trust and such attitudes as uncritical and persistent overconfidence or arrogance[27]: the significance of critical thinking in self-trust is underscored, for instance, by Goering (2008; for further discussion, see below), Atkins (2006, 212), or Kukla (2005, 40).

The previous paragraph has steered the discourse in the direction of the relational aspect of self-trust: as shown above, the trust of a parent (or a teacher) in a child's ability to handle a given situation breeds the child's own self-trust. As expressed by Kong, these types of positive messages received in childhood "encourage the type of self-reading and trust in ourselves that is conducive to embodied poise and self-knowledge, thus enabling a more responsive, confident stance to be adopted towards environmental, social forces in relation to our personal identity" (2017, ch. 3, sec. IV, par. 5). In contrast, "exposure to, and internalization of, negative messages in our formative years give cause for us to distrust the absorbed coping of our bodies, our reflective judgment, and ourselves more generally; in turn, greater challenges are encountered in the process of constituting an authentic self" (2017, ch. 3, sec. IV, par. 5).

Some feminist theorists show that self-trust has a relational aspect also in the case of adults, and that this has a bearing on the development and maintenance of autonomy competency. Sara Goering says that "the ability to trust oneself is linked to how others perceive one's capacities and commitments too, both in terms of how other individuals react to our self-trust, and in terms of how social norms shape our attitudes of self-trust" (2008, 15; see also Anderson, 2014, 141–142). Moreover, the ability to trust ourselves often depends on experiencing other people trust us (Goering, 2008, 18). In the context of medical ethics, this means that respecting patients' (sometimes compromised) autonomy is a much more complex task than merely ensuring that their consent is informed; rather, it is about "helping patients develop the skills and confidence to monitor their own health, evaluate their needs, and assess when their trust in themselves or in their health care providers should be questioned" (12). In fact, physicians should help patients develop self-trust—thus, respecting and enhancing patient autonomy—and for that, Goering underscores, physicians themselves have to be trustworthy (12). "Developing self-trust is not a personal odyssey; it requires the support and encouragement of others", trustworthy others, to be precise (19).[28]

---

27 Govier discusses the idea that it is possible to have too much trust in oneself. See Govier, 1993, 115–116.

28 In her paper (2008), Goering applies this relational view of the development of self-trust to the situation of new parents who might have problems to trust themselves and

Complementarily, Goering also writes that "a physician who challenges a patient regarding difficult decisions may also encourage self-trust," provided that this is done in a way which demonstrates the physician's "respect for the patient's abilities to think through the issues and recognize the significance of various consequences" (19).

In a similar vein, Annette Baier says that "we all need others' frank estimates of our perceived character traits, (…) of our faults" (2009, 201), and of our trust or distrust in ourselves (200). Approaching the relationality of self-trust by means of the Humean term "sympathy" (meaning "empathy"), she believes that "we all need others' sympathy with our self-trust (…), if we are to sustain such states" (200). She also upholds that we "sympathize" with others' trust or distrust in us. She gives an example of her driving teacher, who—by trusting Baier to drive safely—was able to show her that she is a competent driver; thus, he gradually transformed her fear and distrust of herself (as a driver) to a state of self-trust (193–194). Baier elaborates on this in the following way: "Good coaches in sports have (…) a meta-skill, the skill of getting others to become skilled, and to have trust in their skills. Their expressed trust in those they train (…) is replicated in the eventual self-trust of their charges" (194). Like Goering, Baier also underscores that people whose judgment we choose to sympathize with concerning our trust in ourselves must be trustworthy (193), because a trustworthy person will not lead us to have false confidence in ourselves: their trust in us will always be "reason-backed" (195). As stressed by McLeod, "[a] supportive environment for good self-trusting and self-distrusting is one in which people receive truthful and constructive feedback about themselves" (2002, 77).

2.2.8. Self-Knowledge and Self-Discovery

In the previous section, I have signaled that self-trust plays an important role in gathering self-knowledge. Producing new pieces of self-knowledge necessitates trust in oneself as the observer and interpreter of one's current responses, while the maintenance of the already existing pool of self-knowledge requires, for instance, trust in one's memory regarding past events and one's past responses to these events.

As to the connection between self-knowledge and autonomy, Meyers affirms that "self-ignorance is one of the principal enemies of autonomy" (2000, 158). In

---

see themselves as an authority on caring for and making appropriate decisions about the health of their newborn baby.

a similar vein, Sneddon states that "the more one knows about one's own nature, the more autonomous a person one will be," and he emphasizes that particularly relevant to the topic of autonomy is the awareness of one's motivations, because without such knowledge one cannot control one's actions (2013, chap. 3, sec. *Autonomy of persons: Self-knowledge,* par. 2). Ideally, a person should be aware of the sources of motivation particular to them, which includes personal values, and the sources of motivations that are typical to human beings as a species: "To acquire this sort of self-knowledge is to learn about the type of thing one is, in contrast to one's individual identity" (chap. 3, sec. *Autonomy of persons: Self-knowledge,* par. 2). Following Meyers (2005), Sneddon says that these general sources of motivation arise from different aspects of the self: thus, a person can be motivated (1) "by explicit, conscious, rational reflection" (this arises from the "self-as-unitary" dimension of the self), (2) by the culture one was raised in ("self-as-social"), (3) by relationships with family, friends, neighbors, etc. ("self-as-relational"), (4) by the subconscious ("self-as-divided"), and finally (5) by one's bodily instincts, reflexes, etc. ("self-as-embodied") (Sneddon, 2013, chap. 3, sec. *Autonomy of persons: Self-knowledge,* pars. 3–14; Meyers, 2005, 29–30). The more knowledge a person accumulates regarding the nature of their motivations, the more capable they are of exercising control over them (chap. 3, sec. *Autonomy of persons: Self-knowledge,* par. 15).

Sneddon favors Meyers' complex and multi-dimensional view of the human self and motivation, because such a view gives access to much more autonomy-relevant self-knowledge than a view based on an assumption that all motivation stems from explicit thought which is accessible to the rational self, called the "self-as-unitary" in Meyers' parlance (Sneddon, 2013, chap. 3, sec. *Autonomy of persons: Self-knowledge,* par. 16). Subscribing to the former view has important implications. The first implication is that "it might well take hard work, other people and principled practices and resources of, for example, psychological inquiry to gain knowledge of the workings of our own minds" (chap. 3, sec. *Autonomy of persons: Self-knowledge,* par. 16). The second implication is that Meyers' multidimensional view allows for self-discovery and, thus, for self-expansion (provided that a person chooses to endorse a newly discovered motivation). In contrast, the implications of the latter view would be that—for a rational agent—attaining self-knowledge is a fairly simple and straightforward task, and that other people are redundant to its accomplishment. Also, the latter view does not allow for self-discovery and self-expansion: if we assume that all motivation derives from explicit thought accessible to the self-as-unitary, then whatever desires and motives appear in a person in a surprising manner should automatically be classified as unwanted intrusion from outside of the self, without the agent having any say in this matter. This sounds like a view that allows for less autonomy than Meyers' view.

The implication of Meyers' view that I want to stress as particularly relevant to the argumentation in this chapter is that relationships with other people play a significant role in attaining self-knowledge. As stressed by Meyers, "self-knowledge should not be identified with introspective revelations" (1989, 179): "instead of pretending that self-knowledge depends exclusively on one's privileged access to a strictly private realm of mental states, people need to solicit and attend to others' impressions and suggestions" (183).

The practical application of the relational approach to self-knowledge of an autonomous agent is well illustrated by Susan J. Brison (1997/2018, sec. *The Self as Narrative*). Brison shows how the selfhood of trauma survivors, whose memory is severely disrupted by traumatic events, defies Locke's (1694/1974) famous definition of the self as a set of continuous memories (Brison, 1997/2018, sec. *The Self as Narrative*). To illustrate this kind of an epistemological crisis, Brison quotes Charlotte Delbo, a Birkenau survivor: "The survivor must undertake to regain his memory, regain what he possessed before: his knowledge, his experience, his childhood memories, his manual dexterity and his intellectual faculties, sensitivity, the capacity to dream, imagine, laugh" (1995, 255). But in order to do that, the survivor of a trauma, needs attentive and compassionate audience that will support the survivor's endeavor to reconstruct their self-knowledge, self-narrative, and ultimately their capacity of being an autonomous agent: "by constructing and telling a narrative of the trauma endured, and with the help of understanding listeners, the survivor begins not only to integrate the traumatic episode into a life with a before and after but also to gain control over the occurrence of intrusive memories" (1997/2018, sec. *The Self as Narrative*; see also sec. *The Autonomous Self*). Brison corroborates her thesis by referring to written testimonies of other survivors, such as Primo Levi or Jonathan Shay, as well as the psychoanalytical work of Dori Laub, all of whom—like Brison—demonstrate that reconnecting with other empathic humans makes the reconstruction of personal identity and continuation of a self after trauma possible (Levi, 1993, 172; Shay, 1994, 188; Laub and Feldman, 1992, 68–70).

Lisa Goldberg—another feminist autonomy theorist—provides examples of how the relational approach to self-knowledge works in practice in her field of expertise: perinatal nursing. Sharing findings from her study of birthing women, she shows that a trusting relationship with a perinatal nurse makes it possible for a woman to discover "the birthing powers embedded within her own body," thus adding a new element to her self-knowledge (2008, 74–75). Even when unexpected complications occur during the birth process, a nurse can foster greater knowledge concerning the birthing woman's embodied self, making it possible for the woman to take ownership of what is happening within her body and autonomously integrate it into her experience and knowledge of the self (77).[29] Goldberg expresses a realization that her study of birthing women and their knowledge of themselves—facilitated by the relationships with perinatal nurses—gives empirical support to Jean-Paul Sartre's existentialist observation about the crucial role of interaction with other people for self-knowledge: "I cannot obtain any truth whatsoever about myself, except through the mediation of another. The other is indispensable to my existence, and equally so to any knowledge I can have of myself" (1946/1973, 45).

2.3. The Argumentative Part: A Critique of the Omnipresence of Advertising

2.3.1. The Omnipresence of Advertising Influencing Autonomy of Choice

As noted by Cunningham (2003), when advertising gets criticized, advertisers often react by saying "if you don't like advertising, don't watch it," implying that we have a choice in this matter (229; see the Ethical Appendix for more details). In this section, I would like to critically examine—in the context of the omnipresence of advertising—whether, indeed, we can always make an autonomous choice not to be exposed to advertising when we do not wish such exposure to be the case. I will do so by referring to the term "captive audience" from the American legal doctrine.

2.3.1.1. The Argument from a Captive Audience

1. *People who are held captive by speech (in certain environments/locations) are unable to act on their choice not to listen to the speech in question in that environment/location: in other words, they cannot make their choice effectual in the production of behavior. These people constitute what the American legal doctrine calls a "captive audience."*

---

29 For instance, one participant in Goldberg's study, Abby, had an encounter with a nurse who took the time to help her fully understand the meaning of an unexpected complication and "situated the facts about her HELLP syndrome in the context of Abby's life": by doing so, Abby says, "the nurse made her situation 'more real' by entailing that she was not jettisoned from her own bodily knowledge" (Goldberg, 2008, 77).

The captive audience doctrine states that a listener qualifies as a captive audience when they are unwilling to receive the speaker's speech, but are "practically helpless to escape" it (Strauss, 1991, 85; quoting *Kovacs v. Cooper* 1949, 336 U.S. 77; see the Legal Appendix for a more detailed discussion): people who constitute a captive audience do not *really* want to be exposed to certain kind of speech (in certain environments/locations), but no practical solution is available to them to act on their choice to avoid exposure.

2. *Being able to make a choice effectual in the production of behavior is an important ingredient of autonomy of choice.*

As stressed by both Meyers and Sneddon, for a choice to count as autonomous it has to be made effectual in the production of behavior (Meyers, 1989, 52; Meyers, 2000, 156; Sneddon, 2013, ch. 2, sec. *Autonomy of choice*, par. 7; see Section 2.2.5 of this chapter). Therefore—as it has also been observed by philosophers who write about oppression—an environment/location which is not conducive to making an agent's choice effectual in the production of behavior causes the degree to which an individual is able to act autonomously to be lower: in short, the agent's autonomy of choice is limited (see, for instance, McLeod, 2002, 112; McLeod, Sherwin, 2000, 260–261; Barclay, 2000, 56; Sherwin, 1998, 26–27).

3a. *The global omnipresence of advertising produces captive audiences in the following manner.*

As illustrated in the previous chapter, one of the manifestations of the global omnipresence of advertising is the advertisers' strategy to place advertising in such types of locations to which a person is in some way temporarily confined. Good examples of locations of this sort are public toilets, airplanes, airports, taxis, cinema auditoriums, jails, or classrooms, to which a person is confined (one way or another) for the duration of a trip, journey, film, arrest, one's daily portion of education, or a visit to the toilet. The advertising strategy of placing advertisements in such places is based on the notion of captive audience, and the advertisers often affirm this in a direct manner. Here is a quote from Richard Deutch, CEO of Wizmark, referring to the agency's trademark audio-visual advertising placed inside the urinals: "Advertising in the bathroom provides the quintessential captive audience. You can't look left. You can't look right. You have to look at the ad and listen to it" (Johnson, 17 Sep 2006). Similarly, in an article entitled "Marketing to a Captive Audience," Jeff Eberlein, ad agency managing partner from Strata-G Communications in Cincinnati, Ohio, uses the term "captive audience" to talk about passengers waiting to board a plane at an airport (Tice, 15 Oct 2009). Sometimes, it is the activists who point out the captive audience element of advertising in a particular location: take, for instance, the film about advertising at schools entitled *Captive Audience: Advertising Invades the Classroom*. In the written materials accompanying the film (meant to be distributed to teachers at schools), the authors say that the film "lays out (…) a practical blueprint for challenging the incredible cynicism of corporate advertisers who see our young people as a captive market demographic" (Media Education Foundation, 4).

All in all, since what the advertisers are exploiting in the case of the captive audience advertising strategy is a person's temporary confinement to a certain location, this advertising strategy constitutes the most conspicuous counterexample to the advertising industry's thesis that a person who does not wish to be exposed to advertising can simply cease to watch it.

Two objections come to mind in response to this. First, that people come to the abovementioned locations willingly, and thus that they are not really held captive in any way. Second, that people *can* in fact get out of the abovementioned locations at any moment, which—again—leads to the conclusion that the term "captive audience" is not really appropriately used in this context.

As to the first objection, it is indeed the case that people typically come to the abovementioned locations willingly. However, they do not come to these locations to watch advertising. If they willingly agree to come to the locations in question, their consent regards performing a particular action in these locations: an action connected with the main purpose of a given location. This is similar to the medico-legal issue of consenting to a particular medical procedure, an important attribute of which is that it has a particular purpose: the attribute of purpose is one of the elements that differentiates one medical procedure from another, and therefore, if a medical procedure with a different purpose (than the purpose of the procedure which was expected and consented to by a patient) were to be performed, it would require obtaining a different, separate consent (see, for instance, Maclean, 2002).

For example, the purpose of a taxi—as a location that a person enters—is to offer transportation from one destination to another. So, when a person uses a taxi, they want to and agree to be transported in a taxi from one destination of their choosing to another destination of their choosing. Wanting and agreeing to commute by a taxi, however, does not imply wanting and agreeing to watch advertisements inside the taxi cab: notice the difference in the attribute of purpose. More generally, the fact that a person has agreed to perform action A in place x does not automatically entail that this person would or should also agree to perform action B the moment they find themselves in place x. The consent for performing each action should be obtained separately.[30]

According to the second objection, people can get out of the abovementioned locations at any moment: they can leave the public toilet, leave the taxi/bus/subway, leave the airport, etc. To this objection, the following answer could be formulated. First of all, it is not really the case that leaving many of such locations is possible at *any* given moment, but it could be said that it is possible to leave a majority of the abovementioned locations at certain moments. More importantly though, the notion of captive audience should not be understood literally (see, for example: Strauss, 1991, 86; Sadurski, 1999, 92; see the Legal Appendix for a more detailed discussion): the American legal doctrine has clearly spoken against adopting an "impossibility" standard, according to which a person could qualify as a captive audience, if and only if it were literally impossible for the audience to escape from unwanted speech. Conceived in such a way, the notion of captive audience would almost never be applicable to reality, as there is nearly always some possibility of avoiding exposure to the message: in an extreme scenario, one could, for instance, become a hermit (see Black, 1953, 968; see the Legal Appendix). Instead, when defining the term "captive audience," the

30 This approach to consent is perhaps most clearly visible in sexual ethics, especially on the level of practical guidelines. As specified on the webpage of Amnesty International, this feature of consent is referred to as it being "specific," which means that "[c]onsenting to one thing (e.g. kissing) does not mean consenting to everything else" (Amnesty). In a similar vein, Rape, Abuse & Incest National Network provides the following practical rule to be followed in order to contribute to the flourishing of consent culture: consent "should happen every time for every type of activity. Consenting to one activity, one time, does not mean someone gives consent for other activities or for the same activity on other occasions" (Rape, Abuse & Incest National Network). On the level of academic discussion, the question that arises is to what extent should a sexual act be dissected: into separate "levels of sexual escalation," each of which would demand a separate consent, or—in a more detailed manner—into separate (sub-)acts, each of which would demand a separate consent (Cowling, 2016). In medical ethics, an akin topic is the so-called "sectionalization" of consent—a concept introduced in *Davis v. Barking, Havering and Brentwood Health Authority* (1993) by Justice McCullough. The questions that arise in connection to this topic are how to decide that a medical procedure is different and separate from another medical procedure—and therefore demanding a separate informed consent from the patient—but also what components of one medical procedure should be treated as demanding a separate informed consent (and why), i.e., to what extent should consent for one medical procedure be "sectionalized" (see, Maclean, 2002).

Supreme Court has adopted a standard of "impracticality": the degree of captivity has to be such that in order to escape from unwanted speech, the unwilling audience would have to employ a very impractical solution, disruptive of their everyday functioning (*Erznoznik v. City of Jacksonville*, 1975, 422 U.S. 205, 209), for example, they would have to leave a means of transport without getting to the desired location (*Lehman v. City of Shaker Heights*, 1974, 418 U.S. 320-01; see Sadurski, 1999, 93), or leave the toilet without using it, or leave the school without having had the chance to participate in the daily lessons. Black's idea of becoming a hermit in order to avoid exposure to commercial speech (1953, 968) would also count as a very impractical solution.

3b. *The local omnipresence of advertising produces captive audiences as well.*

The most obvious sense in which one can be a captive audience to advertisements is that one is somehow (though not literally, as discussed above) stuck in a certain place where a particular advertisement is situated; it is this sense of the term "captive audience" that I have referred to in point 3a. Nevertheless, I believe that there is also another sense in which one can be a captive audience to advertisements: a person can be a captive audience because the amount of advertising messages in that person's immediate surroundings is such that turning away from one advertising message only leads to being exposed to another. As discussed in the previous chapter, this would constitute the case of the more local manifestation of the omnipresence of advertising, i.e., omnipresence limited to a certain area, like a subway station.

A popular subway station in Warsaw, Poland—Świętokrzyska—would be a good example of this new sense of the term "captive audience": a person standing on the platform is exposed to around thirty six advertising billboards on the walls of the station (plus some LCD screens): averting one's eyes[31]—or walking away—from one billboard only leads to exposition to other billboards on this station, and thus—effectively—the passenger is held captive by advertising that pervades the walls of this subway station.

31 I am purposely using the expression "avert one's eyes," which is typically used in the American captive audience doctrine. See, for example: (1) Justice Brennan's Brennan's dissenting voice, as well as the remark expressed by one of the commentators who agreed with Justice Brennan by saying that "even though individuals were not 'free' to leave the bus, they could still avert their eyes and look elsewhere" *Lehman v. City of Shaker Heights*, 418 U.S. 320-01 (1974), discussed in Sadurski, 1999, 93; or (2) *Bolger v. Youngs Drug Products Corp.*, 463 U.S. 60 (1983), quoted in Strauss 1991, 91. For details of those cases, see the Legal Appendix.

The following objection to this application of the term "captive audience" could be formulated: we cannot speak of being a captive audience in such situations, because the addressee of the advertising messages is never held captive by any one particular advertising message; therefore, that person is free to pass by and look the other way. However, the crucial point to underscore in response to this objection is that even if in such situations one is not a captive audience to one particular advertisement *token*, one is nevertheless a captive audience to advertising as *type*, i.e., to advertising communication in its entirety in that area. One is no longer free to avert one's eyes and look the other way, because—in relation to all advertising in that area—there is no "other way." Differently put, in ad-laden surroundings, one's mind is forced to process the advertising communication, even if one's mind is not forced to process any one particular advertising message. As emphasized by Armand Mattelart, the author of *Advertising International: The Privatisation of Public Space*: "(…) many debates on the 'effects of advertising' on society are affected by a serious flaw. They remain too close to the individual advertisement (…), while our society is immersed in advertising as the dominant mode of communication" (1991, 214).

As an extension of the above-mentioned objection, it could also be said that one is not really a captive audience if one can close one's eyes, or look at one's shoes or the ceiling, while waiting for the subway to come. This is reminiscent of the objection discussed in point 3a, and it could be tackled in a similar way by appealing to the impracticality standard underlying the notion of captive audience. Although it is *possible* to avoid eye contact with the surrounding advertisements by closing one's eyes or by looking at one's shoes or ceiling, while waiting for the subway to come, all of these actions seem to be forced, uncomfortable, and therefore highly *impractical* solutions (in addition, as shown in Chapter 1, the floor or the ceiling may also be covered in advertisements). The ability to visually explore one's immediate surroundings and to do so primarily by looking ahead—as this keeps the head in the most physiologically neutral position—is a non-negligible part of everyday comfort of functioning and coping for the majority of human beings. Within urban planning theory, Jan Gehl points out that "Homo sapiens are a linear, frontal, horizontally oriented upright mammal" (2010, Chapter 2, Section 2.1) and he makes a normative claim that "good city quality at eye level should be considered a basic human right wherever people go in cities" (Chapter 4, Section 4.1; see also Czyński, Ostrowski, 2011, 220–221). In the philosophical tradition, it was Samuel Todes (2001) who—building upon Merleau-Ponty's account of the lived body[32]—underscored the importance of

32 In the words of Hubert Dreyfus, "Todes goes beyond Merleau-Ponty in showing how

"our capacity for effective orientation toward objects in our horizontal field of experience in the world" (124).[33] According to Todes, while the vertical field is connected with the upright posture and good balance of the human body, which are the conditions of effective action in the horizontal field, it is within the horizontal field that the body effectuates action, perceives and handles circumstantial objects, experiences its needs in connection with its surroundings, and experiences the world in general (124–126). In the words of Jasper van Buuren, "in our everyday lives, we are *primarily* concerned with the things surrounding us in the horizontal plane" (2018, 274).[34] Thus, being forced to avoid visual exploration of one's surroundings at eye level seems to be a highly impractical solution, disruptive of everyday functioning and coping of any human being.

Similarly, leaving the subway station, when one is just about to use the subway in order to commute, would also be highly impractical. A subway station is a particularly challenging example because—according to the American legal doctrine—it is much more controversial, as a place that could produce a captive audience, than a means of transport itself (a subway, a plane, a taxi, a bus). In contrast with the 1974 verdict of the Supreme Court, which stated that bus passengers are a captive audience to the posters inside a bus (*Lehman v. City of Shaker Heights*, 1974, 418 U.S. 320-01), in a different case that did not reach the Supreme Court, the court declared that the passengers exposed to advertisements on the subway station walls, passways, and platforms should not be seen as a captive audience (*Penthouse International, Ltd. v. Koch,* 1984, S.D.N.Y., 599 F. Supp. 1338, 1347–1349; Strauss, 1991, 97, ftn 50). Some American legal scholars see this contrast as showing a lack of consistency within the captive audience doctrine: the presence of passengers both in a bus and at a subway station is driven by a similar necessity, and "the same ability to turn the eyes from the offensive message exists" (Strauss, 1991, 97, ftn 50). The difference is that—at least at certain times of the day—the subway station users seem to have more

---

our world-disclosing perceptual experience is structured by the structure of our bodies. Merleau-Ponty never tells us what our bodies are actually like and how their structure affects our experience. Todes points out that our body has a front/back and up/down orientation. It moves forward more easily than backward, and can successfully cope only with what is in front of it" (2007, 1147, ftn 52).

33 Todes refers to this capacity as "poise" (2001, 124).

34 Van Buuren says this as a part of a counterargument against Todes' statement that the vertical field has "priority" over the horizontal field (Todes, 2001, 124). However, this particular sentence of van Buuren does not really conflict with Todes' own view of the horizontal field, which he deems to be the primary realm of human experience.

possibility of moving around the station and thus more opportunity to avert their eyes from a particular message (Strauss, 1991, 97, ftn 50). By the same token, students have more possibility of moving around an entire school building than they have when confined to a single classroom. According to this logic, placing advertisements within the school building, but not in the classrooms, would not count as a captive audience case.

However, the new perspective that I offer, according to which one can be held captive by advertising as type (present in a given area through multiple advertising tokens), helps to justify why the subway station users—or users of other spacious locations, like an entire school building—could also, in certain circumstances, be classified as a captive audience despite the fact that they can move around more than a person sitting in a taxi, a plane, a bus, a subway wagon, or a classroom. I claim that being able to move around more and thus not being forced to be exposed to *one* particular message does not automatically mean that one cannot be classified as a captive audience. More spacious locations, within which people can move around quite freely and avoid exposure to *one* particular message, can produce captive audiences, when these audiences are subjected to the (local kind of) omnipresence of advertising.

4. *To conclude, the omnipresence of advertising, both the global and the local kind, tends to produce captive audiences and this results in people (who constitute these captive audiences) enjoying less autonomy of choice.*

The global kind of omnipresence of advertising manifests, i.a., in advertisements being placed in such types of locations to which a person is in some way temporarily confined (like public toilets, airplanes, airports, taxis, cinema auditoriums, jails, or schools). In small-scale locations, this results in a person being held captive by a particular *token* of advertising. In more spacious locations, this is typically not the case: provided the location is not very crowded, a person can move around more and, thus, is not forced to be exposed to one particular message. However, when in these more spacious locations the local omnipresence of advertising is also the case, an agent can be said to be held captive by advertising as *type*, i.e., moving around the more spacious location enables the agent to escape exposure to a particular advertising token, but it does not make possible escaping exposure to advertising as type—moving away from one token only leads to exposure to another token.

Coming back to premise 2, an agent can either have a desire to watch or not to watch advertising in the above-mentioned, temporarily confining locations, and that agent can either endorse or not endorse that desire. The options are as follows: (1) the agent wants to watch advertising in these locations and endorses that desire (for example, the agent is a shopping vlogger, who likes exposure to commercial advertising and considers it beneficial to the development of their career); (2) the agent wants not to watch advertising in these locations and endorses that desire (for example, the agent is aware of the system of valuing behind the consumerist culture and feels that it does not align with their preferred system of valuing: perceiving commercial advertising as a direct manifestation of the consumerist culture, the agent wants to avoid being constantly exposed to it); (3) the agent wants to watch advertising in these locations but does not endorse that desire (for example, the advertisements are a tempting distraction, but the agent knows that whenever they engage in watching advertisements, this results in a general loss of concentration which is detrimental to the agent's intellectual performance); (4) the agent wants not to watch advertising in these locations but does not endorse that desire (for example, the agent generally dislikes watching advertising, but needs to watch it in some amount for a research project). What is problematic is that only decisions (to watch advertising) that result from options 1 and 4 can be made effectual in producing behavior, because what the agent *really* wants coincides with the forced exposure to advertising. Decisions (not to watch advertising) that stem from options 2 and 3, on the other hand, cannot be acted on since not being exposed to advertising in these locations is not an option which is available to the agent who, according to the Supreme Court's standard of impracticality, constitutes a captive audience. Because making a choice effectual in producing behavior is an important ingredient of considering the choice to be autonomous (as stated in premise 2), an agent is blocked from making an autonomous choice not to watch advertising in the above-mentioned, temporarily confining locations. Consequently, the tendency of the omnipresence of advertising to produce captive audiences leads to a lesser degree of autonomy of choice of contemporary individuals.

Reaching such a conclusion is possible due to the application of the standard of impracticality, recommended by the Supreme Court as realistic (as already mentioned, the standard of impossibility would almost never be applicable to reality). Thus, the existence of a highly impractical solution (such as not going to school, not using the public toilet, leaving the airport, leaving the taxi/bus/subway that one was going to use in order to commute) does not entail that the agent's autonomy of choice has not been negatively impacted by the forced exposure to advertising resulting from the omnipresence of advertising.

2.3.2. The Omnipresence of Advertising Influencing the Development, Maintenance, and Exercise of Autonomy Competence

The two arguments presented in this section will focus on the development, maintenance, and exercise of autonomy competence, and how these are impacted by the omnipresence of advertising. When autonomy competence of an individual is in bad shape, this will affect both autonomy of choice and autonomy of persons, i.e., the individual will be less equipped to make any autonomous choice, and less equipped to make autonomous choices about themselves to express the kind of person they want to be.

2.3.2.1. The Argument from Hindering Critical Reasoning

1. *Critical reasoning is one of the autonomy skills that are essential to the development, maintenance, and exercise of autonomy competency.*

The development, maintenance, and exercise of autonomy competency requires that we remain open to critical interrogation—from ourselves and others—regarding our decisions, attitudes, commitments, and values we hold dear.

In the words of Kukla, exercising autonomy competency conscientiously means that we have "enough critical skills and distance from our commitments to give us the *capacity* to question and assess them": Kukla also mentions that it is this sort of critical attitude that allows us to trust our own judgment (2005, 40, emphasis in original). As discussed in Section 2.2.7, developing self-trust requires being skilled at critical reasoning: it is through trying to make optimum decisions concerning oneself, critically examining one's performance (as well as critically examining the input from other people concerning one's performance), and then self-correcting that a person becomes more and more worthy of their own trust as an agent that can make autonomous choices and shape their own identity. As Section 2.2.7 further elucidates, it is the well-developed skill of critical reasoning that makes it possible for the agent to adroitly assess the trustworthiness of others, which—given the relational nature of autonomy—is highly relevant to the development, maintenance, and exercise of autonomy competency.

That being open to critical scrutiny is crucial for the development, maintenance, and exercise of autonomy competency—and entails being able to articulate and critically assess the reasons behind our decisions, attitudes, commitments, and values we hold dear—has been stressed, for instance, by Benson

(2005), Meyers (1989, 2005), Westlund (2009), Goering (2008), or Atkins (2006). As mentioned in Section 2.2.6, for the assimilation of social norms, values, and attitudes to be classified as self-shaping, and not an imposition, a person needs to be able to critically examine these norms and values. It is noteworthy that a lower ability to critically reflect on the social norms, values, and attitudes that are assimilated into a person's identity (as well as on desires and thoughts that emerge in the process of self-discovery) implies less knowledge about the kind of person one is and wants to be. Less self-knowledge, on the other hand—as discussed in Section 2.2.8—translates into a lower degree of autonomy competency.

2. *The global omnipresence of advertising negatively affects the cultivation of the critical reasoning skill.*

In Chapter 1 of this book, the intrusive presence of advertising has been illustrated with descriptions of such everyday experiences as learning at school, working, relaxing in a park, watching a sports event, reading a book, listening to a song, playing a videogame, watching a film, commuting by means of public transport. In addition, some more rare and special life experiences like giving birth at a hospital, starting to breastfeed a baby, or naming a newborn have been shown to be intruded upon by advertising as well. If everyday reality—with its everyday spaces and events—is permeated with advertising, it becomes increasingly difficult to mentally distance oneself from advertising, its persuasive pressure, and the commercial values it embodies. The underlying psychological mechanism at work here would be that of chronic exposure to a certain type of stimuli leading to habituation and desensitization (e.g. Mrug et al., 2016; Brockmyer, 2012; American Academy of Pediatrics, 2009; Bartholow et al., 2006; Alhadeff, 2015). As Wolfgang Welsch famously commented on the overwhelming presence of advertising stimuli in human environment, "our perception (*aisthesis*) also needs zones of interruption, of alterity and quiet" (1997, 121) because—as underscored in Maria Gołębiewska's interpretation of Welsch—without such interruptions in the influx of stimuli, we can no longer exercise our sensitivity to sensations, and that sensitivity is what we need to be able to perceive, get to know the world, and make judgments (Gołębiewska, 2003, 310).

For instance, protecting certain outdoor public spaces, like the municipal green areas, as sanctuaries from advertising and its persuasive pressure means that people have an opportunity—within the public realm—to pause and reflect critically both on themselves and the world around them. Spence and Van Heekeren comment on the human need for mental retreat from advertising in such spaces: "we need these spaces where we can be ourselves and be by ourselves without being told by advertising messages what to desire or what to eat, drink, drive, wear, or otherwise consume, or aspire to acquire" (2005, 92). As stated by a journalist commenting on advertising invading public parks, "parks are retreats from our urban milieu and the relentless drumbeat of commerce" (Butler, 23 Aug 2011; see Chapter 1 of this book). Exemplary of this way of thinking was Peter Zumthor's *The Serpentine Pavilion* (2011)—a project that catalyzed a London green area's potential to serve as such a retreat, in which busy Londoners could pause, observe, contemplate, reflect, be themselves in the present moment.

Even more emblematic, as a type of space that should actively "create some distance from a popular culture steeped in the ethos of consumerism," are schools (Sandel, 2013, 200): without actively creating this distance, schools leave young people at the mercy of advertisers, and for advertisers a classroom is a place where children can be introduced to new consumer products and where critical reflection about these products and about the desire to possess them should be discouraged (200–201). In Chapter 1, I have quoted an activist saying that "schools exist to teach children to read, write, add and think, not to shop. So what are we teaching them with big corporate ads on civic institutions?" (Pennington, 18 Oct 2004); I have also discussed an organized form of protest against advertising in schools called *Campaign for a Commercial-Free Childhood*, which promotes the ideal of schools as ad-free types of space and the ideal of childhood as a stage of life that should be under special protection from advertising and the resulting commercialization. Moreover, I have quoted Wright saying that "public schools should honor, express, and embody our democratic values and (…) [they] should, for the sake of those democratic values, retain some critical distance and detachment from all cultural institutions and forces only imperfectly embodying those values" (1997, 10). Sandel comments that creating distance from advertising enables the schools to "cultivate citizens (…), capable of thinking critically about the world around them" (2013, 200). That schools should be held accountable for cultivating critical thinking and "the development of democratic character" is stressed by Nel Noddings (2005, Introduction, par. 22; see also 2012). The philosopher also stresses that schools are a perfect place for young people to train "ad-resistance" and thus to learn how to care for themselves by not conforming uncritically to the norms dictated by advertising, both in terms of what to buy and who to be: for Noddings, practicing ad-resistance is not only an exercise in critical thinking, but also in self-understanding, and thus becoming more grounded in being one's own person (2005, ch. 6, par. 8, 17; see also ch. 9, par. 40, ch. 10, par. 9).

Hospitals are another type of space which should actively create distance from advertising, not only to allow their patients to rest, but also to allow them to think critically. If patients are to decide autonomously about their wellbeing—which is one of the basic tenets of medical ethics—their critical thinking skills should be protected and fostered by the medical personnel on whom this wellbeing depends (see, for instance, Goering 2008; Atkins 2006; Kukla, 2005). Instead, advertisers have already been allowed to exert persuasive pressure on patients in hospitals and to exploit both the trust that patients need to have in the medical personnel, as well as the vulnerable position of patients during a stay at a hospital (see Section 1.3.4 of Chapter 1 of this book).

Similarly, all spaces connected with law enforcement should embody the law's critical distance from advertising and commercial values, thus demonstrating that the law is closely linked with the ability to reason critically: the ability of the law enforcement personnel to reason critically when applying the law, and the ability of citizens to reason critically when obeying the law. Provided that a person is to obey the law as an autonomous agent, this person should be able to critically assess their own performance, to critically assess the feedback from the law enforcement officers, and to be able to self-correct on the basis of these assessments. Common intuitions seem to corroborate the need for the law enforcement (with its spaces) to create distance from advertising. Here is a reminder of some more relevant quotes from Chapter 1 (Sections 1.3.1 and 1.3.2): I) an attorney-at-law commenting on advertising in jails, saying "it strikes me as inserting a commercial aspect into something when I don't feel there is any place for it" (Watson, Feb. 2013, 41); II) a professor at Temple University commenting on advertising being integrated into the work of police force, stating that "American society has really gone beyond the pale in turning every part of the environment into ad space. There should be some things that are off limits" (Wood, 3 Oct 2002); III) a police officer—quoted by Sandel—saying that advertising on police cars has "been forbidden territory until recently. Now everything is up for grabs" (Sandel, 2013, 195).

As illustrated in Chapter 1, all of the above-mentioned types of space, which are important for the cultivation of the critical reasoning skill, no longer have the status of being off-limits to advertising due to the gradual elimination of ad-free types of space (and events).

3. *To conclude, by having a detrimental effect on the cultivation of the critical reasoning skill, the global omnipresence of advertising has a detrimental effect on the development, maintenance, and exercise of autonomy competency.*

The skill of critical reasoning plays an important role in the development, maintenance, and exercise of such constitutive elements of autonomy competency as self-trust, self-knowledge, and self-shaping. In addition, the level of proficiency in critical reasoning influences how apt a person is at using other autonomy skills like sensitivity to others' feedback and being able to self-correct. Therefore, the cultivation of the critical reasoning skill should be protected and fostered, both in children, as well as in adults. For that, people need to have access to types of space (and events) that retain critical distance from advertising. Spaces (and events) of this kind enable people to experience themselves, their lives, and their systems of valuing as maintaining a certain critical distance from advertising and the commercial values it embodies and promotes. Conversely, when such sanctuaries (or "zones of interruption") are being eliminated as a result of the omnipresence of advertising, the critical reasoning skill has fewer opportunities of being cultivated—and the autonomy competency, of being kept in good shape.

Parenthetically, it could be said that a certain similarity can be detected between my argumentation presented here and that of Spence and Van Heekeren, who talk about "collective 'sacred spaces'" that should be off-limits to advertising (Spence and Van Heekeren, 2005, 93–94; see the arguments summarized in Sections 5.3.1.3, 5.3.1.4, 5.3.1.6 of the Ethical Appendix). And indeed, prescriptively, I am going in a similar direction. An important difference between my argumentation and Spence/Van Heekeren's argumentation is that I draw attention to different consequences of the gradual disappearance of ad-free types of space and events: while the two academics point to the detrimental effect it has on human well-being, I argue that it has a negative impact on autonomy (through the negative impact on the critical reasoning skill). Although in their book Spence and Van Heekeren do mention "freedom of choice" being violated by certain forms of advertising, they do so in a different argument (2005, 90–91; see the argument summarized in Section 5.3.1.1 of the Ethical Appendix) which is very remote in its logic from my approach. Also, I emphasize autonomy of persons, not autonomy of choice.

The emphasis on autonomy of persons is what makes my argument more akin to Sneddon's (2013, ch. 8, sec. *Advertising…*, pars. 12–22; see Section 5.3.3.1 of the Ethical Appendix for an outline of the argument). However, this emphasis is the only significant similarity. Otherwise, the two arguments are different: while Sneddon talks about the growing amount of commercial advertising that promotes one overarching way of living to the detriment of the ability to self-shape, I write about the global omnipresence of advertising changing the status—from ad-free to no longer ad-free—of such types of space (and events) which should retain critical distance from advertising and, as such, are important to the cultivation of the critical reasoning skill. Importantly, Sneddon does not use the term "omnipresence of advertising." Instead, he interchangeably uses two much broader terms—"oceans of information" and "sea of information"—to denote a much broader phenomenon, and he sees commercial advertising as one of the manifestations of this phenomenon (i.e., the "sea" of all information in general). Thus, what he perceives as problematic for autonomy of persons is simply the increasing *amount* of commercial advertising in people's everyday lives, as a particularly abundant source of the influx of information. In contrast, I focus specifically on commercial advertising, and in the two-pronged definition of the omnipresence of advertising, I go beyond discussing the growing quantity of commercial advertising. In the argument above, I concentrate on the threat to autonomy of persons caused by the *global* omnipresence of advertising, which consists in the gradual disappearance of ad-free types of space and events: this approach to critiquing the pervasiveness of advertising is entirely different from the one presented by Sneddon. Finally, at the centre of my argument lies one particular autonomy skill: the critical thinking skill. Sneddon, on the other hand, speaks more generally about the reflection and decision-making process involved in self-shaping.

Finally, it is worth noting that the focus of my argument on the critical thinking skill has a certain resonance with the reflections of such Frankfurt School philosophers as Erich Fromm. Fromm points out that both political propaganda and commercial advertising have a highly negative impact on the development and maintenance of the critical thinking skill (1976/2008, 152–153), and he also says that "this assault on reason and the sense of reality pursues the individual everywhere and daily at any time: during many hours of watching television, or when driving on a highway, or in the political propaganda of candidates, and so on" (153). The quote can be interpreted as suggesting that Fromm appears to notice the *everywhereness* of advertising. However, he seems oblivious to the idea that the everywhereness in itself might pose a threat to critical reasoning (because certain kinds of space are of particular importance to the development, maintenance, and exercise of the critical thinking skill). Instead, what Fromm identifies as problematic in both commercial and political advertising are the brainwashing methods they apply (152–153). Therefore, the solution he proposes is that "*all brainwashing methods in industrial and political advertising must be prohibited*" (152, italics in original). Fromm's underscoring of the brainwashing methods stands in sharp contrast to this book's emphasis on the omnipresence of advertising in itself and to my argument's conclusion that commercial advertising needs to be banned from the kinds of space that are significant to the development, maintenance, and exercise of the critical thinking skill. Notice that the argument I flesh out would still apply even if the brainwashing methods were obsolete. Also, it is worth stressing that Fromm focuses equally on political and commercial advertising, while my argument is restricted to commercial advertising only. As will be discussed in Chapter 3, the fact that this book talks about the omnipresence of *commercial* advertising (and not about the omnipresence of noncommercial advertising or any other noncommercial messages) is meaningful.

In a like vein, certain similarities can be detected between my line of reasoning and that of Herbert Marcuse, another Frankfurt School philosopher. Most importantly, we both discuss the deterioration of the critical thinking skill due to a lack of distance and resistance towards commercial values or "the order of business," as Marcuse calls it (1964/2007, 62–64). This lack of distance and resistance manifests as the Marcusian one-dimensionality of the contemporary reality, which is the main theme of his book *One-Dimensional Man: Studies in the Ideology of Advanced Industrial Society*. Like Marcuse, I also discuss the importance of keeping commercial and noncommercial dimensions of reality distinct (see in particular Chapter 3 of this book). However, Marcuse's analysis focuses on ideology. He identifies the noncommercial realm mainly with the higher culture (1964/2007, 59–64) and the working class (35), and he recommends that these should remain uncontaminated by and antagonistic to the commercial values. In contrast, my analysis focuses on spatiality. As it has been made visible in the argument above, and will be stressed further in the next argument and in Chapter 3, it is certain types of space that I believe should be kept unpolluted by the presence of commercial advertising, and thus by commercial values. Also, it seems that my understanding of what constitutes the noncommercial realm is broader: the types of space I talk about in the argument from hindering critical reasoning, as well as in the next argument and in Chapter 3, are not restricted to those connected with the higher culture or with the life of the working class.

2.3.2.2. The Argument from Non-Benign Objectification and the Erosion of Trust

1. *In order to develop, maintain, and exercise autonomy competency (including one's ability to trust oneself), one needs others whom one can trust to support and promote one's autonomy, i.e., autonomy-promoting trustworthy others.*[35]

35 As will become visible in this premise, I focus on such kind of autonomy-promoting relationships in which trustworthy autonomy-promoting others are supportive of a person's autonomy (and self-trust) in a rather intentional and conscious way. However, Meyers draws attention to the fact that it is possible for a person to feel that their autonomy is enhanced through interaction with others, without the others' intentional, conscious effort in this respect (2005, 33): the word "enhancement" seems to suit this

As adroitly put by Atkins—who interprets Meyers' theory and applies it to the healthcare context—to become more competent in critical self-reading, self-correcting, gaining genuine self-knowledge, and ultimately to become more self-trusting, self-directing, and "authentic," we need "the critical involvement of other people (…) in conversation with whom we test out our theories and beliefs about ourselves, learn things about ourselves and are forced to confront things about ourselves" (Atkins, 2006, 212). However, the autonomy-fostering dialogue of this sort requires a *trusting* relationship between a person whose autonomy is being promoted and the autonomy-promoting others (214).

In a similar vein, Goldberg talks about a trustworthy other mediating and promoting a person's ability to interpret her own experiences and make them appear "more real" (2008, 81, 77), to discover her own embodied potential (75), to feel self-trusting and integral within her own body (74, 77, 79–800, and consequently to expand her embodied self-knowledge[36] (75, 77; see also Goldberg, 2003, 585–587). This kind of a relationship offers a person "an opportunity to enact her agency and self-direction" (Goldberg, 2003, 585).

As already described in Section 2.2.6, a strikingly similar stance to that of Atkins and Goldberg, portraying trustworthiness of the autonomy-promoting other as a precondition to nurturing another person's skills connected with the development of the autonomy competency (including the cultivation of self-trust) is presented by Goering (2008, 12, 15, 18). Goering, in turn, admits to being inspired in her views by Kukla (2005) and McLeod (2002).

In *Self-Trust and Reproductive Autonomy*, McLeod states that "other people and the norms of society can have a profound effect on whether we can trust ourselves. By recognizing that fact moreover we can fully appreciate how health care providers can be morally obligated to respect patient self-trust as a part of their duty to respect patient autonomy" (2002, 56). To be exact, health care providers should "respect and promote the trust of patients in their ability to further their own goals and values, and to determine what those goals and values should be" (133). McLeod elaborates that a vital part of fulfilling the duty to preserve and

kind of autonomy-promotion well, while the word "support" is better suited to describe the conscious and intentional promotion of autonomy discussed in this argument.

36 For interesting research on "embodied identity," in which it is the physiotherapist who can act as "the important other" and help develop higher embodied self-awareness, integrity within oneself, self-trust, self-knowledge, and therefore empowers a person by making them experience an "increased ability to act," see Gyllensten et al. (2010, 444).

promote patient self-trust—and consequently to preserve and promote patient autonomy—is to create a bond of trust with the patient (6, 148–149).

Complementarily, Kukla adds that establishing a trusting relationship with a patient and making room for patient self-trust enables the patient to defer to trustworthy expert authority on certain decisions and yet remain autonomous, provided that the patient (a) trusts her own judgment regarding the deference, and (b) is able to "take a critical, committed stance on her own trust and deference" (2005, 40). Importantly, in Kukla's view, clinicians' obligation to respect and foster patient autonomy entails a responsibility for cultivating patients' critical skills, especially their "critical engagement with their own health care practices" (40), but also—in the words of Goering who interprets Kukla's theory—their critical assessment of their self-trust and the trust they place in their health care providers: "To do this successfully, physicians must be trustworthy, as well as helping their patients to develop self-trust" (Goering, 2008, 12).

2. *A relationship of trust between a person whose autonomy (including their ability to trust themselves) is being promoted and the trustworthy autonomy-promoting other entails that the latter does not objectify the former in a non-benign way.*

The trust between a person whose autonomy and self-trust are being promoted and the autonomy-promoting other constitutes a particular variety of trust. Thus, it might somewhat differ from other varieties of trust and display certain distinctive features of its own. For the purpose of this argument, I wish to stress one particular feature of trust between a trustworthy autonomy-promoting other and a person whose autonomy and self-trust are being promoted. In all the above-mentioned accounts, this particular variety of trust seems incompatible with treating the person whose autonomy and self-trust ought to be supported as an object (Atkins, 2006, 213–214; Goldberg, 2008, 78–79; Goering, 2008, 16–17; McLeod, 2002, 3–4, 120, 154, 157–159; Kukla, 2005, 42–43). In turn, when the individual in a position of the autonomy-promoting other objectifies a person whose autonomy and self-trust are in need of assistance, the relationship of trust is either precluded or broken (see, in particular, McLeod, 2002, 3–4, 148, 154, 157–159; Goldberg, 2008, 78–79).

However, it must be noted here that, in "Objectification" (1996), Martha Nussbaum gives a counterexample to the thesis that *any* objectification of the person in need of autonomy assistance by the person in a position of the autonomy-promoting other *must* lead to the relationship of trust being precluded or broken: this counterexample shows the need for more nuance and clarity regarding this topic. Nussbaum discusses a literary example of an intimate relationship between Constance Chatterley and Olivier Mellors from D.H. Lawrence's novel: even though Mellors objectifies Lady Chatterley as his sexual partner, he is a trustworthy autonomy-promoting other, whose attitude genuinely enhances Constance's autonomy competency. Why is objectification in this case, as Nussbaum calls it, "benign"?

First, in an analysis of objectification, it matters what features of objectification are displayed (Nussbaum, 1995, 257). Nussbaum lists seven possible features of objectification: (1) *instrumentality*, (2) *denial of autonomy*, (3) *inertness*, (4) *fungibility*, (5) *violability*, (6) *ownership*, (7) *denial of subjectivity*. In her conclusions, Nussbaum confirms an important insight of Kant (1924/1997),[37] as well as that of Catharine MacKinnon (1987, 1989) and Andrea Dworkin (1974, 1987): namely, that out of all these features, "instrumental treatment of human beings, the treatment of human beings as tools of the purposes of another, is always morally problematic; if it does not take place in a larger context of regard for humanity, it is a central form of the morally objectionable" (Nussbaum, 1995, 289). Thus, the presence of instrumentality—unmitigated by regard for humanity in a larger context—will always point to a non-benign form of objectification. In contrast, none of the other features are always morally objectionable (290), and therefore their presence does not automatically point to a non-benign form of objectification. Thus, the analysis of whether a given cluster of objectification features constitutes a benign or non-benign form of objectification has to take into account the context, because "in the matter of objectification, context is everything" (271).

Coming back to Nussbaum's counterexample, Mellors' objectification of Lady Chatterley as his sexual partner is benign due to the following reasons. First, it displays no trace of instrumentalization (275): without a doubt, Mellors sees Constance Chatterley as an end in itself (277–278). Second, the objectification that happens between the two characters in the novel is "symmetrical and mutual" (275), i.e., Lady Chatterley sexually objectifies Mellors as well. It is also important that both lovers voice consent to being objectified: feeling safe due to mutual respect and concern for each other makes the characters trust one another enough to willingly put themselves in a vulnerable position of surrender of one's autonomy, agency, and subjectivity (275–276). Moreover, as Nussbaum points out, the objectification happens "in a context of (…) rough social equality" (275), i.e., the social power of both characters is roughly comparable (ftn 42).

37 As adroitly argued by Barbara Herman, the core notion of objectification is Kantian. See Herman (1993, 55).

Interestingly, Nussbaum stresses that the kind of objectification that takes place between Mellors and Lady Chatterley is not only benign, but actually constitutes a profoundly positive influence on the autonomy competency of Lady Chatterley: "Lawrence shows how a kind of sexual objectification (…) can be a vehicle of autonomy and self-expression for women, how the very surrender of autonomy in a certain sort of sex act can free energies that can be used to make the self whole and full" (277).

Faced with Nussbaum's counterexample, I do not wish to claim that *any* objectification of the person in need of autonomy assistance by the person in a position of the autonomy-promoting other *necessarily* leads to trust in this kind of relationship being precluded or broken. Rather, for the purpose of this argument, I uphold that it is the non-benign sort of objectification—i.e., non-consensual, non-mutual, lacking the foundation of respect, including instrumental treatment of the person in need of autonomy support, in the context of social inequality[38]—that is destructive of the trustworthiness of the person in a position of the autonomy-promoting other, and therefore destructive of trust in the domain of autonomy-promotion.

To annotate, I also do not wish to uphold a stronger claim that all possible varieties of trust require the absence of non-benign objectification in order to endure: there might be varieties of trust that may survive the truster being objectified by the trustworthy other in a non-benign way.[39] In the analysis that follows I will focus only on the variety of trust which is required between an autonomy-promoting other and a person whose autonomy and self-trust are being promoted, and I will elucidate what features of objectification manifest when the global omnipresence of advertising exerts an influence on a relationship of this kind.

3. *The global omnipresence of advertising erodes relationships of trust necessary for developing, maintaining, and exercising autonomy competency: it undermines*

38 It appears that, according to Nussbaum, to be classified as non-benign, objectification may display only some of these characteristics, not necessarily all of them. This is visible when she discusses non-benign—and yet seemingly consensual—objectification from James Hankinson's novel (1989, written under the pseudonym Lawrence St. Clair; see Nussbaum, 1995, 280).

39 In fact, Nussbaum gives a literary example from James Hankinson's novel (1989, written under the pseudonym Lawrence St. Clair), in which a certain variety of trust—i.e., trust restricted to the domain of sadomasochistic sexual acts—may be preserved despite the presence of non-benign objectification (Nussbaum, 1995, 280).

the trustworthiness of autonomy-promoting others by encouraging non-benign objectification.

By gradually eliminating types of spaces and events that are ad-free, the global omnipresence of advertising seems to be gradually eliminating types of relationships that are ad-free, and therefore free from the influence of commercial values that advertising promotes and embodies. To elucidate, what is meant by the gradual elimination of ad-free types of relationships here is the loss of types of relationships that would be free from an underlying agenda of brand-expression, meant to generate brand recognition, brand loyalty, and eventually brand revenue.

One example of a type of relationship which is no longer ad-free is the student-teacher relationship: in Chapter 1, I have shown how teachers were supposed to use the so-called “sponsored educational materials,” manufactured by companies, in order to make children remember the names of the brands (see Sandel, 2013, 197); I have also quoted a psychologist from Harvard commenting on advertising placed on test sheets in schools, stating that “it crosses a line (…) When teachers start becoming pitchmen for products, children suffer and their education suffers as well” (Bonner, 25 Mar 2009).

Teachers play an important role in developing young people’s autonomy competency: Meyers, for instance, suggests that teachers should instruct students “about how common informal reasoning practices can lead to a serious error” and how students can “monitor their own reflection” to reduce the occurrence of errors in judgment; according to Meyers, this would help students avoid self-deception and attempt to produce more accurate self-concepts (Meyers, 1989, 183). Teachers can also teach students how to identify one’s own needs and express them, how to judge the trustworthiness of one’s own judgment, or how to judge the trustworthiness of other people and their feedback. To play that role though, teachers themselves must be trustworthy as autonomy-promoting others, i.e., they have to actively and positively respond to students’ dependency as developing autonomous agents.[40] It is on this condition that the students are able to take the teachers’ feedback seriously and benefit from it to develop autonomy competency, including their ability to trust themselves.

However, a favorable environment is needed to cultivate and encourage teacher trustworthiness necessary for students’ autonomy competency to

---

40 In my explanation of trustworthiness, I am following Karen Jones’ (2012, 73–75) account of trustworthiness.

flourish. In contrast, schools that legitimize the omnipresence of advertising by allowing advertising to become an integral part of the school premises and of the teacher-student relationship create an environment which is not conducive to being trustworthy and creating bonds of trust with students. To elaborate, when school teachers become "pitchmen for products" and students become the "target audience," trust is eroded: teachers—and schools in general—start to have a connotation of being driven by commercial values and commercial interests related to brand-expression, not by caring for students as evolving autonomous agents. In an ad-laden school environment, students are sold to advertisers as a "target audience"—or even worse as a "captive audience" (see the argument in Section 2.3.1.1)—and therefore objectified in a way which is incompatible with autonomy-assistance.

Applying Nussbaum's methodology discussed above,[41] this type of objectification caused by the global omnipresence of advertising displays (at least)[42] five out of seven features mentioned by the philosopher (1995, 257): (1) *instrumentality*, (2) *ownership*, (3) *denial of subjectivity*, (4) *denial of autonomy*, (5) *fungibility*. To elaborate, in 2004, Patrick Le Lay famously said that what the television was selling to advertisers was "the available time of the human brain" (Les Associés d'EIM, 2004, 92–93). Analogously, for the purpose of making money (*instrumentality*), schools that engage in on-campus advertising are treating students' cognitive resources[43] as something that can simply be sold to advertisers (*ownership*), without regard to how the students feel about it (*denial of subjectivity*), what the students really want and how it influences their personal growth as evolving autonomous agents (*denial of autonomy*). Also, as "units" of

41 I refrain from discussing the other possible features of objectification added to Nussbaum's list by Rae Langton (2009), as they do not seem to be of such relevance to the analysis undertaken here as the features proposed originally by Nussbaum (1995). Parenthetically, it could possibly be argued that students are identified with their brains, and thus *reduced to body, or body parts*.

42 It might be additionally argued that students are also treated as inert, but I choose not to elaborate on this possibility, as this point seems to involve some ambiguity: on the one hand, students could be said have a certain inertness due to being a captive audience who have little power over their exposure to advertising; on the other hand, it could be argued that students are perceived by the advertisers as having the power to buy commercial products.

43 My understanding of "cognitive resources" is that of Goldstein (2011, 87): "Cognitive resources refers to the idea that a person has a certain cognitive capacity, which can be used for carrying out various tasks."

target audience to advertising, students are treated as interchangeable (*fungibility*). What is of relevance to the current argument, is that with the objectification manifesting as a cluster of these features, the trustworthiness of schools and teachers who engage in such practice is eroded: they can no longer claim to positively respond to students' being dependent on the school and its teachers for furthering the development of students' autonomy competency. In fact, students are treated as objects that can be used and influenced in a random way and with a random intention, as long as it is profitable. As commented by Noddings, "schools are not businesses (…). Schools, like homes, are special places in the lives of children. They should be centers of stability and community" (Noddings, 2005, Introduction, par. 27) where "strong relations of trust upon which to build" are enabled and protected (ch. 5, par. 3). In short, by objectifying the students in the way described above and therefore undercutting the trustworthiness of teachers, these schools are denying young people the opportunity to benefit from trust-based relationships with their teachers to further develop their autonomy competency, including the students' ability to trust themselves.

The problem of the erosion of interpersonal trust in autonomy-promoting relationships is not restricted to the context of young people and their education. Adults also need trustworthy others in order to preserve and further develop autonomy competency, including their ability to trust themselves. An example of a relationship in which this is profoundly important is the relationship between a patient and a health care professional. That the health care professionals' duty to respect patient autonomy should involve being trustworthy, as a precondition of nurturing autonomy competency—including the patient's ability to trust themselves—has already been shown (see premise 2 of this argument) to be voiced by such feminist autonomy theorists as Goering (2008), Goldberg (2008, 2003), Atkins (2006), Kukla (2005), and McLeod (2002). All of these authors have also implied that being a trustworthy autonomy-promoting other entails not objectifying the patient (see premise 3).

In the empirical material in Chapter 1, it could be observed that the omnipresence of advertising has already eliminated not only clinics, but also hospitals as a type of place which is off-limits to advertising: among the popular forms of in-hospital advertising are sampling packages and health care manuals, in which the content written by health care professionals is interspersed with advertisements. These materials are either left for patients in hospitals rooms or handed to patients by a health care professional: either way the credibility of the advertised commercial products is meant to be parasitic on the credibility of health care professionals as individuals who are competent in health care (see, for instance, Pelargos Family Service). Thus, health care professionals are, in fact, pitching commercial products to patients—either directly, by handing the advertising materials to patients, or indirectly because their professional reputation and credibility as experts in health care is meant to heighten the credibility of any products advertised within the hospital premises.

The objectification that takes place when hospital patients are treated as a target audience to advertising displays the same cluster of features as the in-school objectification of students: hospitals that aim to make money off in-hospital advertising (*instrumentality*) treat patients' cognitive resources as a commodity that can be sold to advertisers (*ownership*), without regard to how the patients feel about it (*denial of subjectivity*), what they really want and how it influences the development, maintenance, and exercise of patients' autonomy competency (*denial of autonomy*). Furthermore, as a target audience to in-hospital advertising, patients become non-individualized, interchangeable (*fungibility*).[44] Objectifying patients in these multiple ways, a hospital and its health care professionals can no longer claim to positively respond to patients' being dependent on the hospital and its health care professionals for supporting the patients' autonomy competency. Thus, in health care environments which are no longer ad-free, health care professionals lose their trustworthiness as autonomy-supporting others. Such erosion of trust constitutes a hindrance to patients benefiting from the autonomy assistance of their health care providers.

It could be objected here that even though schools/hospitals treat students/patients instrumentally—as tools for making money—this instrumentalization is nevertheless mitigated by regard for the students'/patients' humanity in a larger context. What could be added to this objection is that schools/hospitals make money off the presence of students/patients either way: after all, teachers and health care professionals are paid because students/patients come to schools/hospitals to be taught/treated; therefore, there is nothing special in making money off students/patients as a target audience to advertising. I will not argue against this objection directly: it is possible that, apart from partaking in treating students/patients as a target audience to advertising, teachers and health care professionals could indeed be doing their best to treat students/patients as ends in themselves in a larger context of educational/medical interactions. Due to this possibility, I will not claim that the objectification inspired by the global

44 Abstracted from the context discussed here, fungibility/non-individualization in a hospital environment is not ethically problematic. In the context discussed here, it is the most benign of the entire cluster of objectification features, but it makes sense to list it as a part of the analyzed cluster.

omnipresence of advertising is automatically non-benign and trust-eroding because it contains the element of instrumentality. Nor will I argue that no form of respect is possible in the relationships affected by the omnipresence of advertising, despite the presence of the objectification in question.

However, the analysis of the context in which such objectification takes place shows that this objectification is non-benign and trust-eroding for different reasons. Most of all, what points to the non-benign and trust-eroding character of this objectification is the combination of the features of denial of autonomy and ownership, in the context of non-consensuality, non-mutuality, non-symmetry, and the imbalance of power. Notice that students/patients do not freely and willingly surrender to being objectified, as was the case with the Lawrentian benign sort of objectification. Rather, they are treated as *owned*—as if their cognitive resources were *owned*—simply by the virtue of the fact that they find themselves in a certain location, i.e., a school, a hospital. Thus, not only are students/patients denied autonomy in the sense that they have no say regarding (I) the exposition to advertising at schools/hospitals (see the argument in Section 2.3.1.1) and (II) the influence of that exposition on the development, maintenance, and exercise of their autonomy competency (see the argument in Section 2.3.2.1), but they are also denied autonomy in the sense that they have no choice concerning (III) being treated as objects and having their cognitive resources sold as mere commodities to advertisers. This stands in sharp contrast with Constance Chatterley freely and joyfully choosing to be treated as a sexual object to be "used" by another person for their mutual pleasure, and being freely and joyfully allowed to objectify that person in return in a symmetrical way. In the above-depicted examples of objectification caused by the omnipresence of advertising, no such reciprocity can be found. The objectification is non-mutual, non-symmetrical, and characterized by a lack of social equality: on one side there is a powerful institutional objectifier and people who represent it, while on the other side there is a person in a position of vulnerability who is assigned the object-status, without being given a genuine opportunity to freely decide regarding this matter. The vulnerability in this case is a double vulnerability. First, the objectified is in need of educational/medical services provided by schools/hospitals. Second, the objectified is additionally in need of autonomy assistance. This second type of vulnerability could be named—borrowing and molding some of Joel Anderson's terminology (2014, 149)—"a vulnerability to not having access to (certain) autonomy-enriching-and-supporting social practices."

Instead of positively responding to the autonomy dependency born out of these vulnerabilities, schools/hospitals that allow advertising to become a part of their practice exploit these vulnerabilities and undermine student/patient autonomy (see points I, II, III in the previous paragraph). Thus, these schools/hospitals—and the teachers/health care professionals who work for these institutions—forfeit their trustworthiness as autonomy-promoting others, when trustworthiness is defined as positively responding to a dependency, as I assume to be the case following Jones (2012, 73–78). Furthermore, since trustworthiness of autonomy-promoting others is a prerequisite for having access to autonomy-enriching-and-supporting social practices, the erosion of trustworthiness of autonomy-promoting others entails that students/patients are effectively denied access to certain autonomy-enriching-and-supporting social practices.[45] This is the fourth way (IV) mentioned in this argument, in which the student/patient autonomy is being negatively impacted by the global omnipresence of advertising.

4. *Therefore, the global omnipresence of advertising is detrimental to the development, maintenance, and exercise of autonomy competency.*

As stated by Jones, trustworthiness needs to be signaled not through words, but actions: the best way for people to signal their trustworthiness is "by showing us that they are competent and can be counted on by actually doing something that anticipates the ways in which we would want to be able to count on them, if only we knew we could" (Jones, 2012, 75; see also Baier, 1986, 244). Trustworthiness in the domain of autonomy assistance needs to be signaled by demonstrating that one is able to support the autonomy of a person in a position of autonomy dependence. Conversely, one cannot claim to be trustworthy in the domain of autonomy assistance if one objectifies—in a non-benign way—the person who needs autonomy support (see premise 2), particularly if non-benign objectification manifests in denying that person's autonomy in the first place (in ways I, II, and III described in premise 3). In fact, partaking in the denial of autonomy of a person in need of autonomy support is a signal of untrustworthiness in the domain of autonomy assistance.[46]

When autonomy is understood relationally, its efficient operation depends not on how well one socially isolated individual functions, but how well individuals

45 For the importance of access to autonomy-enriching-and-supporting social practices, see, for instance, Anderson (2014, 148–149).

46 Whether forfeiting one's trustworthiness as an autonomy-promoting other might also entail forfeiting one's trustworthiness in other domains is a possible venue for further research. Since the focus of this book is the influence of the omnipresence of advertising on autonomy, the only kind of erosion of trustworthiness that I am discussing here is the erosion of trustworthiness in the domain of autonomy assistance.

function in networks to promote one another's autonomy. In fact, we should talk of autonomy in terms of *networks of autonomy* and the autonomy-enriching-and-supporting social practices that the good functioning of these networks makes possible. Relevantly, it should be stressed that the good functioning of these networks is predicated on (i.a.) how trustworthy people within a network are as autonomy-promoting others: in other words, the trustworthiness of the autonomy-promoting others is a vital resource for the development, maintenance, and exercise of autonomy competency, including the development of one's ability to trust oneself (see premise 1).

The fact that the global omnipresence of advertising induces people in a position of autonomy-promoting others to forfeit their trustworthiness as autonomy-promoting others, means that this important resource is being depleted, and individuals in need of autonomy assistance enjoy fewer opportunities for having their autonomy competency supported and enriched. Therefore, the global omnipresence of advertising has a detrimental impact on autonomy.

Two objections come to mind in connection with this argument.

First, it could be objected that even though the global omnipresence of advertising leads to an erosion of *trustworthiness* of certain autonomy-promoting others, it need not necessarily lead to an erosion of a relevant variety of *trust*:[47] people in a position of autonomy dependency might still place trust in these untrustworthy autonomy-promoting others (despite the untrustworthiness). Some people, who are in need of autonomy assistance, might remain completely unaware of *being* objectified in a non-benign way described above, and therefore they will not *feel* objectified and will continue to trust their teachers, health care providers, etc.; consequently, their opportunities for autonomy support and enrichment would not be negatively impacted by the global omnipresence of advertising in the way described above.

I would reply that it is, of course, possible to place trust in a way which is unjustified, despite the untrustworthiness of the trusted person (for an excellent analysis of unjustified trust and self-trust, see McLeod, 2002, ch. 5). Thus, some people in a position of autonomy dependency could place *unjustified* trust in untrustworthy individuals who are in a position of autonomy-promoting others; in this sense, the relationship of *unjustified* trust might exist, instead of being precluded or broken, in spite of the non-benign objectification described above

47 Below, whenever I use the word "trust" in the response to this objection, I will mean "a relevant variety of trust," i.e., trust in the domain of autonomy assistance.

and the resulting untrustworthiness of the trusted others.[48] However, the mere existence of a relationship of *unjustified* trust, does not entail that this relationship is beneficial for autonomy in the same way that a relationship of *justified* trust would.

In fact, the existence and continuation of a relationship of unjustified trust suggests that certain autonomy competency skills of the truster are in bad shape, i.a. that the truster is unable to critically assess the trustworthiness of people in the position of autonomy-promoting others, as well as her own trustworthiness as a judge of others. Moreover, the existence and continuation of a relationship of *unjustified* trust indicates that the untrustworthy individuals in a position of autonomy-promoting others are not doing their job properly as autonomy-promoting others.[49] If they were, they would notice the above-mentioned error of judgment of the person in need of autonomy assistance and help that person develop the skills needed to critically assess the situation: the importance of autonomy-promoting others supporting the development of the autonomy-dependent person's critical stance towards her self-trust and trust in others is underscored particularly strongly by Kukla (2005, 40) and Goering (2008, 12). In other words, if the relationship of unjustified trust were to be beneficial for autonomy in the same way that a relationship of justified trust is, the untrustworthy individual in the position of an autonomy-promoting other—let us call that untrustworthy individual "U"—would have to help the person in need of autonomy assistance—"A"—to notice the untrustworthiness of U through a critical examination of the situation and, as a result, develop justified distrust of U, thus ending the relationship of unjustified trust. This would support A in becoming a better, more trustworthy judge of others, and enhance her autonomy competency. Therefore, the fact that the relationship of unjustified trust continues to exist is a proof of the autonomy-competency *not* being supported or enriched by the untrustworthy individuals in a position of autonomy-promoting others; in other words, the opportunities for autonomy support and enrichment

48 For instance, an individual might be socially conditioned to expect domination rather than autonomy support from people who are teachers or health care professionals.

49 Hopefully, there might still be other autonomy-promoting individuals in the life of the truster—some family members, friends, etc.—who will nevertheless point out the non-benign objectification present in these types of situations, and question the trustworthiness of teachers/health care professionals as autonomy-promoting others, as well as the trustworthiness of the truster herself as a judge of others.

are still negatively impacted by the global omnipresence of advertising in the way described in the argument above.

The second objection to this argument could be formulated in the form of the following questions. Does the argument have a hidden assumption that an autonomy-friendly environment is necessary for autonomy? Is it not sometimes the case that oppressive conditions might—by stimulating resistance—promote the development of the oppressed individuals' autonomy competency?

I would begin the answer by agreeing with Meyers who says that oppressive environments "need not defeat autonomy" (Meyers, 2000, 152): my argument does not contest that. Meyers even implies that—despite facing much more obstacles on the way—multiply oppressed individuals may be "better positioned" to eventually gain more self-knowledge and attain a higher level of self-definition than multiply privileged individuals (152, 156–158; for instance, multiply oppressed individuals may display more willingness to accept the complexity of their self, while multiply privileged individuals may have a tendency to avoid embracing the complexity within their self due to idealizing unity, coherence, and constancy, 156, 161). However, this is not to say that oppressive conditions promote autonomy. It is the existence of supportive, autonomy-promoting others that makes it possible for a person to resist oppression. If this were not the case, why would dictators like Hitler or Stalin want to isolate people into an organized form of loneliness in order to control them (Arendt, 1951, especially 407–409, 412–413, but also, for example, 371–373, 384, 392)? Conversely, it is the lack of trustworthy outside support that makes people stay in oppressive conditions and avoid help-seeking, even if these conditions pose a threat to their life (see, for example, Chantler et al., 2022, 16–19; see also Burman, Chantler, 2005). In short, living in an autonomy-friendly environment is not a necessary condition of autonomy, but the existence of autonomy-promoting others, before, and/or during, and/or after living in an oppressive environment is.

2.4. Conclusions

As explained by Meyers, autonomy is the *exercise* of a competency which comprises a set of skills (1989, 20). One can exercise that competency to make one particular choice effectual in producing behavior (thus realizing one's autonomy of choice), or one can exercise that competency in an ongoing process of making and effectuating several choices related to the kind of person one wants to be (thus realizing one's autonomy of persons). In any case, autonomy is not merely about *making* choices, it is also about *effectuating* them; therefore, if the agent cannot effectuate autonomously made choices, that agent cannot fully exercise autonomy competency. In the *argument from a captive audience* (Section 2.3.1.1), I have attempted to show that the omnipresence of advertising—manifesting both globally and locally—promotes the creation of such physical environments which produce captive audiences and therefore disrupt the effectuation of an autonomously made choice not to be exposed to advertising. Thus, the first conclusion to be drawn from this chapter concerns the advertising industry's thesis that a person who wishes not to be exposed to advertising may simply cease to watch it: if what I have argued in the argument from a captive audience is correct, this thesis is false.

Conversely, the other two arguments in this chapter (Section 2.3.2) move beyond that part of the exercise of autonomy competency which consists in being able to effectuate an autonomously made choice not to be exposed to advertising. Importantly, in these arguments I tried to show that the omnipresence of advertising undermines not only the exercise, but also the development and maintenance of autonomy competency, as well as the development and maintenance of self-trust, which is a foundation of autonomy competency. I argued that this undermining happens by hindering the cultivation of the critical reasoning skill (Section 2.3.2.1)—which is vital to the development, maintenance, and exercise of autonomy competency, including the element of self-trust—and by exerting a disruptive influence on the social and relational scaffolding meant to support the development, maintenance, and exercise of autonomy competency, including the element of self-trust (Section 2.3.2.2).

In the empirical material in Chapter 1, I have signaled the existence of common intuitions about the omnipresence of advertising: people often tend to think that advertising which aims to be ubiquitous is invasive, as if it somehow intruded upon the sphere of their autonomy. The current chapter offers a plausible philosophical explanation that could corroborate these intuitions: if the arguments presented herein are correct, the omnipresence of advertising exerts a complex negative influence on autonomy. However, offering this potential explanation would not have been possible, if I had tried to follow substantive accounts of autonomy, which are focused mainly on what is going on inside the agent. In contrast, the relational accounts are characterized by a strong focus on external factors, perceived as playing a major role in the development, maintenance, and exercise of an individual's autonomy. It is precisely such approach that was necessary to analyze the way in which ubiquitous advertising—itself an external factor—could exert an influence on autonomy, understood as rooted in and dependent upon what is outside of an agent, i.e., what is contextual, environmental, relational.

3 Conclusions: Towards Ad-Freedom

> "Thus the form of advertising has imposed itself and developed at the expense of all other languages as an increasingly neutral, equivalent rhetoric, without affects, as an 'asyntactic nebula,' (…) which envelops us from every side (…)."
> J. Baudrillard, *Simulacra and Simulation (1981)*

3.1. Definition-Related Conclusions

3.1.1. A Brief Summary of the Definitional Exploration

The subject of this book has been the omnipresence of advertising—a phenomenon that began approximately in the 1990s and continues until present day. Under different names, it has been discussed by other scholars—R. George Wright, Edward Spence and Brett Van Heekeren, Michael Sandel, Andrew Sneddon (see the Legal Appendix and the Ethical Appendix)—but none of these scholars have provided a definition of the phenomenon. Consequently, an important part of the original input in this book has been to fill this definitional gap in a way which is theoretically and empirically well-grounded.

My approach has been to allow the definition to evolve and take shape throughout the book: in a way, I have taken the readers on a journey of definitional exploration with me. The first step, taken in Chapter 1, has been to analyze the scholarly usage of the term "omnipresence" in contexts not pertaining to the topic of advertising; the second step, also in Chapter 1, consisted in extracting and exploring the empirical material that illustrates the phenomenon in question. The combination of steps one and two has led to the third step of attempting to draft (the first approximation at) a definition. The fourth step consisted in bifurcating the general definition into two sub-definitions: of the more local and the more global kind of omnipresence of advertising, which constitute two ways in which the phenomenon can manifest. Steps three and four conclude the work undertaken in Chapter 1. In Chapter 2, the bifurcated definition has been applied to the construction of arguments in an attempt to show the negative impact of the omnipresence of advertising on autonomy competency: observing the bifurcated definition in action has been the fifth step of the definitional exploration. This step has made me realize that the definition of the omnipresence of advertising should include a relational component (apart from the spatial and temporal one).[50] Moreover, combined with all the steps from Chapter 1, the fifth step from Chapter 2 showed the need to elaborate on the topic of types and tokens in relation to how the omnipresence of advertising affects the contemporary human reality. Section 3.1.2 will serve to address these issues and to remodel the general definition proposed in Chapter 1 accordingly. This will be the sixth, final step of the journey of definitional exploration.

3.1.2. The Final Step of the Definitional Exploration

Initially, I proposed to understand the omnipresence of advertising as "a high potentiality for advertising to appear anywhere, anytime"; I also mentioned that "omnipresence of advertising understood in this way can sometimes manifest as high saturation of certain areas/domains of reality with advertising" (Chapter 1). Looking back at the previous steps of the definitional exploration, it is now possible to elaborate on this first approximation in order to produce a more fine-tuned version of the definition. This elaboration will include (a) the relational component, (b) a discussion of types and tokens in the context of how the omnipresence of advertising affects the contemporary human reality, and (c) some final deliberations about the two ways in which the phenomenon manifests—globally and locally.

Manifesting globally—i.e., in the contemporary reality of daily human experience taken as a whole—the omnipresence of advertising affects two levels of everyday human reality: the level of types (of space, events, relationships) and the level of tokens (of space, events, relationships). On the level of types, the omnipresence of advertising operates by gradually eliminating ad-free types of space, events, relationships, the goal being that *all types of space, events, relationships can serve as "advertising carriers."* This has consequences on the level of tokens as well: it implies high potentiality for advertising to appear in every token of space, event, and relationship within the everyday reality of human beings. It is this compilation of progressive elimination of ad-free types of space, events, relationships—on the level of types—and the resulting high potentiality for advertising to appear everywhere on the level of tokens which is central to the phenomenon of the omnipresence of advertising as a whole, not just to its global

50 For some supplementary empirical data showing how the omnipresence of advertising has been affecting the way contemporary human beings relate to one another through language, see the Short Linguistic Appendix. These data provide an additional stimulus for including a relational component in the definition of the omnipresence of advertising.

manifestation. In other words, the global manifestation of the phenomenon—understood in the way described above—is the necessary characteristics of the omnipresence of advertising (as a whole): it is not possible to imagine a reality in which this characteristic is the case, and the omnipresence of advertising is not the case. In a similar vein, it is not possible to imagine a reality in which the omnipresence of advertising is the case, but its global manifestation is not.

On a local scale, on the other hand, the omnipresence of advertising manifests through a high saturation of a limited area of reality with advertising, meaning that a large number of tokens of space, events, relationships is being used as "advertising carriers" in this particular area. This kind of manifestation is more visually obvious and thus more easily detectable than the global manifestation, but it would be a mistake to limit the understanding of the omnipresence of advertising as a whole to the most conspicuous way in which it can materialize. Moreover, the local manifestation constitutes a part of the mechanics of the omnipresence of advertising which seems contingent. Namely, it is possible to imagine a reality without the omnipresence of advertising, but with specific areas (virtual or physical) of that reality purposely designated to be highly saturated with advertising on the level of tokens—areas, like today's trade fairs, that people would enter consensually and intentionally to get information about commercial products. It is also possible to imagine a reality in which the omnipresence of advertising manifests only on a global scale, but does not manifest in the form of specific smaller areas being highly saturated with advertising on the level of tokens.[51]

To conclude, what needs to be underscored and spelled out explicitly is the following. (1) The local manifestation is not necessary for the existence of the omnipresence of advertising, as well as to the process of characterizing the phenomenon in its entirety. (2) In contrast, the global manifestation is necessary for the existence of the omnipresence of advertising, and therefore it is the defining part of the phenomenon as a whole. (3) The general definition of the omnipresence of advertising should reflect the difference described in points 1 and 2.

---

51 In such a reality, it may be the case that the omnipresence of advertising does not *yet* manifest in the form of specific smaller areas being highly saturated with advertising on the level of tokens, but eventually it will. Or it may be the case that the tokens will simply remain more scattered (or more evenly distributed) within that possible reality, never really reaching the point of high saturation on the level of tokens within any specific smaller section of that reality.

In line with the reflections presented above, the general definition could be enriched and remodeled in the following manner. The omnipresence of advertising is a phenomenon which manifests globally in the form of progressive elimination of ad-free types of space, events, relationships, and this state of affairs results from the advertisers' striving towards a reality in which all types of space, events, relationships could serve as "advertising carriers." An accompanying global effect is the high potentiality for advertising to appear in every token of space, event, and relationship within the everyday reality of human beings. Additionally, the omnipresence of advertising may also manifest locally in the form of a high saturation of a specific area of reality with tokens of space, events, relationships converted into "advertising carriers."

Providing a more fine-tuned and complex definition of the omnipresence of advertising equals bringing the definitional exploration in this book to a conclusion. However, I hope to leave this concluding step open to critique and further enquiry by other scholars. The conclusion offered here simply adds another arrow to our collective quiver, thus enabling and encouraging more dialogue about the omnipresence of advertising.

3.2. Objection-Related and Argument-Related Conclusions

3.2.1. The Objection

It seems that a general objection could be raised in connection with the fact that the argument presented in this book does not focus on the omnipresence of *irrational* advertising, or *manipulative* advertising, or *misleading* advertising, or advertising containing *falsehood*—instead, the focus is on the omnipresence of *advertising messages, irrespective of their contents*. This gives rise to an important question: What makes the omnipresence of advertising special and different as a subject of enquiry in comparison to the omnipresence of something else, especially the omnipresence of another kind of message(s)? What if—instead of being subjected to the omnipresence of advertising messages—people were subjected to the omnipresence of messages that communicated high culture,[52] like

52 In the discussion that follows I will be guided by the understanding of the term "high culture" found in Oxford University Press' *A Dictionary of Media and Communication*. According to this source, "high culture" refers to "'[a]uthentic' works of art and individual creativity and the aesthetic pleasures associated with their appreciation which require the demonstration of taste, discrimination, and sophistication derived from and contributing to the cultural capital of an elite as distinct from the 'mere

fragments of films by Andriej Tarkowski or Michelangelo Antonioni, pieces of art by Auguste Rodin, Leonardo da Vinci, Mary Cassatt, or Frida Kahlo, excerpts from the works of Albert Einstein, Marie Curie-Skłodowska, Charlotte Brontë, or W.H. Auden, with the musical accompaniment of the Goldberg variations or the most renowned opera pieces composed by Handel, Gluck, Mozart, Rossini, Wagner, Puccini, or Strauss? Would not this kind of omnipresence also violate autonomy, and would not these violations be the same as the ones presented in the arguments in Chapter 2?[53]

3.2.2. Answering the Objection

The answer to this objection is complex. I will begin by admitting that my intention has been indeed to remain neutral with regard to contents of the advertising messages: I did not want to focus on any particular kind of advertising that would be considered ethically problematic in virtue of its contents being manipulative, irrational, misleading, false, racist, sexist, etc. In fact, it has been my intention to take these ethical issues out of the equation, so that the ethical considerations connected with them would influence neither my analysis, nor the resulting conclusions. My only reservation was that the kind of advertising under scrutiny in this book is *commercial* advertising (see Chapter 0, Section 0.6; see also the Legal Appendix).

This reservation might seem insignificant, but it is not. In fact, it is key to answering the objector's questions and demonstrating that there is something special and different about the omnipresence of *commercial* advertising, in contrast to the omnipresence of noncommercial messages, as in the hypothetical high-culture-messages example.

What is special and different about the omnipresence of commercial advertising is that it uses commercial speech, i.e., a type of speech that is qualitatively different from noncommercial speech. As discussed in detail in the Legal Appendix, the *raison d'être* of noncommercial speech is the interactive interchange of thoughts and ideas within public discourse, through which speakers express who they are; an important part of this interactive interchange is that speakers respond to one another and challenge one another's thoughts and ideas, as well as the values expressed in these thoughts and ideas. Commercial speech, on the other hand, is not the vessel for individual self-expression—it is not the vessel

entertainment' values associated with popular (mass) culture, commercial commodification and uncritical consumption."

53 I owe the idea of this objection to Professor Marcin Poręba (University of Warsaw).

for the expression of one's thoughts, ideas, and personal values, which are likely to be responded to, challenged, or corrected by other participants of the public discourse.[54] In other words, commercial speech is neither expressive of any *self*, nor interactive in the sense in which a *self* in its self-expression can be challenged by another *self*.[55] Rather, the *raison d'être* of commercial speech is to provide the potential consumer with information about commercial products, commercial brands, commercial lifestyles, thus promoting the sales of commercial products.

The example of omnipresence of high culture messages is counterfactual: it is not the case within the contemporary reality, and therefore it remains unknown why, how, and by whom it would be brought about, as well as how exactly it would manifest itself. These would be important factors to consider, when analyzing the kind of violations of autonomy this particular omnipresence could produce. Nevertheless, even without the knowledge of these important details, it is possible to say something about the differences between the violations caused by the omnipresence portrayed in the book and the possible violations caused by the omnipresence described in the objection. If the high culture messages were conveyed through noncommercial speech, the violations of autonomy caused by their omnipresence would necessarily be different from the ones caused by the omnipresence of commercial advertising due to the above-mentioned differences between commercial and noncommercial speech.

Regarding the applicability of arguments presented in this book, the argument from a captive audience would still be applicable to the noncommercial kind of omnipresence of high culture messages, provided that this omnipresence had a tendency to produce captive audiences. As far as theoretical possibilities are concerned, both commercial and noncommercial speech can produce captive audiences (see the Legal Appendix).

In contrast, the argument from hindering critical reasoning would no longer be applicable. Of course, it might be rightly pointed out that human beings

---

54 As discussed in the Legal Appendix, this is an important reason behind commercial speech receiving less constitutional protection within the American legal system. Parenthetically, notice how the portrayal of commercial speech that I draw from the American legal doctrine resonates to some extent with Jean Baudrillard's reflections about advertising being the most neutral and superficial mode of communication, without depth, without any distinctions and differences with regard to meaning, without the expression of beliefs and affects (1981/1994, 87–89), without the defying presence of other people (1970, 18).

55 Commercial speech could be linked with *brand-expression*, expressing a commercial brand's identity, history, etc.

sometimes need retreat or distance from high culture as well, but a crucial difference is that high culture messages conveyed through noncommercial speech are an integral and nourishing part of the public discourse—a discourse within which thoughts, ideas, and personal values are exchanged, responded to, and challenged. In fact, as stressed by Marcuse (1964/2007, 59–66), an essential feature of high culture messages is to awaken the critical mind and inspire the critical engagement of its audience. That one might sometimes need (or even have the right to take) a break from the high culture's invitation to critically engage with its *oeuvres* is an interesting point that could potentially constitute a premise in a different argument, but it does not fit as a premise in the argument from hindering critical reasoning because it does not demonstrate that the omnipresence of high culture messages would have the effect of hindering the cultivation of the critical reasoning skill. In comparison, as argued in Chapter 2, the omnipresence of advertising is a phenomenon which is hostile to the development and exercise of the critical reasoning skill: a vital element of that hostility is the non-interactive commercial mode of communication invading the interactive realm of noncommercial communication in which human beings exercise critical reasoning to challenge one another's thoughts, ideas, values, and selves. When a mode of communication which is non-interactive (i.e., not connected with selves critically engaging with and challenging other selves, their thoughts, ideas, values) is allowed to invade the everyday reality of human experience—eliminating types of space which are important for the cultivation of critical reasoning—then this has a negative impact on the level of critical reasoning skill of human beings subjected to this kind of omnipresence. If a mode of communication which, in principle, is interactive—like high culture messages—were allowed to invade the everyday reality of human experience, this might be problematic for other reasons, but it would not have a negative effect on the critical reasoning skill of human beings subjected to this kind of omnipresence. Such omnipresence could still allow for people's exposure to many kinds of values (not excluding the commercial values[56]), provided a variety of *oeuvres* were showcased and not just a very narrow selection. Moreover, such omnipresence would not be aimed at making people acquire commercial information about commercial products, brands, and lifestyles, at the expense of noncommercial interactions of human beings with themselves, with one another, or with nature.

---

56 Commercial values could be mediated, for instance, by such paintings as Andy Warhol's *Campbell's Soup Cans* (1962) or Richard Hamilton's *Just What Is It That Makes Today's Homes So Different, So Appealing?* (1956).

It could be objected that not all high culture messages seem to be interactive, or equally interactive, in the sense that not all high culture pieces will elicit—in each person—the same willingness to interact with the message conveyed (or with the judgment of other people who have classified a particular piece as a high culture piece). However, a person can be picky about which oeuvres to interact with (just as they may be picky about which people, which opinions, which judgments to interact with), and this does not falsify the general rule that high culture pieces use a mode of communication which is interactive. A simple proof of the interactivity of high culture is that in order to be classified as a "high culture piece," an *oeuvre* has already had to be a subject of much critical debate and—as a result of the interaction with the piece and with each other—many people have reached a consensus concerning the cultural value of that piece (a consensus that does not exclude a possibility of some individual's *votum separatum* in the debate, or indifference towards the subject of the consensus).

Moving on to the applicability of the last argument to the noncommercial kind of omnipresence of high culture messages, a preliminary reservation must be made: namely that it is impossible to give a satisfactory analysis of the kind of objectification that could result from the omnipresence of high culture messages conveyed through noncommercial speech because, as a counterfactual phenomenon, it lacks an empirical foundation, and therefore lacks genuine context. Nevertheless, it is possible to point to some key elements of the argument from non-benign objectification that would be absent in the case of the noncommercial omnipresence of high culture messages (for similar reasons to the ones discussed in the previous paragraphs), thus making the argument from non-benign objectification non-applicable.

Most importantly, without the element of commercial speech and thus without the commercial interest described in the argument from non-benign objectification, the omnipresence of high culture messages would not be aimed at making people acquire commercial information at the expense of noncommercial interactions, including autonomy-supportive interactions. The omnipresence of high culture messages would be a noncommercial phenomenon within the noncommercial realm of human interactions, and therefore it would not inject the pressure of commercial interests and commercial values into those interactions—autonomy-support included—where noncommercial interests and noncommercial values are key. As a result, people in the position of autonomy-promoting others would not be pushed to be a part of the non-consensual process of selling the cognitive resources of individuals in need of autonomy support. Therefore, the instrumentality and ownership features of non-benign objectification—as portrayed in the argument from non-benign objectification—would not be the case for the noncommercial omnipresence of high culture messages. Moreover, the fungibility, the denial of subjectivity, and the third kind (III) of autonomy denial that are described in the argument would also be absent. This does not mean no objectification might be involved.[57] But it means that the kind of objectification (if any) caused by the noncommercial omnipresence of high culture messages would be qualitatively different—in a significant way—from the nonbenign objectification caused by the omnipresence of advertising that leads to an erosion of trust in autonomy-promoting relationships, and there seems to be no *a priori* reason to believe that the objectification (if any) caused by the noncommercial omnipresence of high culture messages would lead to the erosion of trust in autonomy-promoting relationships.

The only way for the violations of autonomy caused by the omnipresence of high culture messages to be the same as the violations caused by the omnipresence of commercial advertising would be for the high culture messages to be conveyed *via* commercial speech. This could be brought about by injecting high culture content into advertising messages selling commercial products. These might be commercial products which have a genuine connection with high culture (books, paintings, musical records, etc.), or commercial products which have nothing or little to do with high culture, for which a parasitic connection with high culture would be created by advertisers (for instance, in order to make the potential customers associate the high quality or uniqueness of well-known and esteemed *oeuvres* with commercial products). In any case, if messages evoking high culture were used to sell commercial products, their omnipresence would, in fact, be equal to the omnipresence of commercial advertising, which is the subject matter of this book. Other things being equal, all arguments presented in Chapter 2 could be as applicable to the omnipresence of high culture messages conveyed *via* commercial speech as they are to the omnipresence of commercial advertising.

I will now proceed to formulate some conclusions from the discussion in this section.

Although supporters and enablers of the omnipresence of advertising might try to convince us that commercial advertising integrates perfectly well with the noncommercial elements of human everyday reality (see Chapter 1 for some examples of such persuasion attempts), it is important to remember that no

57 Some objectification features could be present—for instance, the first (I) and/or the second (II) kind of autonomy denial, and/or a different kind of fungibility than the one described in the argument, etc.

matter how well-integrated commercial advertising might *appear* within the noncommercial reality, it never ceases to connote and evoke a qualitatively different reality—a reality of commercial interests instead of noncommercial interests of human beings *vis-a-vis* themselves and one another, a reality of commercial values instead of noncommercial values, a reality of non-interactive[58] and non-challengeable brand-expression instead of interactive and challengeable self-expression. When this commercial reality is allowed to dominate the noncommercial reality in the form of omnipresence of advertising, this is detrimental to the development, maintenance, and exercise of autonomy competency for the following reasons.

1. Incessantly evoking a commercial reality within the noncommercial realm of human everyday experience causes an injection of commercial values and commercial interests into human interactions and relationships—such as autonomy-promoting relationships—in which noncommercial values, noncommercial interests, and an interactive, challengeable mode of communication are key. In autonomy-promoting relationships, this leads to non-benign objectification which causes an erosion of a fundamental and necessary element of autonomy-promoting relationships: the trustworthiness of autonomy-promoting others. This trustworthiness is an important resource of relationally conceived autonomy competency, and depleting that resource is detrimental to the development, maintenance, and exercise of autonomy competency.
2. Moreover, an unrestrained and overwhelming use of a non-interactive and non-challengeable mode of commercial speech *via* the omnipresence of advertising causes a significant depletion of time and space that ought to be allocated to witnessing and partaking in a mode of communication in which selves—along with their thoughts, ideas, values—can be expressed and critically challenged by other selves. Being provided with a considerable amount of time and space to witness and partake in the interactive and challengeable mode of noncommercial communication is an important element of the development, maintenance, and exercise of the skill of critical reasoning. Therefore, depleting the resources of time and space allocated to witnessing and partaking in the interactive and challengeable mode of noncommercial

58 As already stated earlier in this section, I use the word "non-interactive" in the sense of not being connected with selves critically engaging with and challenging other selves, their thoughts, ideas, values.

communication is detrimental to the development, maintenance, and exercise of the critical reasoning skill—an autonomy skill which (as described in the argument from hindering critical reasoning) is essential i.a. to critically evaluate the trustworthiness of people in the position of autonomy-promoting others, to critically evaluate one's own trustworthiness, to critically evaluate the structure of one's life against other possible ways of living, and to critically evaluate one's system of values against other possible ways of valuing. When such critical evaluations cannot be performed skillfully, a person has lower self-trust, lower self-knowledge, and lower ability to shape their self.

3. Furthermore, the development, maintenance, and exercise of autonomy skills other than the critical reasoning skill are also dependent on being provided with a sufficient amount of time and space devoted to the daily practice of witnessing and partaking in self-expression of oneself and others. When witnessing and partaking in the expression of commercial brands becomes a dominating everyday experience that takes over the time and space for witnessing and partaking in self-expression (of oneself and others), one has less sensitivity to one's felt self-referential responses, especially to inner discord; less ability to communicate with other people concerning one's needs, desires, values, concerns; less sensitivity to others' feedback; and less ability to self-correct. Similarly to the aforementioned hindrance of the critical reasoning skill, the hindrances of other autonomy skills also translate into lower self-trust, lower self-knowledge, and a lower ability to shape the self.

3.3. Solution-Related Conclusions

3.3.1. Solution-Related Concluding Thoughts and Guidelines

It is now time to give shape to some concluding thoughts regarding solutions to the ethically problematic consequences of the omnipresence of advertising described in this book.

As a result of the advertisers' striving towards a reality in which all types of space, events, relationships can serve as "advertising carriers," the omnipresence of advertising has been shown to negatively affect the spatio-tempo-relational resources people need—as a part of their everyday experience—in order to develop, exercise, and keep their autonomy competency in good shape. Therefore, if what we consider valuable and worth preserving is not an abstract, purely theoretical notion of autonomy, but autonomy as a practical competency that needs a sufficient number of spatio-tempo-relational resources to be developed, exercised, and kept in good shape, then a phenomenon that depletes these important autonomy resources—and does so on a daily basis—has to be curbed in a way that prevents these depletions.

One solution-related conclusion is the following: some types of space, events, and relationships need to be kept entirely ad-free and legally protected as such. As to *which* types of space, events, and relationships should be kept entirely ad-free, I believe that reasonable guidelines can be deduced from this book. First, these should be types of spaces, events, and relationships that play an important role in interpersonal autonomy-support. Second, these should be types of spaces, events, and relationships that have a particularly important connection with the development, maintenance, and exercise of the critical reasoning skill—and other autonomy skills. Reflecting on these two criteria, which are comprehensible and justified (see Chapter 2, especially Sections 2.3.2.1 and 2.3.2.2), it becomes clear that the types of space, events, and relationships that should be treated and protected as fundamental components of human ad-freedom are especially those connected with education and personal development, with achieving and maintaining critical distance from commercial values, with critical assessment of oneself and others (by oneself and others), and with such circumstances in which autonomy might be somewhat compromised, especially those connected with personal health and safety. To be more specific, the pool of ad-free types of space, events, and relationships should include education-related environments and events, teacher-student (and teacher-parent) relationships and interactions; law-enforcement-related locations, events, relationships and interactions; medical, social, and psychological care locations, events, relationships and interactions; as well as the time and locations connected with achieving and maintaining critical distance from commercial values, such as public green areas, nature reserves, spaces and events which are devoted to or which embody high culture.[59]

Another solution-related conclusion of this book would be that the types of space, events, and relationships which are not significant from the point of view of interpersonal autonomy-support or the development, maintenance, and exercise of the critical reasoning skill (and other autonomy skills) need not be classified as off-limits to advertising.[60] Not unconditionally, however. As implied

59 To give a spatial example, a museum or an art gallery are spaces devoted to high culture, while the architectural creations of Antonio Gaudi or Peter Zumthor constitute spaces that embody high culture. Some spaces devoted to high culture might at the same time be spaces that embody high culture.

60 Of course, there might also be other ethically important, compelling reasons—not connected with the value of autonomy—to keep some other type(s) of space, events, and relationships entirely ad-free, but my point of focus in this book is solely on the value of

in the argument from a captive audience, people should be able to act on their choice not to be exposed to advertising in situations that are not entirely ad-free (see Chapter 2, Section 2.3.1.1). In other words, even if a type of space, event, or relationship is not off-limits to advertising, this should not entail the lack of autonomy of choice of the target audience of advertising. On the contrary, those spatio-tempo-relational circumstances which are not entirely ad-free *have to be conducive to autonomy of choice*, i.e., they have to provide favorable conditions for the use of practical everyday tactics for avoiding exposure to advertising.

3.3.2. Solutions Are Possible: An Example

I will now give an example of a spatially-oriented solution in order to show that it is possible for an everyday environment to *not* be off-limits to advertising, and yet to be highly conducive to autonomy of choice (and autonomy of persons) at the same time. The solution is inspired by an idea presented in the film *Anon* (2018). During the first minutes of the film, the spectator witnesses the main protagonist taking a walk through a futuristic urban space which—as a physical reality—is entirely ad-free: on the buildings, city furniture, streets, sidewalks, vehicles, not a single advertisement or even commercial signboard can be found. However, this space has an additional layer—an "augmented" layer of reality—which is not ad-free. This is due to the fact that everyone, including the main protagonist, has an ocular implant that provides an Augmented-Reality head-up display that allows the user to see and read all kinds of information, including commercial advertisements, commercial signboards, as well as information about particular commercial products that the user of the implant becomes interested in.

Let us now imagine a modified, much more desirable and attainable version of that idea,[61] involving the use of an already existing and non-invasive device, called Augmented Reality glasses (AR glasses).[62] The key elements of the idea

---

autonomy, and therefore the solution-related conclusions presented in this chapter are autonomy-oriented. However, as already underscored, the discourse presented here is not meant to exhaust the discussion of the omnipresence of advertising, and therefore it leaves room for solution-related conclusions from different ethical perspectives than the one presented here.

61 I am proposing a modified version, because by no means do I want to suggest that an entire humanity should get such implants: it seems neither technologically possible at this point in time, nor desirable, as that would be a very invasive solution.

62 For a good scholarly introduction to and exploration of the topic of AR glasses, see, for instance, Rauschnabel, Brem, Ro (2015), Rauschnabel, Ro (2016), Rauschnabel (2018), Rauschnabel, Felix, Hinsch (2019).

that I offer as an example of a solution to the problems caused by the omnipresence of advertising discussed in this book would be the following. (A) *All* advertising information would be relegated to the AR level of reality. (B) Each member of the target audience would be provided with a free-of-charge pair of AR advertising glasses[63] allowing the user to easily access all advertising information in the AR mode, but also to always be able to act on the choice not to be exposed to advertising. (C) Consequently, the only actions required to avoid exposure to advertising would be to take off (or turn off) the AR glasses or not put them on in the first place—these are very simple and practical tactics, the exercise of which would not be disruptive of everyday functioning. (D) Even in the AR mode there would be types of space, events, interactions, relationships that are off-limits to advertising—the ones mentioned in the third paragraph of Section 3.3.1. Thus, within the framework of this particular idea, being "entirely ad-free" would mean being ad-free on both the non-augmented and the augmented layer of reality, while "not entirely ad-free" would mean being ad-free on the non-augmented layer of reality and not ad-free on the augmented layer of reality.

Realizing this idea would mean that: (a) noncommercial speech, noncommercial interactions, noncommercial relationships are prioritized within our everyday reality as crucial to everyday human functioning, relating, and self-expressing, to the flourishing of public discourse, and to the development, maintenance, and exercise of autonomy competency; (b) commercial speech, commercial interactions, commercial relationships are curbed within clear spatial confines which are ethically-justified; (c) at the same time, commercial information conveyed via advertising remains easily accessible to the advertising

63 I am assuming here that the advertising industry would provide their target audience with the AG advertising glasses for free. Financially, this seems to be a feasible solution, considering a huge amount of money spent on advertising worldwide every year (Statista, 2021). By the end of 2023, the world spending on advertising was projected to reach 691 billion U.S. dollars (Statista, 2021). The population of the world at that point in time was around 8 billion people (Worldometer), including children that need not and should not be equipped with the AG advertising glasses. 8 billion people minus 1,9 billion children under the age of 15 (Gapminder) equals 6,1 billion people to be equipped with the AG advertising glasses. If 6,1 billion people were to be equipped by the advertising industry with the AG advertising glasses at the price of 50 dollars per a pair of glasses (which is a reasonable price considering the current prices of AG glasses on Amazon.com), it would cost the industry 305 million dollars—less than half of the money that was projected to be spent on advertising by the end of 2023.

audience[64]; (d) ad-freedom (i.e., freedom from advertising) is not a limited (finite) good that there might not be enough of for everybody; (e) switching between being exposed to advertising and not being exposed to it is always a matter of effectuating an autonomous choice (to put/turn on the AR glasses).

3.3.3. Less Than Ideal Solutions: The Satisfactory Level

The example from the previous section is an attempt to show that it is possible to realize a certain ideal in terms of autonomy protection and support. However, less than ideal solutions are also imaginable. The question is where to draw a line between satisfactory and unsatisfactory solutions. The guidelines described in Section 3.3.1 are helpful.

The method of finding satisfactory solutions proposed here is based on perceiving the surrounding reality spatially—composed of types of space, as illustrated in Chapter 1. An important part of a satisfactory solution is that it ought to include protecting some types of space as entirely ad-free, based on ethical analyses such as the one conducted in this book. Combining the empirical exploration from Chapter 1 and the ethical analysis from Chapter 2, the following classification of types of space to be protected as *entirely* ad-free could be proposed. (1) Types of space connected with health and immediate safety: hospitals, medical clinics, ambulances (Section 1.3.4); fire and rescue service buildings, equipment, vehicles (Section 1.3.3). (2) Types of space connected with law enforcement and civil service: jails (Section 1.3.1), police stations, equipment, and vehicles (Section 1.3.2); courts; city halls. (3) Types of space connected with education, personal development and contemplation (secular or spiritual): schools (Section 1.3.5); churches and temples (Section 1.3.10); green areas (Sections 1.3.11, 1.3.13); buildings and areas connected with (or embodying) high culture. It would be best if all three categories of these types of space were legally protected as *entirely* ad-free. However, if—for some reason—this might not be feasible, the

64 As expressed by the American Supreme Court: (1) a "commercial advertisement is constitutionally protected not so much because it pertains to the seller's business as because it furthers the societal interest in the 'free flow of commercial information'" (*First National Bank v. Bellotti*, 1978, 435 U.S. 783, quoting *Virginia State Board of Pharmacy*; quoted in Post, 2000, 14); (2) "the primary purpose for protecting commercial speech is to ensure the free flow of commercial information to benefit the listener to support intelligent and well-informed consumer decisions" (Pomeranz, 2012, 401, paraphrasing the verdict in *Virginia State Board of Pharmacy v. Virginia Citizens Consumer Council, Inc.*, 1976, 425 U.S. 748, 764–765).

classification implies a hierarchy. In the least ideal solution, if only one category of these types of space were to be legally protected as *entirely* ad-free, it should be category 1, due to the fact that circumstances connected with health and immediate safety are the most autonomy-compromising. If only two categories were to be legally protected as *entirely* ad-free, it should be categories 1 and 2, as category 2 also typically involves autonomy-compromising circumstances.[65]

It ought to be explicitly stressed here that if a category of types of space were to be legally protected as *entirely* ad-free, this would imply that no advertising whatsoever would be allowed within an entire category of types of space (in each and every type of space belonging to that category) without exceptions.

Other types of space—those not protected as entirely ad-free—would contain "pockets of ad-freedom": this would be the complementary part of the formula for a satisfactory solution. A "pocket of ad-freedom" would be a variation of an architectural concept of a space within a space. To elucidate, within a space which—in itself—is not off limits to advertising, a smaller space would be created, entirely free from advertising: an ad-free section of an ad-laden subway station, or ad-free relaxation rooms/areas in a shopping mall, etc.

The formula for a solution presented here is not ideal. It would not allow the agent to execute their choice not to be exposed to advertising *at will*: the agent could not switch modes—from advertising to non-advertising mode—as easily and instantaneously as in the example solution from Section 3.3.2. Sometimes it could be altogether impossible to execute one's choice not to be exposed to advertising; for instance, there would be too many people on the subway station to use the ad-free section of the subway. However, the agent would have the certainty that some types of space are entirely off limits to advertising, and that—in principle—it is possible to not be exposed to advertising within ad-laden spaces, even if this option is not always realizable.

3.4. To Close and to Inspire

3.4.1. Ad-Freedom

The discussion conducted in this book sheds light on a new concept: ad-freedom. The adjective "ad-free," which has been in use for quite some time now, refers

65 If only two categories were to be legally protected as ad-free, it might be considered whether public schools ought not be included in category 2, since they are a kind of service provided by the state, and school attendance in the majority of countries around the world is mandatory.

to things external to human beings, like an ad-free website, an ad-free green area, an ad-free sports event, an ad-free book. However, in Chapter 1 I suggested that it might make sense to start conceptualizing and actively using a noun "ad-freedom," derived from the adjective "ad-free," and I proposed that ad-freedom would refer to the type of freedom enjoyed due to the existence and accessibility of ad-free spaces and events. Ad-freedom would therefore be *a person's* freedom from advertising, and not a freedom ascribed to an object, an event, a space.

That ad-freedom is *a person's* freedom from advertising was further underscored in Chapter 2, where a relational approach to autonomy was applied and I discussed human relationships and interactions as being ad-free or not. Consequently, ad-freedom would refer to the type of freedom enjoyed by human beings due to the existence and accessibility of ad-free spaces, events, relationships, and interactions, or—more generally—due to the existence and accessibility of ad-free contexts of human everyday functioning.

What could be added here, based on the entire argument presented in this book, is that ad-freedom is not only a freedom *from* commercial advertising—and everything it stands for—but also a freedom *to* experience the everyday reality primarily as a noncommercial reality, with its multitude of noncommercial spaces, events, human interactions and relationships.

All in all, conceptualizing ad-freedom as a person's freedom constitutes a significant shift of focus, which allows for a formulation of the following conclusion: as a person's freedom, ad-freedom cannot be treated as a consumption good, meaning it cannot be bought, sold, or exchanged for any consumption good. Rooted in the noncommercial reality, ad-freedom can only be attained by noncommercial means. Thus, the concept of ad-freedom stands in sharp contrast to the concept of *paid* non-exposure to advertising.

3.4.2. Paid Non-Exposure to Advertising

Within the current reality of the omnipresence of advertising, it is often the case that one faces a choice between being exposed to commercial advertising and paying for not being exposed to it. In such a reality, the state of not being exposed to advertising becomes a consumption good, and a person who has to pay for her non-exposure to advertising is still *de facto* subjugated to the overwhelming presence of commercial advertising because having to choose a commercial way out of being exposed to commercial messages means that one continues to be trapped within the commercial realm that operates according to the rules and logic of commercial advertising. In other words, paid non-exposure to advertising is an option that materializes commercial values and serves commercial interests; it belongs to the commercial realm and does not really offer freedom from commercial advertising and everything that commercial advertising stands for. What is (literally) on offer is merely non-exposure, not ad-freedom.

In Section 3.3.2, I have given an example solution to the problems presented in this book in order to show that solutions are conceivable. Drawing attention to the contrast between ad-freedom and paid non-exposure could be helpful to others who will continue the search for *good* solutions; a good solution, I claim, must not confuse these two terms. To be blunt, there is no place for paid non-exposure within any good solution to the problems discussed in this book, because paid non-exposure is just another facet of the objectification discussed in the argument from non-benign objectification and the erosion of trust: just like people's cognitive resources were shown to be treated as a consumption good that can be bought and sold, so is non-exposure to advertising. If one has to pay for non-exposure to advertising, and it is no longer possible to take non-exposure to advertising for granted (i.e., to simply enjoy it in the form of ad-freedom), then one is objectified in a non-benign way: what ought to be a person's freedom is treated as a sellable good which is owned by another, the advertiser, who does not care how the objectified person feels, what that individual really wants, and how it influences the development, maintenance, and exercise of that person's autonomy competency.

3.4.3. Paths for Further Study

The argument presented in this book is composed of two main parts—the definitional exploration and the fleshing out of novel argumentation concerning the topic of the omnipresence of advertising—both of which open new paths for further study: philosophical, extra-philosophical, multidisciplinary.

The definitional exploration provides a solid basis for further study of the omnipresence of advertising. Ethics-wise, more ethical violations could be investigated—those that are connected with personal autonomy (for instance, violations regarding other autonomy skills than those investigated herein), as well as those connected with other ethical values. But the definitional exploration in this book can also be useful for other disciplines, like urban studies (to critically examine how the current spatial arrangements of the cities enable the omnipresence of advertising), law (to critically examine the current legal regulations that make the omnipresence of advertising possible), linguistics (to investigate the linguistic consequences of the omnipresence of advertising[66]), or

66 A small sample of what such research could involve is provided in the Short Linguistic

political studies (to study the antidemocratic character of the omnipresence of advertising).

The argumentative work in this book generates some paths for potential future study as well. For instance, the argument from non-benign objectification and the erosion of trust has touched upon the ethical theme of trust and trustworthiness. However, I have intentionally limited my interest in this topic to the kind of trust and trustworthiness which are autonomy-relevant in a direct and explicit manner because they take place between a person in need of autonomy support and an autonomy-supporting other. The influence of the omnipresence of advertising on other kinds of trust and trustworthiness have been left unexplored and could constitute material for future study.[67] In fact, it would be of high value if social psychologists researched to what extent the main purpose of a given type of space (or event) is being corrupted by the presence of advertising, and how this might erode relationships of trust connected with this type of space (or event).

Another ethical theme that has emerged during the analysis of the omnipresence of advertising conducted through the lens of relational autonomy is vulnerability. Although vulnerability is intertwined with relational autonomy and I have embraced this intertwinement in my analysis, vulnerability has not been my primary focus and I believe that more remains to be said regarding this topic, for instance, at the intersection of the themes of vulnerability and embodiment. Consider, for example, a local kind of omnipresence of advertising in a city, with a lot of large format advertisements diverting a person's attention, obstructing the full view of the surroundings, and covering the facades of the buildings: when certain visual cues which allow to identify the buildings are concealed or made less visible, making sense of one's immediate surroundings becomes much more challenging and stressful, especially when a heightened kind of vulnerability might be involved (for instance, a person is a child, an elderly person, a non-resident of that area).

The argumentative work in this book has also shed light on a new facet of the notion of captive audience, thus making it applicable to new sets of circumstances which involve the audience's mobility. This fresh perspective offered in the argument from a captive audience might inspire legal scholars to revisit and

---

Appendix.

67 For example, the empirical data gathered in Chapter 1 seem to suggest that it might be worthwhile to investigate the impact of the omnipresence of advertising on the trustworthiness—and also integrity—of people as skilled professionals.

further develop the captive audience doctrine to make it fit more contexts of everyday human experience.

Hopefully, the definitional exploration and the argumentative work combined together can also stimulate the legal scholars to look for legal solutions to the problems caused by the omnipresence of advertising. In a similar vein, the problems discussed in this monograph call for new urban planning solutions. Finding such solutions is beyond the scope of this volume, but it would be an important extension of the work presented herein.

What is also beyond the scope of this book is studying the full extent of the corrosion of public discourse caused by the omnipresence of advertising and the invasion of everyday reality with commercial speech, commercial values, and commercial interests. But the definitional exploration and the argumentation presented herein may serve as a springboard for political scientists and sociologists to undertake the analyses necessary for such a study.

Furthermore, it would be a natural extension of both the definitional exploration and the argumentative work in this volume to study how the discussion and conclusions presented herein could be applied to the virtual reality, which has not been the explicit focus of this book.

Another natural extension of the definitional and the argumentative work would be the study—especially by ethicists and media scholars—of different kinds of advertising than commercial advertising, especially in the context of my postulate of entirely ad-free spaces. For instance, should political advertising and social advertising also be banned from these "entirely ad-free spaces" or not?[68] If yes, then for what reasons? With all probability, these would not be the exact same reasons as those discussed herein.[69] A related, much more general question that arises is whether it could be ethically justified to put spatial confines on other kinds of persuasive speech; should there be some publicly accessible "sanctuaries" from all kinds of persuasion?

Finally, what I wish to share with other scholars is the concept of ad-freedom, which stems largely from the definitional exploration, but which has also profited from the discussion in the argumentative chapter. As this book draws to a close,

---

68 This could, *inter alia*, depend on the existence of a hidden commercial agenda behind certain political or social advertisements.

69 It could also be discovered that social advertising and/or political advertising foster the development, maintenance, and exercise of autonomy competency, instead of working against it.

I leave the concept of ad-freedom open to further theorization, critique, and practical application by scholars from all disciplines to which it may be relevant.

3.4.4. Final Remarks

I wish to close this book with two general conclusions, the first one being that the omnipresence of advertising is characterized by complexity—both on the ontological and on the ethical level. In the process of definitional exploration, I have emphasized that the omnipresence of advertising is an ontologically complex phenomenon, not reducible to the mere issue of the amount of advertising: this is an important shift in the way that the omnipresence of advertising has been perceived. In addition, if what I have argued in Chapter 2 is correct, then the omnipresence of advertising is complex also because of its multifaceted corrosive influence on the entire tissue of personal autonomy, i.e., on what is external to the agent, meaning the spatio-tempo-relational circumstances in which one develops, maintains, and exercises autonomy competency, as well as on what is internal to the agent, like self-trust and autonomy skills.

The second conclusion is that the omnipresence of advertising has a counterpart—its nemesis, we might say—and that is ad-freedom, construed as a freedom of persons. However, this counterpart, or counterpower, will not materialize *ex nihilo*. It has to be actively created through prioritizing the noncommercial everyday reality of human beings over the reality of commercial interests, commercial benefits, and commercial values. Prioritizing noncommercial interactions with oneself, others, and the environment in the everyday human experience would create favorable conditions for the flourishing of critical interchange of personal thoughts, ideas, and values between self-expressing individuals, and for people's engagement in autonomy-enriching-and-supporting social practices, both as trustworthy givers of autonomy support and as trustworthy receivers within autonomy-supporting networks. This is the kind of thriving that human beings need to practice autonomy skills on a daily basis, and therefore to be skilled in shaping their selves and being themselves.

4 The Legal Appendix

4.1. Introduction

The purpose of this appendix is to present selected topics from the scholarly discourse concerning the notion of commercial speech within the American legal system. Due to the notion originating from the American legal discourse, the American scholarly debate on commercial speech is rich and in many respects pioneering: for instance, it was an American legal scholar who first took the topic of the pervasiveness of commercial speech seriously before any philosophical scholars did.

I begin the appendix by differentiating commercial speech from noncommercial speech. Then, I go on to discuss why commercial speech is seen as valuable from the point of view of the American Constitution—this elucidates the rationale behind protecting commercial speech under the First Amendment. After that, I present the typical reasons for limiting the freedom of commercial speech, which are connected with the contents of the advertising message or with a particular target audience of commercial speech. In the consecutive sections, I discuss the captive audience doctrine in the context of commercial speech, as well as the topic of the pervasiveness of commercial speech. In these sections, I point to the connection between the subject of commercial speech and the ethical values of privacy and autonomy.

All of the topics presented below have been a valuable source of inspiration for writing this book.

4.2. Commercial Speech in the American Legal Discourse

4.2.1. Commercial Speech Versus Noncommercial Speech

The notion of commercial speech has originally been developed in the United States. At first, "purely commercial advertising" was declined the First Amendment protection (*Valentine v. Chrestensen*, 1942, 316 U.S. 52, 54; see Post, 2000, 2), but in 1976 the Supreme Court[70] reversed its position on this issue and declared that commercial speech—just like noncommercial speech (often

70 Hereinafter the American Supreme Court is referred to as "the Court" since this is the common practice in the relevant academic discourse. Whenever the word "court" is written *without* the capital letter, it refers to a lower-level court.

referred to as "core speech")—falls under the protection of the First Amendment (*Virginia State Board of Pharmacy v. Virginia Citizens Consumer Council, Inc.*, 1976, 425 U.S. 748). The 1976 verdict gave rise to the so-called "commercial speech doctrine."

However, the fact that both kinds of speech are now protected under the First Amendment does not entail that they are protected to the same degree. In fact, commercial speech gets reduced constitutional protection (*United States v. Edge Broadcasting Co.*, 1993, 509 U.S. 418; see Post, 2000, 2, 46–47), meaning that it is easier to put legal restrictions on commercial speech (Ruane, 2014, 15; Post, 2000, 3). Although some Justices and legal scholars disagree with such different treatment of the two kinds of speech and support the view that there is no "philosophical or historical basis for asserting that commercial speech is of 'lower value' than 'noncommercial' speech" (*44 Liquormart, Inc. v. Rhode Island*, 1996, 517 U.S. 484, 522, Thomas, J., concurring; see Post, 2000, 2, and Pomeranz, 2012, 407, ftn 101),[71] the justification for treating the two kinds of speech differently can be found in the relevant literature. At the core of this justification lies the claim that commercial speech and noncommercial speech are qualitatively different. I will now try to explain how.

First of all, the flow of information in commercial speech goes only one way: from the seller to the prospective consumer. In the words of Victor Brudney, "commercial speech is much less likely to be challenged by, responded to, or corrected by third parties" (Brudney, 2012, 1223). Noncommercial speech, on the other hand, is interactive in its nature: speakers can become listeners and listeners can become speakers (Pomeranz, 2012, 401). Second of all, the *raison d'être* of the two kinds of speech is different. The *raison d'être* of noncommercial speech is the interchange of thoughts and ideas within public discourse. As stressed by Jennifer Pomeranz, "this type of exchange only occurs in the realm of core speech [= noncommercial speech]" (2012, 401). In contrast, the *raison d'être* of commercial speech is to propose a commercial transaction[72] (Ruane, 2014,

---

71 Good examples of scholars who advocate the view that commercial speech should not be regarded as having lower value are Martin H. Redish and David F. McGowan. See Redish, 1982, 630–635; McGowan, 1990.

72 This definition of commercial speech derives from a leading commercial speech case, *Virginia State Board of Pharmacy v. Virginia Citizens Consumer Council, Inc.*, 1976, 425 U.S. 748, 762, where the Court referred to commercial speech as "speech which does 'no more than propose a commercial transaction'" (The Court quoted *Pittsburgh Press Co. v. Pittsburgh Commission on Human Relations,* 1973, 413 U.S. 376, 385). In a different case, the Court has also referred to commercial speech as "expression related solely to the economic interests of the speaker and its audience." See *Central Hudson*

14; Pomeranz, 2012, 395) and provide the potential consumer with information about the object of the potential transaction. In the light of these differences, commercial speech in itself is not considered to be a part of the public discourse (Post, 2000, 4).[73]

It might be mentioned here that some legal scholars—R. George Wright, for example—find defining commercial speech as speech that proposes a commercial transaction problematic. Wright points out that numerous "commercial forms of speech often do not fit neatly into the category of proposals": these are, *inter alia*, certain proxy statements, reports to shareholders, accounting or budget reports, corporate financial statements, product safety brochures, warranties (Wright, 1997, 55).

4.2.2. The Value of Commercial Speech

In order to establish a point of contrast for the constitutional value of commercial speech, I wish to start by briefly describing the value of noncommercial speech. When it comes to noncommercial speech, both the speaker's and the listener's interests are considered important (Pomeranz, 2012, 400): the value of noncommercial speech is connected with the speaker's right of self-expression and with the listener's right to be well-informed. Noncommercial speech is constitutionally valuable because the interchange of thoughts and ideas is key to democratic decision-making and to "the discovery and spread of political truth" (*Kleindienst v. Mandel*, 1972, 408 U.S. 753, 775, Marshall, J., dissenting; quoted in Pomeranz, 2012, 401)

Conversely, the protection of commercial speech under the First Amendment is characterized by laying stress on the listener's interest and the lack of focus on the speaker's (the seller's) interest. As emphasized by the Court in 1976 (*Virginia State Board of Pharmacy v. Virginia Citizens Consumer Council, Inc.*, 1976, 425 U.S. 748, 764–765),[74] "the primary purpose for protecting commercial speech is to ensure the free flow of commercial information to benefit the listener to

---

Gas and Electric Corp. v. Public Service Commission, 1980, 477 U.S. 557, 561. However, this second definition did not really gain much popularity within the legal discourse connected with commercial speech.

73 Post discusses the contrast between commercial speech and what has been referred to by the Court as 'public discourse' in such cases as *Rosenberger v. University of Virginia*, 1995, 515 U.S. 819; *Hustler Magazine, Inc. v. Falwell*, 1988, 485 U.S. 46; *Murdock v. Pennsylvania*, 1943, 319 U.S. 105; *Thomas v. Collins*, 1945, 323 U.S. 516.

74 For the discussion of the Court's verdict in this case, see, for example, Post, 2000, 8–14.

support intelligent and well-informed consumer decisions" (Pomeranz, 2012, 401, paraphrasing the verdict of the Court). In 1978 the Court made this position even more explicit by saying that a "commercial advertisement is constitutionally protected not so much because it pertains to the seller's business as because it furthers the societal interest in the 'free flow of commercial information'" (*First National Bank v. Bellotti*, 1978, 435 U.S. 783, quoting *Virginia State Board of Pharmacy*; quoted in Post, 2000, 14). The 1980s verdicts reiterate this position: in 1980, the Court declared that the "First Amendment's concern for commercial speech is based on the informational function of advertising" (*Central Hudson Gas & Electric Corp. v. Public Services Commission*, 1980, 447 U.S. 557, 563; quoted in Post, 2000, 14), and in 1985 the Court made it clear that the "extension of First Amendment protection to commercial speech is justified principally by the value to consumers of the information such speech provides" (*Zauderer v. Office of Disciplinary Counsel*, 1985, 471 U.S. 625, 651; quoted in Pomeranz, 2012, 401). Finally, in the 1990s, the "Court's emphasis on the First Amendment interests of the listener in the commercial speech context" was underscored by Justice Blackmun (*City of Cincinnati v. Discovery Network*, 1993, 507 U.S. 410, 432; quoted in Pomeranz, 2012, 401, ftn 68). All in all, when it comes to commercial speech, "the First Amendment goes beyond the protection of (…) the self-expression of individuals" (*First National Bank v. Bellotti*, 1978, 435 U.S. 765, 783; quoted in Post, 2000, 14) and becomes very listener-oriented (Post, 2000, 14). In other words, the constitutional value of commercial speech is connected with the listener's right to be well-informed.

This right of the listener is considered important because it enables the listener to make intelligent consumer decisions. However, Robert Post gives an additional reason for the importance of the right of the listener to be well-informed in the context of commercial speech. The scholar points out that although commercial speech is not a part of the public discourse, the information conveyed by means of advertising *may* be of relevance to democratic decision-making and democratic self-governance: for instance, Post says, advertising may provide citizens with information that the cost of gasoline is rising, and this affords the citizens a possibility to organize themselves politically to advocate—within public discourse—for government action to control the prices. In this sense, even if commercial speech is not a part of the public discourse, it *may* contribute to the formation of public discourse (2000, 11).

Without Post's argument, the constitutional value of commercial speech seems to be connected merely with the listener's right to be well-informed as a consumer. With Post's argument, however, comes a new argumentative force: the constitutional value of commercial speech becomes connected with the listener's right to be well-informed also as a citizen, not only as a consumer.

4.2.3. Freedom of Commercial Speech and Its Limitations

In the previous sections, commercial speech has been shown to be qualitatively different from noncommercial speech, but still constitutionally valuable. Now I would like to focus on the views regarding how and why freedom of commercial speech should be restricted.

Generally speaking, the Court has been limiting the freedom of commercial speech in two ways: (1) the advertiser can be compelled to disclose some kind of information (such instances are referred to in the doctrine as "compelled speech"; see, for example, Ruane, 2014, 18), or (2) the advertiser may be compelled to refrain—partially or fully—from speaking (such instances are referred to in the doctrine as "compelled silence"; see Ruane, 2014, 18). As to the most typical reasons why methods (1) and (2) may be applied, they are as follows. The advertiser can be compelled to disclose some kind of information because the content of the advertising message is somewhat incomplete, inaccurate, or misleading, or because the advertising message contains false information.[75] As to the compelled silence measure, this measure can be imposed on the advertiser when the contents of the advertising message is aggressive or when the advertised product is illegal (McGowan, 1990, 364; Post, 2000, 46, Ruane, 2014, 15). However, the advertiser can also be compelled to be wholly or partially silent due to targeting a particular audience, like children, for instance (Browne, Biksacky, Frondorf, 2009). To give another example, in 1995, the Court upheld as constitutional a law that prohibited injury lawyers from direct-mail solicitations of accident victims for thirty days following an accident or disaster (*Florida Bar v. Went For It, Inc.*, 1995, 515 U.S. 618; mentioned in Ruane, 2014, 15, ftn 99); it has been argued that such advertising practice was "intrusive" upon "the privacy and tranquility of personal injury victims" (Moore, Murray, 2008, 267).

75 "Advertising that is false, deceptive, or misleading of course is subject to restraint." *Bates v. State Bar of Ariz*, 1977, 433 U.S. 350, 380. Quoted in Pomeranz, 2012, 415, ftn 153; see also Pomeranz, 2012, 400, ftn 63, 403–404; Corbin, 2009, 985; Brudney, 2012, 1175, ftn 71. It should be mentioned that it is also possible to apply the compelled silence measure in the above-mentioned cases, especially when commercial speech is false.

4.2.4. The Captive Audience Doctrine

Another reason why the commercial speaker can be forced into silence or partial silence is connected with the speaker holding the audience "captive" to speech.

To elucidate, the captive audience doctrine states that a speaker imposes speech on an audience and holds them captive when the audience is unwilling to receive the speech but "practically helpless to escape" it (Strauss, 1991, 85; quoting *Kovacs v. Cooper*, 1949, 336 U.S. 77).[76] Also, in order "to qualify as a captive audience, the unwanted message must invade the audience's privacy in an 'essentially intolerable manner'" (Corbin, 2009, 946, quoting *Cohen v. California*, 1971, 403 U.S. 15, 21). The connection with privacy touches the very roots of the captive audience doctrine, which are said to go as far as the landmark paper on privacy by Samuel Warren and Louis Brandeis (1890).[77] To elaborate, what the captive audience doctrine invokes is "the right to be let alone" (Strauss, 1991, 86, see also ftn 6), considered by Warren and Brandeis to be crucial for the development of an "inviolate personality (1890, 194–195, 205)."

One more thing that should be said concerning the definition of a captive audience in the American law is that this notion is *not* conceived in such a way that in order to qualify as a "captive auditor" one literally has to have no way out. An "impossibility standard" dictating that speech should be silenced only when it is impossible for the audience to escape from the speech would almost never be applicable to reality.[78] As Marcy Strauss remarks, a person is very rarely (if ever) genuinely captive to speech; in fact, there is almost always some alternative by means of which the audience can avoid the message (Strauss, 1991, 86). Therefore, as Wojciech Sadurski stresses, the notion of captive audience cannot be taken literally. He says that the doctrine mainly rests on the principle of respect for an agent's autonomy: if the agent is put in circumstances where it is impossible for them to make a choice regarding whether or not to listen to a given token of speech, or the choice would entail "high personal costs, then the law should support the audience against the speaker" (Sadurski, 1999, 92). In fact, the Court has formulated, what might be called, a standard of "impracticality."

76 Captive audience doctrine is not limited to commercial speech. As far as noncommercial speech goes, captive audience doctrine can be applied to such contexts as employer free speech, for instance (see, for example, Hartley, 2010).

77 For the background story on what stimulated the writing of Warren and Brandeis' paper, see Prosser, 1960.

78 The "impossibility standard" was proposed by Franklyn S. Haiman in the following paper: Haiman, 1972, 182–184, 194–195.

According to the captive audience doctrine, a person is held captive by speech when "the degree of captivity makes it impractical for the unwilling (…) auditor to avoid exposure" (*Erznoznik v. City of Jacksonville*, 1975, 422 U.S. 205, 209; quoted in Corbin, 2009, 946).[79] For example, a person using a bus is held captive by what is communicated on the posters inside the bus not because there is no way to avoid looking at the messages on the posters—this individual could simply get off the bus, and that would be a very simple way out of this situation. Instead, this person is held captive because they *need* to use the bus for their everyday functioning; having to get off earlier than planned would be disruptive to that person's everyday functioning and thus impractical.[80]

The most emblematic place, according to the Court, where one can be held captive by speech is one's home. A commercial speech case that illustrates this is *Breard v. City of Alexandria*. In *Breard*, the Court upheld as constitutional a local statute prohibiting uninvited commercial door-to-door solicitation. The Court stated that "the exigencies of trade are not ordinarily expected to have a higher rating constitutionally than the tranquility of the fireside (…) To force a community to admit the solicitors of publications into the home would be a gross misapplication of the First and Fourteenth Amendment guarantees" (*Breard v. City of Alexandria*, 1951, 341 U.S. 627, 645; quoted in Alton, 1976, 5).[81] Guided by a similar logic, in a later case of *Rowan v. U.S. Post Office Department*, the Court unanimously upheld a federal law authorizing householders to say "no" to being sent advertisements containing sexual materials which the householders found offensive; in the justification of the verdict, Chief Justice Burger stated that "the right of every person 'to be let alone' must be placed in the scales with the right of others to communicate" (*Rowan v. U.S. Post Office Department*, 1970, 397 U.S. 728, 736; quoted in Heyman, 2008, 151).

---

79 It might be added here that apart from the Court's standard of impracticality and Haiman's proposed standard of impossibility, there are other propositions regarding the notion of a captive audience. Douglas G. Lichtman, for example, has put forward a proposition that the existence of a captive audience should rather be a reason for imposing *lesser or no restrictions* on speech because the existence of a captive audience is an "asset" that should be utilized and not wasted away. See Lichtman, 2006.

80 This discussion concerns the case of *Lehman v. City of Shaker Heights*, 1974, 418 U.S. 302, which shall be invoked later in this section.

81 It should be noted though that the *Breard* verdict dates back from the time before commercial speech was explicitly granted First Amendment protection in *Virginia State Board*.

However, in the commercial speech cases connected with the domestic environment the scales have not always leaned in favor of the right to be let alone. In *Bolger v. Youngs Drug Products Corp.*, the Court declared unconstitutional a statute which put a ban on sending unsolicited advertisements for contraceptives to the home. The Court justified the verdict by saying that the recipients of mail were not powerless but could "effectively avoid further bombardment of their sensibilities simply by averting their eyes"; the Court also stated that the "short, though regular, journey from mail box to trash can (…) is an acceptable burden [for the recipients of mail], at least so far as the Constitution is concerned" (*Bolger v. Youngs Drug Products Corp.*, 1983, 463 U.S. 60; quoted in Strauss, 1991, 91). As noted by Strauss, the problem with the notion of "an acceptable burden" is that, looking at the captive audience doctrine cases, one notices that "the Court has not consistently explained when it will impose on the unwilling recipient some burden, even a minimal one, to turn away from the message, rather than silence the speaker" (Strauss, 1991, 91). What makes the verdict in *Bolger* even more surprising is that in a noncommercial speech case that took place just five years after *Bolger*, the Court stated that "the State's interest in protecting the well-being, tranquility, and privacy of the home is certainly of the highest order in a free and civilized society,"[82] and "there simply is no right to force speech into the home of an unwilling listener" (*Frisby v. Schultz*, 1988, 487 U.S. 474, 484–85).[83]

Anyhow, it is important to stress that the captive audience doctrine is not limited to the domestic environment. Even though the right to privacy outside of home is somewhat diminished, it does not mean that it is completely inapplicable to the outside-of-home locations. A good example of a noncommercial speech case in which the Court ruled that an audience is captive in a non-domestic location is *Hill v. Colorado*. In *Hill*, the Court upheld as constitutional a statute that limited the freedom of speech of activists who were protesting in front of an abortion clinic and engaging the clinic's patients in unwanted conversations: a part of the justification of the verdict was the protection of "the unwilling listener's interest in avoiding unwanted communication," which the Court recognized

82 Here the Court in *Frisby v. Schultz*, 1988, 487 U.S. 474, 484–85 is quoting *Carey v. Brown*, 1987, 447 U.S., 471.

83 *Frisby* concerns antiabortion speech. For a discussion of this case, see Heyman, 2008, 151. The quoted statement of the Court makes the *Bolger* verdict even more surprising because the Court is meant to be more strict regarding the noncommercial speech cases, as has been explained in the section *Commercial Speech Versus Noncommercial Speech*.

as an aspect of the broader right to privacy (*Hill v. Colorado*, 2000, 530 U.S. 703, 707–710).[84]

In turn, a good example of a commercial speech case in which an audience was declared captive in an outside-of-home location is *Lehman v. City of Shaker Heights*. In *Lehman*, the Court upheld a local ban on political advertising on buses, stating that "the streetcar audience is a captive audience. It is there as a matter of necessity, not of choice" (*Lehman v. City of Shaker Heights*, 1974, 418 U.S. 298, 302; quoted in Strauss 1991, 98).[85] Also, the Court famously remarked that whilst the radio with its advertising broadcast can be turned off, "not so the billboard or street car placard" (98). In his dissenting opinion in this case, Justice Brennan expressed a view that the bus audience was *not* a captive audience since the travelers could easily avoid looking at the advertising posters by averting their eyes (*Lehman v. City of Shaker Heights*, 1974, 418 U.S. 298, 320–21; see Sadurski, 1999, 93). Commenting upon the dissenting voice of Brennan, Sadurski wrote: "This may be true, though perhaps rather artificially so; written messages in places where we do not expect them (that is, which are typically not fora for communication) in a sense 'trap' us and the reality of a lengthy journey on a train or a bus may be such that the tired travelers stare, willy nilly, at the advertising messages and it takes a lot of force of will to avert one's eyes" (Sadurski, 1999, 93).[86]

Interestingly, in contrast with the *Lehman* verdict, in *Penthouse International, Ltd. v. Koch*—a case that did not reach the Supreme Court—the court decided not to treat the subway station users as an audience captive to the advertisements on the station walls, passways, and platforms (*Penthouse International, Ltd. v. Koch*, S.D.N.Y. 1984, 599 F. Supp. 1338, 1347–1349; discussed in Strauss 1991, 97, ftn 50). In her comment on this case, Strauss expresses surprise at the court not following the *Lehman* verdict since the bus and the subway situations seem similar. Strauss says: "The distinction between the bus and the subway is not obvious. The same ability to turn the eyes from the offensive message exists. Individuals 'need' to be on the platform for the same reasons they need to take the buses. Although there may be greater ability to move around the platform, that

84 For a discussion of the case, see, for example, Heyman, 2008, 150.

85 It seems that the verdict in Lehman might have been inspired by Justice Douglas' dissenting voice in *Public Utilities Commission v. Pollak*, 1952, 343 U.S. 451, 468. For more discussion on this, see Strauss 1991, 97, ftn 50.

86 Sadurski is commenting on the dissenting voice of Justice Brennan, but also on the voice of another commentator (Strauss, 1991) who supports the view of Justice Brennan.

is not always true, as anyone who has taken the subways in New York or Chicago during peek hours can attest" (Strauss, 1991, 97, ftn 50).

In her discussion of the captive audience doctrine outside of home, Strauss also brings attention to a more general but important matter: namely that most courts invoke the fact that we are inevitably captive audiences in society, forced to endure many unwanted stimuli.[87] But, Strauss says, "the descriptive statement that people are subjected to unwanted stimuli is not the same as saying that normatively they *should* be forced to endure them" (Strauss, 1991, 95). Even if it is indeed the case that people encounter unwelcome messages on a daily basis, it does not change the fact that some circumstances may arise when the law should intervene because people *should not* be forced to endure certain kinds of captivity to unwanted stimuli. Discerning these kinds of captivity that ought to trigger some kind of intervention is ethically and legally significant.

4.2.5. The Pervasiveness of Commercial Speech

4.2.5.1. Charles Black: An Early Intuition (1950s)

As mentioned in Chapter 0, the seeds of the omnipresence of advertising are scattered all over the 20th century. Thus, it is reasonable to assume that even before the last decade of the 20th century, some presentiment concerning the increasing presence of commercial speech in people's everyday lives might have been expressed. A good example comes from the 1950s paper of an American legal scholar, Charles Black.

Black begins by warning against underestimating the seriousness of the harm connected with being captive to commercial speech: "the triviality (…) of commercials tends to no extent whatever to imply the triviality of being forced to listen to them" (Black, 1953, 968). According to Black, freedom *from* unwanted speech[88] is as important as freedom *of* speech, and what is at stake if any of these freedoms were to be taken away from a person is that person's dignity: "Few shafts could strike with more on-target insult at the very manhood of humanity than its degradation into a collectivized *object* of speech, powerless to escape and powerless to answer (…) What is perfectly clear is that the claim to freedom

---

87 Strauss quotes the following case as an example: *Erznoznik v. City of Jacksonville*, 1975, 422 U.S. 205, 210; Strauss, 1991, 95.

88 That freedom *from* speech is one of the freedoms protected under the First Amendment has been postulated by such prominent First Amendement scholars as Thomas I. Emerson or Roger C. Hartley. See Emerson, 1970, 710; Hartley, 2010, 79–83.

from unwanted speech rests on grounds of high policy and on convictions of human dignity closely similar to if not identical with those classically brought forward in support of freedom of speech in the usual sense" (967).

Black then goes on to admit that the commercial speaker ("the adman") has the right to speak, but that having this right cannot imply that the audience is forced to hear the commercial speaker out: "The adman has every right to preach his Gospel, and to insinuate advocacy of the following of his Way. But is it consonant with any notion of free competition among ideas, or, indeed, of freedom of any kind, that all of us should be forced to hear him or become hermits? That is not true, and no one would dare suggest it be made true, of any other Way, or of any other Gospel" (968).

Black draws attention to an important point. Logically speaking, we have a way out of being held captive by the advertising that surrounds us: we could avoid exposure to advertising by becoming hermits. But Black makes a normative claim here: a person should not be put in a position, in which the only way to avoid exposure to advertising is the choice of becoming a hermit. This, he claims, is incompatible with the idea of freedom.

It is interesting to note here that becoming a hermit is a pretty drastic—not to say unnecessary—measure to avoid advertising if we consider the way advertising has been typically discussed in the captive audience doctrine: no one would really have to become a hermit to avoid one particular advertisement, or even a group of advertisements in one particular location. Therefore, the question is why Black would mention becoming a hermit as a solution to the exposure to advertising, and I believe that the answer is that he did not want to refer to the avoidance of one particular advertisement or a group of advertisements in one particular location. Instead, he wanted to refer to the avoidance of all advertising in general, and in this sense his reasoning might be applicable to the discussion of the pervasiveness of commercial speech because the solution of becoming a hermit is relevant precisely to such circumstances in which commercial speech becomes pervasive on a more global scale.

4.2.5.2. R. George Wright: Right on Time (1990s)

As Chapter 0 makes clear, it was the 1990s that witnessed the beginning of the phenomenon I refer to as the omnipresence of advertising. Therefore, when in 1997 R. George Wright publishes his legal analyses of what he calls "the pervasiveness of commercial speech," or "the pervasiveness of the culture of commercial speech" (5, 40), he reacts to what is happening around him in real time. In fact, he is the first scholar to react to the phenomenon not by mentioning it briefly or peripherally, but by making it an important topic of his research; philosophy scholars will follow his lead with their ethical analyses only after the turn of the century (see the Ethical Appendix).

Wright begins to describe the pervasiveness of commercial speech by providing a practical example of the manifestation of this phenomenon: an American school that used to be called President Franklin Delano Roosevelt Junior High, and now goes by the name of Arrid-Mentos Junior High (the word "Arrid" refers to a brand of a deodorant, and the word "Mentos" refers to a brand of sweets). Wright adds that the school is situated on a street that used to be called Minerva Street, but now has been officially renamed Ford Bronco Drive (after a type of a Ford vehicle). I will not paraphrase the entirety of Wright's description of the school's premises, but I will provide a sample. When the students go to the school cafeteria during the lunch break, all the tableware (trays, cups, napkins, etc.) are emblazoned with a Pepsi logo, and the school radio programs (including the school's official announcements) are interspersed with commercials. On the walls of the hall, one can see advertising posters, as well as continuously running TV monitors with advertising messages. Even during the lessons, the students are exposed to advertising because a lot of the classroom materials are sponsored: for example, the history lessons are sponsored by Hershey's, and therefore the students have to learn about the history of chocolate (1–3). In a nutshell, "the school has entered into a series of Faustian bargains in return for modest, but desperately needed, cash payments" (1–2), and the advertisers have used this opportunity to appropriate as much of the school's space as possible.

It is worth stressing that the example of Arrid-Mentos school is fictional. However, Wright creates this imaginary example on the basis of facts about American schooling (203), which I have illustrated with real-life examples in Chapter 1 of this book.

I will now quote Wright's immediate comment after invoking the example of Arrid-Mentos Junior High, and I will point to two meanings of the pervasiveness of commercial speech that could ensue. Wright states that "the most serious harm is that the school is teaching a generation of students that there is almost no place where commercial advertising, commercial relationships and commercial values do not belong. This school is in effect ratifying the pervasiveness of our commercial culture (…) Schools should not be in the business of implicitly announcing that commercial forces are deservedly, or at least inevitably, everywhere, and that no sanctuary, no perspective, no integrity, is possible" (5–6, 10).

What Wright says could be interpreted in two ways. Firstly, I believe that Wright wants to point the reader's attention to the fact that Arrid-Mentos Junior High is a school—if advertising is allowed to be present at a place where children receive their education, then this shows that commercial speech can truly be present everywhere. "The commercialization of the public school is nonetheless a betrayal of the students' basic interests. Public schools should reflect popular sovereignty and our democratically expressed will (…) public schools should honor, express, and embody our democratic values and (…), for the sake of those democratic values, retain some critical distance and detachment from all cultural institutions and forces only imperfectly embodying those values" (10). In a nutshell, a public school should serve as a "sanctuary" from commercial speech. If it stops to serve this function for the current and future generations, then advertising is permissible everywhere, and in this sense, we are dealing with the pervasiveness of commercial speech. Not in the sense that it is literally everywhere, but that *its presence is permissible everywhere.*

Whilst the first interpretation of the meaning of the pervasiveness of commercial speech would be connected with permissibility, the second could be connected with the overwhelming presence of advertising within the Arrid-Mentos school's premises. We can say that: (1) commercial speech pervades the school time (lessons, breaks, and lunchtime are all saturated with advertising); (2) commercial speech pervades the school space (it would be very difficult for the students to find a place within the school's premises where they would not be exposed to advertising); (3) commercial speech pervades the school's identity (the name of the school and the name of the street on which the school is situated derive from commercial brands, but also the school's speech to students is not free from commercial speech: the school's official announcements on the radio are sponsored by commercial brands and interspersed with commercials). According to this interpretation, we can also say that there is no "sanctuary" from advertising on a smaller scale: within the school's premises. In the microcosm of Arrid-Mentos Junior High, commercial speech *is present almost everywhere*, although—like with the previous interpretation—we cannot say that it is present *literally* everywhere.

The two interpretations of the meaning of the pervasiveness of commercial speech do not necessarily exclude one another; on the contrary, they may complement one another. However, to be fair to Wright, it seems that the meaning that he wanted to underscore is the one connected with permissibility. The students of Arrid-Mentos Junior High are victims of the pervasiveness of commercial speech because it is their *school*, not their neighboring shopping mall, that is subjected to a flood of advertisements—this experience teaches them that it is permissible for commercial speech and commercial culture to be almost everywhere. Furthermore, the harm comes also from the fact that the students cannot say "no" to this exposure to advertising. Even more importantly, they cannot say "no" to an identity change that this exposure to commercial speech causes in them. By getting used to experiencing commercial speech in more and more places—even such places as the school—the students begin to take it for granted that there is no place where commercial culture does not belong: all relationships and all situations can—in some way—be infused with commercial values.

But Wright wants to take his argument further: what happens to the students of Arrid-Mentos Junior High is something that happens to human beings in general. As more and more spaces fall prey to commercialization and we gradually habituate ourselves and desensitize ourselves to the ubiquitous and chronic exposure to commercial speech, we too absorb the message that it is permissible for commercial speech and commercial culture to be present almost everywhere. Wright's hypothesis is not implausible, since many psychological studies have shown that a lasting exposure to a particular phenomenon leads to habituation and desensitization to that phenomenon: for instance, chronic exposure to violence leads to desensitization to violence (e.g. Mrug et al., 2016; Brockmyer, 2012; American Academy of Pediatrics, 2009; Bartholow et al., 2006) or consistent exposure to environmental degradation leads to desensitization to environmental degradation (Alhadeff, 2015).

Consequently, faced with the ubiquitous and chronic exposure to commercial speech *via* advertising, we start to believe it is normal that no "sanctuary" exists, and this changes us. Whatever parts of our lives and selves used to be noncommercial, they are now becoming more and more commercialized, without us even noticing. "The pervasiveness of our commercial culture is (…) a matter of the ways in which commercialism and commercial values affect how we experience the otherwise noncommercial elements of our lives. That is, personal relationships that might otherwise have been based primarily on friendship, love, respect, legitimate authority, or considerations of dignity have gradually been tainted and transformed, however subtly, by elements drawn from the commercial sphere" (6). As a result, our selves become more and more commercial, and the most important area in which this is realized is the area of values and valuing. This is reflected, for example, in the way human beings judge one another: "we are increasingly judged on the ability—past, present, or future—to contribute usefully to the commercial culture. There are, of course, other ways of judging persons, or of extending and withholding honor and respect. Such ways are, however, currently fading in importance" (202). This kind of a change in valuing is a significant identity change for the human beings to whom Wright's comment is applicable. In the concluding chapter of his book, Wright issues the following warning: "the commercialization process changes not only what we value but also what we are capable of valuing. Thus it may hinder our very capacity for enjoying less commercial values" (199).

Wright connects the topic of the change to human identity with the subject of autonomy. As observed by Wright, some changes to who we are require making a conscious and explicit decision. If we were to become a doctor, even if we were unaware of the multitude of the alternative courses of action to becoming a doctor, at least we would be aware of the alternative of not becoming a doctor, and such an alternative would seem realistic to choose. But when it comes to having our self infused with commercialism, most of us are either unaware of any alternative ways of being or regard such ways of being as unfeasible and unrealistic in the contemporary society. Thus, there is no moment of decision about being infused with commercialism because we can hardly be said to have a choice in this matter. This change just happens to us due to the continuously expanding presence of commercial culture (24–25). In fact, it has already happened to a large number of human beings—Wright says: "by now, it is difficult to imagine a preexisting, noncommercial self to be subsequently affected by the commercial culture" (6). However, provided appropriate tools were in force to keep commercial speech at bay, we could have a say regarding *the extent* to which our self and our life are infused with commercialism: even if a completely noncommercial self is not an option, we could still be given a choice of having a less commercial self as an alternative to a more commercial self. But for such an alternative to exist and for us to be able to exercise our autonomy in this respect, the pervasiveness of commercial speech would have to be regulated. If it remains unregulated, our autonomous critical decision making shall continue to be traded away, just like the autonomous, critical decision making of the Arrid-Mentos students is being traded away "for gym shoes" (11). As Wright stresses, "increasingly, there is a danger of confusing a diversity of choice among market goods and services with freedom itself, in the form of diversity in basic ways of living and thinking. Being able to choose among brands and products is a poor sort of freedom if our culture prevents us, realistically if not formally, from seriously considering less consumption-oriented ways of living" (46). Interestingly, Wright adds that our freedom would also suffer in a culture that would be uniformly against consumption-oriented ways of living. What he advocates is not a society that would reject commercial culture altogether, but such in which one would have a genuine choice between different ways of living, thinking, and valuing (46–47).

The lack of choice between the more commercial self and the less commercial self, according to Wright, is most troubling in the case of poor people. It is the poor children that will most often find themselves in the position of the Arrid-Mentos Junior High students (203), and it is the poor people that will most often find themselves in a situation in which they can pick a highly commercialized version of a product or no product at all, which can hardly be called a choice (131). This social group will therefore be most affected by the pervasiveness of commercial speech.

Wright concludes: "What we can do for the poor in this regard, beyond relieving their poverty, corresponds closely to what we should be doing in our own narrow interests. We should rethink our recent exaltation of commercial speech. Permitting the reasonable regulation of commercial speech might contribute to a broader process of 'denaturalizing' the currently dominant culture of consumption and of legitimizing other approaches to contemporary life" (203). No matter the financial status, it is in the best interest of all people that many different ways of living (not only consumption-oriented ways of living) constitute real options that we as autonomous agents are free to choose.[89] The necessary—though not sufficient—condition to achieve that is the reasonable legal regulation of commercial speech: "the reasonable regulation of commercial speech is merely one step in a complex process of legitimizing and facilitating free choices of either commercial or less commercial styles of life, consistent with democracy, the free speech clause, and the rest of the Constitution" (Wright, 1997, 18).

Parenthetically, it is possible to imagine an alternative line of thinking, according to which it is the rich who are more in danger of having a more commercialized self: having the means to buy all—or a lot of—the advertised goods means that the rich, and their children, are especially prone to acquiring a belief that everything can be bought, everything can be monetized. Conversely, the poor would be less inclined to think this way due to being able to afford a very limited amount of the advertised products. Even more so, being in financial distress could lead to a stronger inclination to contest a way of living which is heavily influenced by commercial values, and an increased drive to look for different values on which an individual's personality could be constructed.

Interestingly, the alternative line of reasoning and the one presented by Wright do not exclude one another: the rich, and their children, might indeed show more inclination to have an excessively commercialized self for the reason mentioned above, but at the same time it is true that the poor, and their children, have more limited options of avoiding exposure to commercial speech—which might have a bearing on the construction of a self—due to not being able to afford paid non-exposure to advertising (see Chapter 3 of this book).

---

89 That decommercialization of public places is beneficial for human autonomy is suggested also by Timothy Zick. Zick writes that the commercialization of public places often drastically reduces freedom of the embodied expression. See Zick, 2009, 98–99.

5 The Ethical Appendix

5.1. Introduction

This appendix is divided into two parts. The first part is devoted to the topic of advertising being a threat to personal autonomy from the perspective of other ethicists. The second part of the appendix is meant give an overview of what has been said by ethics scholars concerning the omnipresence of advertising.

5.2. The Autonomist Analysis of Advertising in the Ethical Discourse

Ethicists who have chosen to discuss the thesis that advertising is a threat to personal autonomy have approached the debate from many different angles, taking different definitions of autonomy as the basis. Below is an overview of four important ethical approaches to the topic of advertising and the value of autonomy. In the names of these approaches, the suffix *-ian* is used to indicate that the definitional basis of the critical approach derives from the philosophy of a particular philosopher: Harry Frankfurt, Charles Taylor, Robert Noggle, Immanuel Kant.

5.2.1. Arrington's Frankfurtian Autonomist Defense of Advertising and Its Criticisms

There is a famous debate between two authors—Robert L. Arrington (1982) and Roger Crisp (1987)—who both take Harry Frankfurt's theory of first-order and second-order desires (1971) as the definitional basis of what they understand as autonomy.

Although Frankfurt did not use the term "autonomy," he did discuss the notion of the "freedom of will." According to Frankfurt, an agent whose will is free has both kinds of desires, and his second-order desires are not just desires about first-order desires: they are desires about the first-order desires being effective (1971, 8–9). An agent who is capable of enjoying the freedom of will wants some of his first-order desires to have bearing on his actions, and thus to constitute his will (8, 10, 14). When the second-order desires of an agent imply the agent wanting some of his first-order desires to constitute his will, Frankfurt calls these second-order desires *second-order volitions* (10), and it is having and exercising second-order volitions that Frankfurt considers essential to having and enjoying the freedom of will (14).

Taking this theory as a foundation, Arrington forms the definition of nonautonomous desires and autonomous desires. About nonautonomous desires he says that these are first-order desires "which one might have but with which one would not identify. They are experienced as foreign to one's character or personality" (1982, 7). The lack of identification with a given first-order desire comes from the level of second-order desires: when one has a second-order desire not to have and not to fulfill some first-order desire, then—Arrington says—this first-order desire is nonautonomous (7). Arrington gives an example of a kleptomaniac who has a first-order desire to steal, but on the level of second-order desires, he does not identify with the first-order desire to steal; he finds it repulsive, wishes to be rid of this desire, and seeks treatment for that purpose (7).

In contrast, Arrington defines autonomous desires in the following way: "When on the contrary a person has a second-order desire to maintain and fulfill a first-order desire, then the first-order desire is truly his own, autonomous, original to him" (7). By defining autonomous desires in this way, Arrington takes a stand against the utilitarian criticism of advertising proposed by John Kenneth Galbraith (1952/1995, 134–136). Arrington interprets Galbraith as suggesting that all desires which are induced by advertising are necessarily nonautonomous (not original to the agent), and in this sense all advertising which persuades its audience to have a certain desire violates the audience's autonomy. Referring to Frankfurt allows Arrington to say that a first-order desire being induced does not automatically entail that it is impossible for the agent to identify with this first-order desire and thus to claim it as chosen autonomously (Arrington, 1982, 7). If such automatic entailment as Galbraith suggests were the case, then—Arrington says—the only autonomous desires would be "the purely physical ones for food, shelter, sex, etc."; in contrast, all the culturally induced desires could never be claimed as our own (6–7). For example, we could never claim the desire to listen to our favorite music as a first-order desire that we have autonomously chosen to identify with.

The idea to disagree with the conclusion (implicit in Galbraith's reasoning) that all culturally induced desires are of necessity nonautonomous was first conceived by Friedrich A. von Hayek (1961). But Arrington enriches Hayek's reasoning by applying the elements of Frankfurt's theory to the argument against Galbraith: Arrington suggests that the autonomy of desires does not consist in having only non-induced desires, but in being able to autonomously choose which first-order desires—induced or non-induced—one wants to (this is the "want to" from the level of second-order volitions) maintain and fulfill as those with which one identifies (1982, 7). By this token, a culture-induced first-order desire to listen to Satie's music or an advertising-induced first-order desire to buy an Esprit sweater may well be autonomous, provided that the agent who has the first-order desire identifies with it, meaning that she has a second-order volition to have and to fulfill the first-order desire to listen to Satie's music or to buy an Esprit sweater.

There are two important autonomist critics of Arrington's defense of advertising: one is Taylor R. Durham and the other is Roger Crisp. Each of them criticizes a different aspect of Arrington's defense, but neither of them undermines Arrington's Frankfurtian way of defining autonomy: this seems to be taken for granted as felicitous.

Durham accuses Arrington of building his defense of advertising on the false assumption that all advertising addresses the mass audience, thus ignoring important threats to autonomy which are peculiar to the more and more popular kind of advertising that targets a particular audience (Durham, 1984, 173). Durham says that "this underlying assumption of one message, one audience is flatly contrary to much advertising since the turn of the century, and ignores the rapid increase in the specialized cultivation of particular customer groups or market segments since the early 1960s" (173).

To illustrate the threats to autonomy that Arrington ignores, Durham describes concrete cases which he believes to be emblematic. A particularly interesting case is that of the tobacco industry developing two different advertising strategies for two different target audiences: the rationale behind this is to keep as high sales results as possible despite consumers' growing consciousness of the health risks connected with smoking and the increasing concern with personal health in general (1984, 177). In order to stop these trends from significantly eroding cigarette sales, the tobacco industry introduces a whole selection of low-tar cigarette brands (including low-tar versions of major traditional brands) and launches advertising campaigns targeted exclusively at the more highly educated smokers, who—according to research—are most likely to take the risk to health seriously and either quit smoking altogether or reduce the number of cigarettes they smoke (177). But this advertising strategy is meant exclusively for this particular audience, while the people whom the research depicts as less likely to be concerned with their health and therefore less likely to change their smoking habits continue to be targeted with the advertisements of the traditional high-tar cigarettes; in other words, the information about the new low-tar alternatives is purposely withheld from them (177).

By presenting cases of this sort, Durham conveys an important message: when it comes to advertising, we should be concerned with more than just the typical instances of deception, meaning such cases in which the claims in advertising messages are false or some important information about the product's safety is not disclosed. Durham wishes to show us that although such cases as the tobacco industry case do not instantiate this typical kind of deception, ethicists should not automatically assume that the advertising employed in these instances is moral. In fact, Durham claims that in cases like the tobacco industry case a different kind of deception is at play, which—using a more contemporary vocabulary—we would call "deception by omission" or "misinformation by omission": "Here the deception might be interpreted as allowing some groups, but not others, to continue holding certain beliefs about the available opportunities to fulfill certain needs or desires. Rather than falsely represent the particular set of attributes obtainable through a specific product, the advertising strategy misrepresents the set of alternative attribute bundles" (179). According to Durham, such structuring of information poses a threat to autonomy: "While such strategies may not in their content undermine or denigrate rational decision making in general, they can constrain the scope of such decision processes for some groups relative to others, and thus in effect restrict the range and value of personal autonomy" (179). And this is the kind of threat to autonomy that Arrington, in his absolution of persuasive advertising, did not consider.

Another important critic of Arrington is Crisp. In his criticism, Crisp adopts Arrington's Frankurtian view and beats Arrington with his own weapon: Crisp says that "many of us have a strong second-order desire not to be manipulated by others without our knowledge, and for no good reason" (1987, 414). Therefore, once we discovered that we have been manipulated by persuasive advertising to buy a certain product or service, we would no longer want to endorse the fulfillment of the first-order desire for that product or service, even if in different circumstances we might want to endorse it (415). In other words, if our first-order desires were manipulated, we would feel resentment towards the manipulators, and we would disown this particular manifestation of our first-order desires which have been aroused by persuasive advertising with the use of manipulation (415).

It is easy to see why Crisp's argumentation makes sense. To understand this, let us take a somewhat analogous case from the field of sexual ethics: one might have a first-order desire to have sex and a second-order desire to endorse the realization of this first-order desire. However, the issue of *how* (in what circumstances) one would realize this first-order desire matters and would most certainly influence one's endorsement of the idea of fulfilling this first-order desire in the particular circumstances in question. Let us imagine that person x—who has the second-order desire not to be manipulated—would have the first-order desire to have sex with a very concrete individual y on a particular day q, but that during the meeting on day q person y would intoxicate person x with a drug added to person x's drink, without x's knowledge and permission; the drug's purpose would be to make person x lose track of what they were doing and induce an intense desire for sexual interaction. As a result, x would have sex with y.

I believe most ethicists would agree that even though person x had a pre-existing desire to have sex with person y on day q, person x would be within their rights to feel great resentment towards person y for having been manipulated and abused in this way; person x would be right to feel that their autonomy has been violated because of the circumstances in which the realization of that pre-existing desire took place. Even more so, one could argue that the situation which resulted cannot be classified as *the realization of the pre-existing desire*, because the pre-existing desire was a desire (1) to have sex with person y, (2) for it to happen on day q, (3) to be aware of what is going on, and (4) be able to voice one's consent on that matter. In other words, the pre-existing first-order desire was quite complex; it was composed of a bundle of elements, all of which were important for the identity of this desire. Therefore, we cannot say that x's pre-existing first-order desire and the drug-induced first-order desire that person x felt during the sexual act with person y are identical. The latter, which is the desire that got realized in the sexual act, is different than the former, which did not get realized. Importantly, it is the realization of the former kind of desire that person y would endorse on the level of second-order desires, not the latter.

By the same token, I may have a first-order desire to buy a certain product and have the second-order desire to endorse this first-order desire, but I may also exhibit the second-order desire not to have my first-order desires subjected to any sort of manipulation without my knowledge and consent (or without my knowledge and for no good reason, as Crisp would put it). In these circumstances, having my first-order desire to buy an Esprit sweater manipulated by persuasive advertising would constitute a violation of my autonomy, no matter if I had or did not have a pre-existing first-order desire to buy an Esprit sweater. To the possible objection that one may not necessarily have the second-order desire not to be manipulated, Crisp responds prescriptively: human beings *ought* to have the desire not to be manipulated—it is in their best interest to have such a desire, and the lack of such desire "is itself evidence of profound manipulation" (415). This thesis of Crisp seems too strong and too imprecise. It seems more reasonable and credible to say that it is only in some contexts that the lack of desire not to be manipulated could be the evidence of manipulation. But it is not the case that—every minute of one's life—one ought to display an incessant second-order desire not to be manipulated: this could, in turn, be the evidence of living in a state of pervasive distrust and fear.

5.2.2. Sneddon's Taylorian Autonomist Criticism of Advertising

A much more contemporary critic of Arrington is Andrew Sneddon. In contrast to Durham and Crisp, Sneddon does not try to directly contest the claims made by Arrington; instead, the critic says that even if Arrington were right, what he discussed has barely touched the tip of the iceberg as to what could and should be debated regarding advertising and autonomy. By focusing solely on the autonomy of desires, Arrington deals with the topic of advertising's threat to human autonomy in a very superficial way. Moreover, this superficial treatment of the topic has influenced the work of other ethicists who followed: "the literature on advertising has been damaged by use of an unduly narrow sense of what autonomy involves" (2001b, 16). In short, due to the widespread use of an overly narrow conception of autonomy, the topic of autonomy versus advertising has not been done justice.

Sneddon refers to the kind of autonomy that Arrington and his followers speak of as *shallow autonomy*, i.e., autonomy which is equal to making autonomous choices (17). According to Sneddon, what these philosophers have ignored when discussing the threats which advertising may pose to autonomy is that autonomy can also signify being an autonomous person (16). Sneddon refers to this second kind of autonomy as *deep autonomy*, and he believes *deep autonomy* to be separate from[90] and ethically more significant than *shallow autonomy* (17). Therefore, "showing that advertising either cannot or does not compromise autonomous choice [i.e., shallow autonomy] is not necessarily to get if off the hook" (17)[91].

So, what does being an autonomous person mean for Sneddon? To be an autonomous person is to have and exercise control over one's life in the sense of shaping one's conception of oneself (17–18). While shallow autonomy would be about asking myself "whether I do in fact want to want the item in question [in

---

90 As Sneddon explains, a person can be autonomous and yet make some choices in her life non-autonomously: for example, she can give other people (like doctors) the power to make particular decisions for her (she may recognize that a doctor may be better equipped than she is to handle particular medical decisions concerning her health) (2001b, 17). Differently put, the fact that certain decisions in one's life may be non-autonomous does not automatically entail that one is not an autonomous person.

91 In his later work Sneddon will abandon the term *shallow autonomy* in favor of *autonomy of choice*; correspondingly, he will abandon the term *deep autonomy* and substitute it with the term *autonomy of persons* (2013; see Chapter 2 of this book for more information on Sneddon's newest work on autonomy).

the current context: a product or service that is the object of my first-order desire]", exercising deep autonomy would consist in (1) "assessing what our values are and whether our 1st order desires are consistent with these," and also (2) "assessing whether our values themselves are desirable" (18). Sneddon underscores that in the case of deep autonomy "more is involved than the matching of 1st order desires with 2nd order ones" since "it is reasonable to think that one's values consist of a web of various levels of desires, beliefs, interests, and needs" (18).

Although (as illustrated above) in his explanation of the term "deep autonomy" Sneddon does not shy away from the Frankfurtian terminology, the connection between his thought and the thought of Frankfurt is not as direct as in the case of Arrington. In fact, the development of the term "deep autonomy" is rooted in the work of Charles Taylor (1985a, 1985b, 1989, 1991)—especially in the Taylorian concept of *strong evaluation*[92]—and it is due to the fact that Taylor makes an explicit link between the notion of strong evaluation and the thought of Frankfurt (Taylor, 1985a, 66; see also 1985b, 15) that Sneddon's work is connected to the ideas of Frankfurt as well.

This is what Taylor says about the notion of strong evaluation: "I want to speak of strong evaluation where we 'evaluate', that is, consider good/bad, desirable/despicable, our desires themselves" (Taylor, 1985a, 65). But the Taylorian strong evaluation is more than just the evaluation of first-order desires—Sneddon emphasizes that it also involves "discriminations of right or wrong, better or worse, higher or lower, which are not rendered valid by our own desires, inclinations, or choices, but rather stand independent of these and offer standards by which they can be judged" (Taylor, 1989, 4; Sneddon, 2001b, 19). Importantly, it is Taylor who inspires Sneddon to claim that being an autonomous person is intimately connected with shaping one's conception of oneself (Sneddon, 2001b, 20): when we strongly evaluate our desires, Taylor says, we are "defining what it is we really are about" (Taylor, 1989, 68), "we are reflecting about our desires in terms of the kind of being we are in having them or carrying them out" (Taylor, 1985b, 25–26). Defining our identity in this way is, in fact, an exercise of self-rule (Sneddon, 2001b, 21).

In Sneddon's interpretation of Taylor, in order to perform strong evaluation well and thus to succeed in the process of forming an authentic identity for

92 It is from Taylor, who uses the metaphor of depth to talk about *strong evaluation*, that Sneddon gets the idea of referring to this kind of autonomy that he describes in his earlier work as *deep autonomy* (Taylor, 1985b, 25-26).

oneself, one must remain open to "horizons of significance" (Taylor, 1991, 66), which are "the horizons against which things take on significance for us" (37). Since we are social creatures, "the source of our horizons of significance is the other people with whom we live" (Sneddon, 2001b, 21), and the openness to these horizons of significance (or horizons of value, as Sneddon also refers to them) involves the "openness to possible ways of living" (21–22). Interestingly, in the process of strong evaluation we need not commit to any one of the ways of living that we see are possible; instead, we can decide to incorporate various pieces of various possible ways of living into our own life (21). What matters is that we remain open; as Sneddon emphasizes in his interpretation of Taylor, "strong evaluation is an on-going process" (21).

But in order to remain open to possible ways of living, we need to have the knowledge that these other ways of living and the values they represent exist (22). The problem with advertising—Sneddon says—is that it does not favor exposure to a variety of possible models of ways of living; instead, it encourages homogeneity (22). And even if some may object to this claim by saying that particular advertisements differ from each other, thus providing us with many models of how we can live, Sneddon replies to this objection in the following way: "The sorts of models of ways of living people are exposed to through advertising are best seen as part of just one over-arching way of living. Turning from particular advertisements to advertising as a whole reveals the reinforcement of a deeper sort of homogeneity" (22). In order to corroborate his thesis, Sneddon mentions the work of Barbara Phillips and John Waide. Phillips argues that advertising lobbies for the capitalist and consumerist way of living and valuing at the expense of any non-capitalist and non-consumerist alternatives (Phillips, 1997, 109); correspondingly, Waide says that associative advertising instills in people a conviction that they are what they own and suppresses the thought that identity could be constructed on a different, not market-oriented basis (Waide, 1987, 75).

To recap the crux of this section, let me summarize Sneddon's argument in an orderly fashion: (1) by encouraging homogeneity, advertising makes it impossible for its audience to develop the knowledge of the variety of possible ways of living (and the values connected with these ways of living); (2) this kind of knowledge is essential to being open to possible ways of living (and the values connected with these ways of living); (3) openness to possible ways of living (and to the values connected with these ways of living) is essential to being an autonomous person, able to construct an authentic identity; (4) exercising *deep autonomy* means being an autonomous person who is able to construct an authentic identity (by assessing and re-assessing the values which constitute the building blocks of one's identity); (5) therefore, advertising compromises *deep autonomy*. (6) Thus, even if advertising poses little threat to *shallow autonomy*, it is still highly problematic from the ethical point of view due to compromising the more significant type of autonomy: *deep autonomy*.

Sneddon ends his paper by saying that developing the concept of deep autonomy helps to fully account for Aldous Huxley's concerns about advertising and autonomy (Huxley, 1958, sec. *The Arts of Selling*). Using his own terminology, Sneddon summarizes Huxley's point in the following way: "Advertising subverts democracy not by manipulating particular choices—not through interference in shallow autonomy—but by dissuading people from developing the skills that would put them into a position to make rational choices" (Sneddon, 2001b, 26). People who are not able or willing to assess their way of living against a background of possible ways of living are "unable to participate in democracy in its fullest sense" (26).

5.2.3. Cunningham's Nogglian Autonomist Defense of Advertising

In her paper *Autonomous Consumption: Buying Into the Ideology of Capitalism*, Anne Cunningham admits that Sneddon makes an important attempt at providing "a philosophical basis for the common and pressing cultural criticism of advertising as a controlling force in American culture," but she believes that accepting Sneddon's analysis would make us draw conclusions which go too far (2003, 231). According to Cunningham, the problematic point of this analysis is that Sneddon defines autonomy in a normative way: in Cunningham's words, Sneddon says that being autonomous means "being thoughtfully engaged in self-reflection" (232) which involves reflection about the possible ways of living. If Sneddon were right in defining autonomy in this way—Cunningham says—we would have to admit that any institution that tries to get to us by curtailing our ability and eagerness to question the values behind the belief system it promotes would be guilty of violating our autonomy (232). Cunningham gives the example of Catholics who are "discouraged from examining their beliefs and seeking other viewpoints" and asks whether Sneddon would contend that Catholicism constitutes a threat to autonomy (232). She then goes on to say that by Sneddon's standards no person in the world could be classified as autonomous, since we all live in "a socially constructed world and tend to abide by, often without questioning, its socially constructed norms and values" (232–233).

I will allow myself a small comment on Cunningham's criticism here. Although Sneddon has not tried to answer Cunningham's attack, it seems plausible that he would consider it to be a logical implication of his reasoning that Catholicism constitutes a threat to autonomy. However, from that it does not follow that no person in the world might be autonomous by Sneddon's standards—Cunningham seems to be committing a slippery slope fallacy here. Even if norms and values are socially constructed, it is not the case that nobody engages in critical reflection regarding these norms and values, and that Sneddon's definition of autonomy is completely inapplicable to reality because of that.

For Cunningham, however, her criticism of Sneddon seems solid, and she believes that such a deficient account of autonomy is not a reliable tool for considering whether advertising violates autonomy. Instead, Cunningham proposes to adopt a belief-based theory of autonomy formulated by Robert Noggle (1995).

According to Noggle, we experience two kinds of desires: *authentic desires* and *alien desires*. Both kinds of desires can cause our behavior and thus play a role in explaining the way we act. Authentic desires are "desires we do not hesitate to call our own" (57), we identify with them, and therefore they do not violate our autonomy when they cause our actions. Alien desires, on the other hand, are more problematic because "they seem to arise from outside the *self* conceived as the source of one's autonomous agency" (57). In order to elucidate this, Noggle introduces his belief-based concept of the self (which leads to the belief-based account of autonomy): he explains that an important (though not essential or fundamental) feature of the self is that it is a believer: "a self is what has the beliefs" (65). Authentic desires arise from *straightforward beliefs*, i.e., from beliefs which (a) are knowable through introspection (60), (b) form an integrated, interconnected web (59), (c) are easily instilled or gotten rid of when exposed to the rest of one's straightforward beliefs (60), and (d) constitute mental assertions (60). Noggle contrasts straightforward beliefs with *quasi-beliefs*, i.e., representational states which can function similarly to straightforward beliefs in their ability to form desires, but which nevertheless lack all of the above-mentioned features of straightforward beliefs (a, b, c, d) (60). Alien desires are caused by a particular kind of quasi-beliefs: Noggle calls them *discordant quasi-beliefs* and explains that they are in conflict with straightforward beliefs of the agent (64).[93] Consequently, since the self is a believer, discordant quasi-beliefs are in conflict with the self, and alien desires caused by discordant quasi-beliefs are separate from the self (64–65).

93 In contrast, *concordant quasi-beliefs* are those that do not contradict any of the agent's straightforward beliefs.

Cunningham (2003) applies Noggle's approach to talk about autonomy and advertising. According to Cunningham, although advertising may create quasi-beliefs, these are not discordant quasi-beliefs, but concordant quasi-beliefs that are not in conflict with the agent's straightforward beliefs (234). In short, Cunningham's argument could be summarized as follows: (1) (following Noggle) the formation of alien desires constitutes a violation of our autonomy; (2) (following Noggle) only by creating discordant quasi-beliefs is it possible to form alien desires in a person; (3) advertising does not create discordant quasi-beliefs; (4) therefore, advertising does not violate our autonomy. As far as the justification of premise 3 goes, Cunningham says the following: "By the very fact that capitalist values are so fundamental to our way of life, advertising is unlikely to condition consumers to act in ways that contradict our larger belief systems. As such, advertising, though it may in other ways detrimentally affect society and consumers' well-being, does not violate our autonomy" (236).

5.2.4. Villarán's Kantian Autonomist Criticism of Advertising

While Cunningham (2003) has made an attempt to criticize Sneddon (2001b) for implying that all ideologies which discourage people from considering alternatives violate human autonomy, Alonso Villarán (2017) has in turn criticized Cunningham's defense of advertising for leading to a conclusion that no ideology-based institution could potentially violate human autonomy. Villarán takes the example of Nazi ideology and says that "if Cunningham is right, it seems unavoidable to admit that Nazi advertising did not violate the Nazis' autonomy, insofar as it did not contradict their larger belief system, Nazism." (485). All in all, the implication of Cunningham's reasoning is a very strong claim that "no ideology-based institution is oppressive" (485). Villarán points out that it is much more reasonable to claim that some ideology-based institutions are oppressive, while others are not—it all depends on the ideology that lies behind these institutions—and it is not impossible that advertising may be one of the oppressive ideology-based institutions that thwart human autonomy (485). In order to consider this possibility, Villarán decides to explore the Kantian account of autonomy applied to the context of advertising (485).

Before constructing a Kantian version of the autonomist criticism of advertising, Villarán emphasizes that he wants to target a particular kind of advertising, which he calls "irrational advertising" (480). In order to explain the term, Villarán invokes the discussion of manipulative marketing techniques by Shlomo Sher. According to Sher, the marketer/advertiser can try to manipulate the audience in two ways: (1) by deceiving them,[94] or (2) by exploiting a vulnerability (emotional, perceptual, cognitive, ethical) in the audience's normal decision-making process (2011, 103, 107). It is this second type of manipulation that is of interest to Villarán (2017), and he proposes to call advertising that uses this kind of manipulation "irrational advertising" because by "playing on a vulnerability the advertiser appeals to something different than the reason of the audience" (481). Here is Sher's example of what Villarán refers to as irrational advertising: "Using a well-regarded spokesperson [=an authority figure] typically makes for an effective marketing tactic because we heuristically place great value in the opinions of people we admire—regardless of whether they have any actual expertise about, or experience with, the product in question" (2011, 108). Examples of irrational advertising can also be found in much earlier business ethics literature: as Villarán points out, the marketing technique referred to by Waide (1987) as associative advertising is another good illustration of irrational advertising (Villarán, 481). All in all, irrational advertising could be defined as advertising which aims to manipulate the audience not by deception, but by a non-rational appeal that exploits the audience's emotional, perceptual, cognitive, or ethical vulnerability.

Having established the target of his criticism—irrational advertising—Villarán goes on to outline Kant's account of autonomy and the differences between that account and the accounts of autonomy applied in the advertising ethics literature so far (485–486). An informative and exhaustive definition of autonomy is given by Kant in the *Critique of Practical Reason*. Kant says that "*autonomy* of the will is the sole principle of all moral laws" and it "consists in independence from all matter of the law (namely, from a desired object) and at the same time in the determination of choice through the mere form of giving universal law that a maxim must be capable of. That *independence*, however, is freedom in the *negative* sense, whereas this *lawgiving of its own* on the part of pure and, as such, practical reason is freedom in the *positive* sense" (CPR, 5:33). One of the important things to notice in this definition is that Kantian autonomy has both the element of freedom in the negative sense, as well as freedom in the positive sense. Villarán quotes Denis G. Arnold and Nelson E. Bowie in order to stress that genuine and fully realized freedom, according to Kant, implies being free to choose the moral law: "Freedom in its fullest realization is the ability to guide

94 Notice that both Sher and Villarán challenge the typical division into deceptive and manipulative advertising. Sher sees deception as a kind of manipulation, and so does Villarán. For a detailed justification of Villarán's decision to do so, see Villarán (2017, 480).

one's actions from laws that are of one's own making. Freedom is not simply a spontaneous event. Free actions are caused, but they are caused by persons acting from laws they themselves have made. This is positive freedom" (Arnold, Bowie, 2003, 223).

Villarán claims that what the advertising ethicists have been discussing so far is mainly the negative element of autonomy, while missing out on "the question if irrational advertising is also a threat to positive freedom, and hence to *moral autonomy*" (Villarán, 2017, 486). It seems debatable whether Villarán is right on this: I believe it can be argued that apart from discussing the importance of freedom from manipulation and coercion, the advertising ethicists have also been advocating for the freedom of the advertising audience to act from the audience's own preferences and desires (e.g. Galbraith, 1952; Arrington, 1982). However, Villarán is right to point out that Kant talked about *moral* autonomy, which is qualitatively different from the kind of autonomy most widely discussed in the business ethics literature on advertising so far. In fact, Villarán boldly claims that when discussing autonomy in the context of advertising, the advertising ethicists have been talking about the nemesis of Kantian moral autonomy: heteronomy (Villarán, 2017, 486). Indeed, the aforementioned freedom of the advertising audience to act from the audience's own preferences and desires looks strikingly similar to heteronomy understood as the satisfaction of one's inclinations (Kant, CPR, 5:73) or "dependence upon the natural law of following some impulse or inclination" (5:33). Therefore, what is interesting and new about Villarán's Kantian autonomist criticism of advertising is that he proposes to think about a qualitatively different kind of autonomy than the one discussed by the advertising critics before; he proposes to think about such autonomy which "comes with honoring the moral law instead of the law of happiness" (Villarán, 2017, 487).

Villarán's criticism is modest: he does not want to prove that—with all certainty—irrational advertising diminishes moral autonomy, but rather that (a) irrational advertising threatens moral autonomy by promoting its opposite, heteronomy, and that (b) the likelihood of this threat being successful is high (487–488). In order to prove that (a) is the case, Villarán quotes several famous advertising slogans, but he focuses particularly on Sprite's "Obey your thirst" and quotes Sandel's comment on this slogan: "Sprite's ad contained (inadvertently, no doubt) a Kantian insight. When I pick up a can of Sprite (or Pepsi or Coke), I act out of obedience, not freedom. I am responding to a desire I haven't chosen. I am obeying my thirst" (2010, 108). But Villarán reads more out of this slogan than Sandel does: "The message is stronger—an imperative: you must obey your thirst. In more abstract terms, Sprite is telling us that we must obey our needs. Now here we are only one step away from our inclinations (…) It is my claim that this is irrational advertising's over-all underlying message, the rule of lawless happiness in our lives, which is just another name for heteronomy" (2017, 488). Villarán's claim that irrational advertising contains an over-all message echoes the claim of Waide.[95] The difference is that Waide believed that the over-all message of (associative/irrational) advertising was "You are what you own" (1987, 65), while Villarán says that this message reads "Obey your happiness" or "Do what you want" (Nike's slogan "Just do it", Puma's "Follow your instinct", or Diesel's "Be stupid" are good examples of that) (2017, 488). The idea behind the over-all message identified by Villarán is to make us, the audience, think less, be less rational in our actions, because "the less we think, the less rational we act, the more chances that we will not restrict our needs and inclinations with an eye to the moral law, but instead give way to them" (488); as a result, heteronomy is promoted and moral autonomy is threatened. Villarán adds that—apart from promoting heteronomy in a subtle and covert way—irrational advertising can also promote heteronomy overtly by validating actions which go against what the moral law dictates. An example that Villarán gives is the 2013 Reebok slogan which endorses dishonesty: "Cheat on your girlfriend, not on your workout" (488).

Parenthetically, Villarán's attempt to provide empirical illustration in support of the thesis that irrational advertising is a threat to moral autonomy (by promoting its nemesis, heteronomy) is not entirely felicitous. The example that Villarán focuses on the most is not completely convincing: obeying one's thirst could be interpreted as indicative of being authentic, and acting authentically could derive its status as a moral duty from the first formulation of the categorical imperative. In a similar vein, Nike's slogan "Just do it" could be interpreted as consistent with the Kantian notion of autonomy. If one passes a judgment that one has a moral duty to perform a certain action, one should just do whatever the duty dictates—one should "just do it."

After the not entirely successful attempt to support his thesis empirically, Villarán mentions three "hints" which seem to suggest that irrational advertising may pose a threat to moral autonomy: the financial hint, the exposure hint, and the cultural hint (488). As to the first hint, Villarán notices that an enormous amount of money goes into advertising today (for a corroboration of this statement, see, for instance, Statista, 2021) and that the rule of the business world is that money goes where it can truly bring profit. These observations, along with

---

95 For a similar idea being voiced by Sneddon as well, see Section 5.2.2, especially (2001b, 16). Like Villarán, Sneddon refers to Waide in this respect.

the fact that irrational advertising constitutes a significant part of contemporary advertisements, suggest that "more and more people are taking the bait and hence acting heteronomously" (Villarán, 2017, 489). As far as the exposure hint is concerned, Villarán quotes the American Association of Advertising Agencies, stating that "a typical adult has potential daily exposure to about 600–625 ads in any form" (American Association of Advertising Agencies, 2015).[96] Remembering (what has been said above) that a significant part of these advertisements is based on the technique of irrational persuasion, "one can safely assume that, like drops of water, if given enough time, can drill through stones irrational advertising can drill through people's moral autonomy, whether by weakening our good will or by damaging our pure practical reason" (Villarán, 2017, 489). By the former Villarán means that irrational advertising encourages us to yield to lawless happiness and disregard the moral law, and by the latter he means that irrational advertising confounds our reason by portraying heteronomy as "the path to a good life" (489). Finally, regarding the cultural hint, Villarán says that our *zeitgeist* consists in a mixture of materialism, hedonism, and consumerism, all of which are tendencies promoted by irrational advertising today (489). Considering the pervasiveness of advertising in general and irrational advertising in particular (the exposure hint), it seems that we can assume that irrational advertising is at least partially responsible for the current popularity of such tendencies as materialism, hedonism, and consumerism, which are in fact "forms of heteronomy" (489). According to Villarán, on the basis of the three hints, it is reasonable to imply that the threat which irrational advertising poses to moral autonomy is likely to be successful.

However, it could be objected that the way Villarán interprets the Kantian notion of autonomy is questionable. He seems to interpret autonomy as a characteristic that could be ascribed to persons, while according to a different reading of Kant, it is not a person who is autonomous, but the moral laws as self-given and self-imposed by that person's will; this reading could be inferred from such

96 The figure is taken from (15 Feb 2007) "Our Rising Ad Dosage: It's Not as Oppressive as Some Think." There has been much debate over the number of advertisements that a typical adult in the West is exposed to. Apart from the number quoted by Villarán, a lower number of 362 ads per day was indicated in a 2014 report, as well as a much higher number of 5000 ads per day, mentioned in the famous Yankelovich Monitor poll from the nineties. Regarding the first figure, see *America's Media Usage and Ad Exposure 1945-2014* (2014) and Johnson (29 Sep 2014). According to Ayres and Funk (2003), Yankelovich Monitor poll results were originally presented in: (13 Nov 1995) "See And Don't Call Back."

passages as GW, 4:440, or CPR, 5:33 (see O'Neill, 1989). The fact that people are "taking the bait" shows that their will is deficient in terms of autonomous law-making, but *not as a result of having the autonomy of their moral laws threatened by external stimuli* (such as irrational advertising). By definition, autonomous law-making is uninfluenced and therefore unthreatened by external stimuli. In other words, it *cannot* be threatened by irrational advertising.

5.3. The Omnipresence of Advertising Mentioned in the Ethical Discourse

Historically speaking, many ethicists have mentioned some aspects of the omnipresence of advertising, although they did not necessarily use the term "omnipresence of advertising" when doing so. Robert L. Arrington, for example, hints at one of the probable reasons behind the amount of advertising that contemporary individuals are faced with. He mentions the advertisers' belief in the effectiveness of an advertising technique called *indirect information transfer* (1982, 5), which relies on exposing the potential consumer to the same advertisement "over and over again, *ad nauseum*" (4). From the point of view of an advertiser, a large quantity of the same advertisement is a good investment, because even if the consumer becomes sick of it, "its repetitiousness has generated what ad theorists call *information*": it is believed that when the consumer goes shopping, they are likely to buy the product which is being advertised *ad nauseum* because the repetition makes them recognize the name of the brand and they typically assume that "any product advertised so often has to be good" (4). Interestingly, following in the footsteps of Philip Nelson (1978), Arrington believes that indirect information advertising is beneficial to the audience. According to Arrington, who paraphrases Nelson, the most heavily advertised products win a market version of the "survival of the fittest" competition and—for that reason—they are the best products the consumer can get: "even when the [advertising] message (the direct information) is not credible, the fact that the brand is advertised, and advertised frequently, is valuable indirect information for the consumer. The reason for this is that brands advertised the most are more likely to be better buys—losers won't be advertised a lot, for it simply wouldn't pay to do so (…) If the indirect information has been received and has had its impact, the consumer will purchase the better buy even if his explicit reason for doing so is silly (…)" (1982, 5). But Arrington's reasoning is far from solid: from the fact that advertisers invest in very frequent and repetitious advertising because they know that consumers will typically think that a heavily advertised product is better and they are more likely to buy it, it does not follow that the heavily advertised product is likely to be a better buy. In fact, David Braybrooke (1967)—whom Arrington refers to in connection with a different matter—observes that it is typical for the potential consumers to develop preferences for heavily advertised products irrespective of their actual quality.[97] Also, since Arrington wrote his paper, the technique he mentioned has become so popular that we can barely talk about a few heavily advertised products truly standing out from the crowd. Rather, it seems that an overwhelmingly big amount of market products these days are advertised very frequently and repetitively, in which case the audience ends up being bombarded with a huge amount of indirectly transferred information that has become difficult to process.

Noticing this quantitative aspect of the exposure to advertising, John Waide warns us that "all the ads put together constitute a cultural bombardment with an ideology of acquisitiveness" and he talks about the "constant exposure to associative advertising" which changes us in such a way that "our characters and conceptions of virtue already largely reflect the result of advertising and we are unlikely to rebel" (1987, 76).

In a similar vein, Villarán discusses the daily exposure to many advertisements—particularly advertisements which resort to irrational persuasion—as a force we should not underestimate in terms of the influence it has on our moral autonomy. The more irrational advertising we are regularly exposed to, Villarán says, the more our pure practical reason gets damaged and our moral autonomy undermined (2017, 489).

Durham, on the other hand, has an interesting observation that while ethicists are typically preoccupied with distinguishing between different kinds of advertising, assuming that particular kinds of advertising (deceptive, persuasive, manipulative, associative, irrational, etc.) are ethically problematic and others are not (purely informative advertising is often mentioned as non-problematic), these scholars do not notice that even if advertising is purely informative—with no harmful function implied—but it comes in an overwhelming amount, this is a form of exerting persuasive pressure on the audience (1984, 176). Thus, a conclusion can be drawn that the omnipresence of advertising—no matter what kind—can in itself be deemed ethically problematic and worthy of ethical enquiry.

And yet, there has been little scholarly interest in making the omnipresence of advertising the focal point of ethical study. Rather, this phenomenon is typically being portrayed as the background to the actual enquiry that is being conducted,

97 The relevant part of Braybrooke is quoted in Durham (1984, 179).

and not as the subject proper. However, three ethicists have devoted more attention than usual to the omnipresence of advertising.

5.3.1. Edward Spence, in Collaboration with Brett Van Heekeren

One of these ethicists is Edward Spence. In order to produce the book *Advertising Ethics* (2005) which, among other topics, touches upon the omnipresence of advertising (although the phenomenon is not called this way), Spence has collaborated with Brett Van Heekeren, a scholar from the School of Communication at Charles Sturt University. Together, they have produced the following tokens of argumentation concerning the omnipresence of advertising.

5.3.1.1. The Freedom of Choice Argument/The Privacy Argument

The first argument fleshed out by Spence and Van Heekeren is called "the privacy argument," although I think it might be more accurate to refer to it as *the freedom of choice argument*, since the two scholars do not seem to elaborate enough on how the violation of the freedom of choice translates into the violation of the audience's privacy: the explanation provided in the beginning of the argument (2005, 90) is too general to consider it satisfactory.

The argument goes as follows. (A) Some forms of advertising do not allow us to execute our right to freedom of choice in situations when we might not want to view or hear unwelcome ads. Billboard advertisements are one example. As stressed by Spence and Van Heekeren, "car drivers (…) may not be able to avert their eyes from the unwelcome billboard ads on the chance of causing a traffic accident" (91). (B) Thus, such forms of advertising violate our right to freedom of choice (and our right to privacy, as the two scholars claim) (91).

5.3.1.2. The Suspension of Discontent Argument

However, even though according to Spence and Van Heekeren the advertising audience is justified in being discontent concerning "the curtailment of their freedom of choice as whether or not to view, listen, watch, or read" the ads "that pervade our private and public spaces," the audience may be willing to "suspend their discontent" (2005, 91). This is possible if the audience is offered some kind of a benefit in exchange for the loss of their freedom of choice. The benefit in question is typically a financial one, like free Internet, free email services, or a part of revenue generated from billboard ads being spent by the government to improve the public roads and pavements. A nonfinancial benefit might also be involved, when the ads that violate the audience's privacy and freedom of choice are particularly clever and humorous, thus providing the audience with witty entertainment that tends to "lighten up our collective and communal mood" (91).

5.3.1.3. *The Time-Out Argument*

The third argument goes as follows. (1) Contemporary advertisers aim at the ubiquity of advertising, and the resulting invasiveness of advertising practices has become a part of the intensity and business of everyday life (2005, 92). In contrast to this descriptive observation, Spence and Van Heekeren emphasize that (2) for the reason of preserving their well-being, human beings need such spaces that give them an opportunity to retreat from the intensity and business of everyday life: "We need these spaces where we can be ourselves and be by ourselves without being told by advertising messages what to desire or what to eat, drink, drive, wear, or otherwise consume, or aspire to acquire" (92). These spaces have a cultural, natural, or spiritual character, like beaches, forests, botanic gardens, public parks, art galleries, museums, and temples. (3) Due to how essential these spaces are for human well-being, they are deemed priceless: "No payoff or trade-off can compensate us enough for implicitly agreeing to suspend our collective discontent at having these spaces open to advertising" (92). (4) Thus, most people would not be willing to accept that their right to the freedom of choice concerning the invasion of these spaces by advertising is being violated, and they would perceive this kind of advertising with particular reluctance. (5) Consequently, advertising in these spaces would be self-defeating and "instrumentally and pragmatically pointless" (92).

5.3.1.4. *The Preservation of Aesthetic Space Argument*

In their fourth argument, Spence and Van Heekeren focus on aesthetic spaces, i.e., spaces in which we can experience art in its many forms. Just like nature, art—whether in the form of literature, music, painting, or sculpture—offers an important kind of cultural retreat "where people can seek enjoyment in the freedom of their imagination, comfort, relaxation, and edification" (2005, 92). Such spaces of retreat should not be invaded by advertising. Rather they should be preserved as "our collective 'sacred spaces,'" which are off-limits to advertising (93). This is because art is perceived to evoke certain "collective aspirational values that we [human beings] share as a community" and the presence of advertising in spaces connected with art taints these values and our understanding of these values (93; for a further elaboration of this line of argumentation, see Spence, 2018, 235–250). In addition, advertisers and the advertising industry have a collective ethical responsibility to participate in the preservation and protection of the collective aspirational values shared by the humanity (Spence and Van Heekeren, 2005, 93, 35–36).

A conclusion that stems from both the time-out argument and the preservation of aesthetic space argument is that the advertising industry is ethically required to respect the sanctity of what Spence and Van Heekeren call "our collective sacred spaces" by staying out of these spaces (93).

Our collective sacred spaces can be natural, spiritual, or aesthetic. Not violating the sanctity of the collective sacred spaces that are aesthetic would mean no more fictomercials (advertisements smuggled into literature), advertorials (advertisements disguised as editorial content, such as a newspaper article), product placement[98] in songs and music videos, and so on (92–93).

5.3.1.5. The Deception Argument

Originally Spence and Van Heekeren do not single this argument out as a separate argument, but they make this reasoning a part of *the preservation of aesthetic space argument*, as well as a part of the overall conclusion of their book. I believe, however, that this argument merits to be fleshed out separately and be given a name "the deception argument." The reasoning within this argument would go as follows.

(I) "Insofar as being trustworthy is both good for one's professional, organizational and personal reputation, trustworthiness is not only ethically but also instrumentally desirable" (2005, 122). (II) One of the consequences of the pervasiveness of advertising is the proliferation of deceptive and misleading forms of advertising, like fictomercials, advertorials, or infomercials (i.e., longer advertisements disguised as an information program or a talk-show), or like "songs, films, or books that are essentially advertising campaigns masquerading as culture" (122, 92–93). (III) It might be the case that a lot of people, especially those who have grown up in the environment where the pervasiveness of advertising has become a norm, have become so accustomed to advertising that they no longer mind it; but even if this is the case, these people do mind being the target of the advertising and marketing attempts to deceive them (122). (IV) Consequently, "in-your-face advertising that does not attempt to deceive consumers by

---

98 In fact, Spence and Van Heekeren use the word "cross-branding" instead of "product placement" in their argumentation. However, I find the word "product placement" to be much more precise in conveying their meaning ("cross-branding" seems too general as a term to be used with reference to such case studies as that of Sting's song *Desert Rose* and the advertisement of the S-type Jaguar placed in the song's music video).

cloaking itself misleadingly and deceptively in content, information, or culture" is much more desirable—both from the ethical and instrumental point of view—than those forms of advertising that involve deception (122). (V) Therefore, advertising should avoid any sort of deception because by doing so it preserves its ethical credibility, trustworthiness, and professional integrity, which is highly desirable not only ethically, but also instrumentally (122).

5.3.1.6. The Overload Argument

In a somewhat similar vein to Wright (1997, 5), Spence and Van Heekeren say that one individual advertisement violating our collective and communal sacred spaces is not what we should be concerned about: one such instance is—ethically speaking—a minor issue (2005, 93). The problem starts with the contemporary tendency of advertising to saturate as much of our reality as possible with brands, as a result of which our sacred spaces are under attack from a multitude of advertisements; the authors refer to this phenomenon as "brand pollution" (93–94). If the trend continues, we may soon find ourselves in a very undesirable situation: "there might not be any sacred spaces left empty of advertising and this outcome could lead to the emptiness of any sort of cultural meaning in society other than the meaning of brands" (93). The undesirability of this situation does not concern only a limited number of people; even those individuals who work in the advertising industry must have a preference that their own favorite sacred spaces of retreat should remain free from advertising (93). Hence, the two scholars propose to formulate this assumed preference of the entire humanity in the form of Kant's Categorical Imperative: "one could not consistently will that the invasion of all our sacred spaces by advertising should become a Universal Law" (93). Therefore, if we assume that the above-mentioned preference is true for the entire human community, then legal measures must be taken against advertising invading our communal sacred spaces. *Brand pollution*—just like any other form of environmental pollution—needs to be regulated (94).

5.3.1.7. Spence's and Van Heekeren's Concluding Remarks

Although the pervasiveness of advertising is not the only ethically problematic issue discussed in Spence and Van Heekeren's book, in the concluding chapter the two scholars state that "the pervasiveness and unrestricted proliferation of advertising that threatens to engulf all aspects of our private and public domains remains the biggest ethical problem in advertising" (2005, 122). As the most realistic solution to this problem, they see some kind of a co-regulation that would be the fruit of the cooperation between the advertising industry and the government (representing the interests of the citizens). The co-regulation would declare spaces that Spence and Van Heekeren call *sacred spaces* to be advertising-free zones, i.e., zones that would be legally protected from any commercial advertising. In the final words of the two scholars, "ethical advertising that is socially responsible and thus sensitive and responsive to the community's needs, demands this protection" (122).

5.3.1.8. Spence's Additional Argument of 2018

In a 2018 anthology of texts devoted to media ethics, Spence has fleshed out an additional argument somewhat related to the topic of the omnipresence of advertising (Spence, 2018, 245–246). One might say that this is an argument which—in a very general way—echoes the concerns of R. George Wright (1997, 5–6, 10–11). Spence points to the consequences of the omnipresence of advertising for children and other vulnerable audiences. Like Wright, Spence is concerned about the lessons we are teaching children by exposing them to the all-pervasive advertising. However, unlike Wright, Spence focuses on a particular aspect of that exposure, namely the fact that a vast majority of contemporary advertisements teaches its audience to associate happiness with the sole acquisition of consumer products. By doing so, the advertising industry diminishes the value of happiness and perverts the significance of this concept. In a reality where "the pervasiveness and ubiquity of advertising can reach children through many different mediums and at different times (…), the effect of that diminution on children over a long period of time could" be a deeply negative one (2018, 245)[99] In other words, the omnipresence of advertising makes it almost impossible for a contemporary child not to be continually exposed to the messages conveyed by the advertising industry; one such message is that the child ought to equate the sole acquisition of consumer products with happiness (which is an important collective aspirational value of the humanity that should be protected). Spence emphasizes that "society at large, including the advertising industry, has an ethical responsibility to safeguard the vulnerable members in our society" (246) and that by encouraging children "through a plethora of ads to associate happiness with the sole acquisition of consumer products," we—collectively as a society—are not treating these children well (245).

---

99 For example, one can imagine some serious repercussions for the well-being of a child who feels acutely disappointed and unhappy when not being able to afford certain goods or when the acquisition of goods does not automatically translate into feeling happy and fulfilled (Spence, 2018, 245–246).

5.3.2. Michael Sandel

Another ethicist who has devoted some more attention to the omnipresence of advertising is Michael J. Sandel. In his book *What Money Can't Buy: The Moral Limits of Markets* (2013), Sandel does two important things regarding the main topic of this book.

Firstly, he draws attention to the phenomenon which he refers to it as "the proliferation of advertising" (185), "the explosion of naming rights and advertising in the 1990s and early 2000s" (184), and he says that the commercialism that came with this onslaught of advertising "has displayed a distinctive kind of boundlessness, emblematic of a world in which everything is for sale" (186). He notes that this phenomenon has raised public alarm and distaste, which has manifested i.a. in the form of several newspaper headlines addressing the issue, like Los Angeles Times' *Nowhere to Run, Nowhere to Hide from Ad Barrage*, The Sunday Times' (London) *Ad Onslaught*, The Washington Post's *Ads Infinitum*, The New York Times' *Anywhere The Eye Can See, It's Now Likely to See an Ad*, USA Today's *Ads Are Here, There, Everywhere* (184). Another form of expressing public distaste and alarm is the voice of critics and activists—who have called advertising "a kind of pollution" and "a pestilence" (185)—as well as the voice of ordinary consumers: for example, one shopper protested against food stickers that serve as movie advertisements by saying "I don't want my apple defiled with advertisements" (185). Finally, Sandel also quotes one advertising executive expressing concern regarding the pervasiveness of advertising by saying "I don't know if anything is sacred anymore" (185).

Secondly, Sandel emphasizes that even though "it is hard to deny the moral force of these concerns (…), it is not easy to explain what is wrong with the proliferation of advertising we have witnessed in the last two decades" (185). Providing such an explanation through philosophical argumentation would therefore be a worthwhile task, which is what Sandel attempts to do to some extent.

5.3.2.1. The Argument from Freedom of Choice or the Laissez-Faire Argument

This is an argument in which Sandel summarizes the position of many people who defend "the unfettered market in advertisements" (2013, 186), i.e., such a market which operates according to the principle that every space can be sold and bought as advertising space. According to Sandel, the advocates of the laissez-faire attitude to the proliferation of advertising claim that as long as the person who sells the particular space owns it (it is their house or a part of their body) and the sale is voluntary, then nobody can object to the space being sold as advertising space (one should be free to sell one's own house or forehead as advertising space, if one wishes to do so); thus, each and every kind of space should be eligible for sale as advertising space, if it is being sold voluntarily by its owner (186). Sandel refers to this claim as *the principle of freedom of choice* (186).

5.3.2.2. The Argument from Coercion and Unfairness

This argument (which could also—maybe more accurately—be called "the argument from the exploitation of people in financial distress") is meant to deliver a polemic against the reasoning presented above. However, the polemic does not consist in undermining *the principle of freedom of choice*, but in attacking the premise of voluntariness of some selling choices. For instance, if a homeowner who faces imminent foreclosure agrees to have the exterior of their house used as advertising space, then we can hardly call this choice a genuinely voluntary one (2013, 186). A similar lack of voluntariness would be true in the case of a parent desperately needing money to buy medicine for their child and—in order to get that money—agreeing to have an advertisement tattooed onto their own body (186). In conclusion, "market relations can be considered free only when the background conditions under which we buy and sell are fair, only when no one is coerced by dire economic necessity" (186).

5.3.2.3. The Argument from Degradation and Corruption

According to Sandel, the two arguments presented above constitute the core of the current debate, in which one side favors *the principle of freedom of choice* and the idea that any space can be sold and bought as advertising space, and the other side opposes this idea with the argument from coercion and unfairness (2013, 186). However, Sandel claims, neither of these ways of reasoning addresses the ethical question of what is wrong with the world in which commercialism is allowed to "invade every human activity" (187).

To fill this gap, Sandel proposes his argument from corruption and degradation, which follows some moral intuitions expressed in the public discourse with the use of such critical terms as "debasement", "defilement", "coarsening", "pollution", the loss of the "sacred" (187). The fact that such language is being used indicates that the presence of advertising can have a degrading effect on "ways of living and being," on "certain attitudes, services, and goods" (187). This happens when the *meaning* of a given thing becomes corrupted due to the influence of advertising. For example, "product placement spoils the integrity of books and corrupts the relationship of author and reader. Tattooed body ads objectify and demean the people paid to wear them. Commercials in classrooms undermine the educational purpose of schools" (201).

Nevertheless, as stressed by Sandel, not all instances of the presence of advertising are corrupting: the advertising signage on stadium scoreboards or banners on the outfield walls are good examples of such presence of advertising which is fitting and which does not corrupt what it comes in contact with (201). However, it is also not the case that any form of advertising at a sports stadium would be all right. Sandel says that "it's different when corporate-sponsored banter invades the broadcast booth and asserts itself with every pitching change or slide into second base. (…) The unrelenting corporate-sponsored slogans uttered by the announcers intrude upon the game and spoil the inventive, authentic narrative that a play-by-play account of a game can be" (201).

Thus, as Sandel tries to show, the presence of advertising may have a degrading effect for two reasons. First, because of the type of practice or good that it comes in contact with, like literature, human body, schooling. Second, because of a particular form of advertising: for instance, a certain form of advertising is fitting for a sports stadium, without corrupting the meaning of the practice that a stadium stands for, while a different form of advertising would already be intrusive and have the corrupting effect.

Therefore, Sandel argues, when wanting to decide "where advertising belongs, and where it doesn't," we cannot content ourselves with the property-rights-versus-fairness debate; we should also consider the question of "the meaning of social practices and the goods they embody" and "ask, in each case, whether commercializing the practice would degrade it" (188).

5.3.2.4. The Argument from Pollution

Apart from the argument from corruption and degradation, Sandel offers another original argument to enrich the public debate about advertising spaces: I have called this argument the argument from pollution.

In this argument, Sandel addresses these cases of advertising which are not corrupting when considered as individual cases in isolation from other instances of advertising (2013, 188). These cases, however, "though not corrupting in themselves," may still be ethically problematic when considered as a part of a bigger phenomenon (188) that we could refer to as *advertising pollution* (187). Sandel explains what he means by using the analogy to carbon dioxide emissions: he says that whilst the emission of carbon dioxide is not wrong in itself (a non-harmful instance of this is, for example, humans breathing out carbon dioxide on a daily basis as a part of the breathing process), an excessive emission of this substance has a destructive effect on the environment (188). Similarly, "otherwise unobjectionable extensions of advertising into novel settings may, if widespread, bring about a society dominated by corporate sponsorships and consumerism, a society in which everything is 'brought to you by' MasterCard or McDonald's" (188). Therefore, an excessive accumulation of instances of advertising which are not corrupting in themselves also constitutes a kind of degradation (188) and—we could even say—pollution.

Notice that the conclusion of Sandel's argument is somewhat reminiscent of a thought already expressed by Wright, who said that the problem lies not in "any particular allegedly harmful instance of commercial speech," but in the dominance and omnipresence of commercial speech in general (1997, 5).

Interestingly, after having made the conclusion, Sandel comes back to the anecdote of the shopper who talked about not wanting the apples she buys to be "defiled" by stickers advertising a movie. The philosopher uses the concluding remarks of his argument to elaborate further on what the lady said. He comments that, taken literally, her words might seem exaggerated: after all, an ordinary fruit bought at a supermarket is not really an item that could be *defiled* by a sticker (2013, 189). However, Sandel argues, "the shopper's objection, presumably, is not to this ad on this apple but to the invasion of everyday life by commercial advertising" (189). What we should interpret as truly being *defiled* in this example is not a piece of fruit, but "the common world that we inhabit, increasingly dominated by market values and commercial sensibilities" (189).

5.3.3. Andrew Sneddon

The third ethicist who has fleshed out a token of argumentation connected with the topic of the omnipresence of advertising is Andrew Sneddon. In the book entitled *Autonomy* (2013), Sneddon further develops and enriches his already existing line of argumentation (2001b), discussed in Section 5.2.2. Importantly, in the earlier version of the argument, there is no connection to the topic of the omnipresence of advertising, whilst in the later version, the connection is observable, although Sneddon does not talk explicitly about what I have termed the "omnipresence of advertising." Rather he discusses a more general phenomenon which he calls the "oceans of information" that flood the minds of contemporary individuals and might pose problems for personal autonomy (2013, ch. 8).

Despite making the problem appear much more broad, Sneddon chooses to focus on commercial advertising as a good example of one of the abundant sources of these "oceans of information," especially since contemporary individuals interact with advertising on a daily basis and in a great number of forms: "This plethora of forms of representation and of interaction with them makes advertising a good place to look to get a sense of some possible effects that living in a sea of information has on our prospects for being autonomous" (ch. 8, sec. *Advertising as a model for autonomy and information-mediated interpersonal relations*, par. 3).

Just like he did in his earlier work, Sneddon underscores that in his critique he will not focus on how advertising might threaten autonomy of choice, but rather on how it might undermine autonomy of persons (see Chapter 2 of this book for more details concerning the distinction): thus, he intends to show that what Waide (1987) and Phillips (1997) have written about advertising affecting who we are as persons is actually autonomy-relevant (Sneddon, 2013, ch. 8, sec. *Advertising...*, pars. 4–7).

5.3.3.1. *The Argument from Cognitive, Volitional, and Ontological Impoverishment*

According to Sneddon, self-shaping—which is a crucial element of autonomy of persons—requires reflecting upon and choosing with regard to the values we hold dear, and with regard to "our lower-order mental states, especially first-order ones, in the light of our values" (par. 9). Sneddon explains that to do this well, a person needs to (1) be open to possible ways of living, and (2) have rich conceptual horizons. "These two components of strong evaluation—openness to possible ways of living and conceptual richness—are threatened by the amount of commercial advertising to which we are exposed" (par. 9).

As Sneddon argues, the problem with commercial advertising is that it exposes people to one overarching way of living (a consumerist way), and so—with its nearly constant presence in people's everyday lives—advertising acts against people having knowledge of other ways of living (pars. 12–13).[100] "Even more deeply, the effect of nearly constant exposure to commercial advertising is the spread of the idea that we should want the things that the market can provide": this is a powerful normative standard, which is very difficult to resist, given the near constancy of people's exposure to advertising (par. 15). Corroborating his line of argument with the thoughts of Waide (1987) and Phillips (1997), Sneddon further argues that through its constant presence in people's

100 A similar point is made by Wright (1997, especially 24–25). Like Sneddon, Wright stresses the importance of openness to other ways of living, thinking, and valuing to personal autonomy (46–47, 203).

lives, advertising changes people's perception of the world, of themselves, and of the possible ways of living: as a result, people gradually lose the willingness to consider ways of life that are different (Sneddon, 2013, ch. 8, sec. *Advertising...*, pars. 16–18). Yet, as Sneddon underscores after Taylor (see Section 5.2.2), considering other ways of living is a crucial element of shaping a person's identity and the course of their life (Sneddon, 2013, ch. 8, sec. *Advertising...*, par. 19). Moreover, "not only does advertising compromise both the knowledge of ways of living and the willingness to pursue and use this knowledge, it also compromises the existence of the objects of such knowledge": some ways of living become impossible, as completely incompatible with capitalism/consumerism (par. 20).

This brings Sneddon to discussing the threat that advertising poses to the richness of our conceptual horizons. First, by threatening the existence of certain ways of living that constitute the background against which we examine our own ways of being and valuing, advertising either directly "impoverishes our conceptual horizons, or it practically does so by making certain ideas harder to think about" (par. 22).[101] Second (a point inspired by Waide's reflection), advertising encourages us to focus on the acquisition of commercial goods rather than on developing and maintaining such relationships with other people (friendship, for instance) that involve "complex, attentive conversation," which enables us to acquire and refine concepts necessary to think about and "articulate our senses of ourselves and the rest of the world" (Sneddon, 2013, ch. 8, sec. *Advertising...*, par. 22).

All in all, the amount of commercial advertising to which we are exposed—as a very homogenous source of information—constitutes a threat (1) to being open to possible ways of living and (2) to conceptual richness, both of which are necessary to shape our identities and the courses of our lives, i.e., to enjoy autonomy of persons.

101 Notice how this line of reasoning is reminiscent of Wright's reflection that "our culture [pervaded with commercial speech and commercial values] prevents us, realistically if not formally, from seriously considering less consumption-oriented ways of living" (Wright, 1997, 46; see Chapter 1).

6 The Short Linguistic Appendix

In the following Appendix, I wish to add some empirical observations about how the omnipresence of advertising is affecting the way people relate to one another through language, a tool of major importance in all human connections. My thesis is that, as a result of the omnipresence of advertising, the language which people use to establish, maintain, and nourish personal relationships is becoming advertisement-laden, i.e., filled with references to advertisements and branded products, through which people express emotions, intentions, attitudes, in order to connect with other people. I will now discuss this on the example of a simile.

It has been a longstanding human tradition to use a simile to pay a compliment to a person whose beauty or personality one admires, likening that person's body parts or features of personality to the weather phenomena, seasons of the year, stars, flowers, fruits, animals, and other furniture of the world. Nowadays, the new trend to be observed is paying a compliment by referring to branded products popularized through advertising. The reference to Coca-Cola (either the bottle or the drink), for instance, is widely used to express admiration either for a person's curvy body shape or for a person's sweetness. The former has even been registered and explained in the Urban Dictionary under the entry "body like a coke bottle" (Shawtybad555, 5 Dec 2010). There are numerous contemporary songs that include the simile of Coca-Cola, like Primeminibeats ft. Gypsy *Body Like a Coke Bottle* (2020), YCee ft. Maleek Berry *Juice* (2017), GAB ft. SouthBoyz *Coca Cola Body* (2017), INNA ft. J Balvin *Cola Song* (2014), Lou Bega *Sweet Like Cola* (2010), Frankie J *That Girl* (2006). Moreover, there are blog entries that illustrate the usage of this simile—for instance, a fitness instructor blogging about *How to Build a Coke Bottle Body With Muscle and Curves*, begins her blog entry with the following words: "Today, I want to dedicate this article to the coveted shape we've all come to know as the 'Coke Bottle Body'" (IFBB Pro Roxie Beckles). Interestingly, the association with a curvy body shape was ingrained in the very design of the bottle: the original Coca-Cola bottle from 1916 "was a tribute in glass to the bounteous ideals of Victorian womanhood" (Ewen, 1988, 179), and when the bottle was being redesigned about fifty years later, Raymond Loewy—the product designer—simply elongated the bottle, "achieving (…) a 'slenderized look'" (180), indicative of the new thinner and fitter female body ideal. As Jon Stratton (2001) affirms, "the Coca-Cola bottle, the phallic signifier in so many youth-oriented Coca-Cola advertisements, is, then, in the first place, the representation of an ideal female body" (49). Thus, the above-mentioned association—imbedded into the product design and popularized by advertising—has been assimilated into contemporary language in the form of a simile.

Another popular contemporary simile rests on a comparison between a person and a Ferrari vehicle: to say to somebody "you are like a Ferrari" implies that a person is powerful and superior—in quality—to other people; conversely, to say that somebody is not like a Ferrari is to imply that they are somewhat inferior. Here are a couple examples of usage to illustrate the meaning of the simile. In a reality show *The Real Housewives of New York City* (2008–), in a conversation with two of her friends, a woman called Bethenny is relaying the words of her father "she's a mustang, and you just have to let her run" (season 1, episode 5). Although her father said it originally about somebody else, Bethenny means to say that now it applies to her: in the turbulent relationship she has with her boyfriend, she is a mustang—a horse—who needs to run. Surprisingly, one of the friends replies "You're a Ferrari, not a Mustang." Clearly, instead of an association with a horse, the friend's first association with the word "mustang" is the brand of the car, and since he wants to raise Bethenny's self-esteem and empower her in the difficult situation she is facing, the friend claims that Bethenny is like a Ferrari, i.e., of superior quality to a Mustang. In response, even though Bethenny points out that there has been a linguistic misunderstanding, she takes the comparison to a Ferrari as a compliment. Another example comes from popular literature: in a book *Love You Two* (Chansikar, 2020), the main protagonist, Aniruddh, is trying to make a woman called Neeti realize that her father would have preferred to have a son instead of a daughter: "I am sorry, but for your father, a boy would have been like a Ferrari, whereas, having you was like Marutti 800" (Chapter 2 *Meeting Neeti*). To give yet another example, in the singing competition *American Idol* (2002–), one of the judges, Luke Bryan, compared a contestant's voice to a Ferrari, while another judge, Katy Perry, complimented the beauty of that contestant by comparing him to another branded product, a Hallmark card. The contestant was thrilled with both comparisons: "'Oh my goodness, Katy Perry just complimented me and called me a little southern Hallmark card. That made my life,' Ward said. 'When Luke started talking to me he said, "Well man your voice is like a Ferrari." And that was like oh my goodness. That's crazy, Luke Bryan did not just compare my voice to a Ferrari'" (Gutierrez, 26 March 2018). From all these examples it is clear that comparing a person to a Ferrari serves the purpose of making a person feel empowered and superior.

In contrast, comparing a person to a Duracell Bunny means that this individual "seems to have limitless energy and endurance" (Your Dictionary). This is a curious simile, because a Duracell Bunny is not even a branded product, but a mascot character from the advertising campaign of Duracell. In a similar vein, a person can even be compared to the advertisement itself. In a reality show *Selling Sunset* (2019–), a wedding officiant marrying a couple said: "Beside the fact that these two look like a walking Calvin Klein ad, the beauty of their union is even greater on the inside" (season 2, episode 8). For the wedding officiant, who was a close friend of the bride, this was a way of saying something warm about the bride and the groom looking beautiful at the wedding, and the compliment was well received by both the couple and the audience. The simile "to look like a Calvin Klein ad" can be found in other contexts as well, but—like in the above-mentioned wedding context—the person to whom it is applied is always physically attractive and often also stylish. Here are some examples from popular literature: "I'm reminded of the first time I saw him and how I thought he looked like that Calvin Klein ad my momma has hanging in her locker at work" (Greenland, 2018, Chapter 53); "He had the kind of face you would see in those Calvin Klein ads" (Byrd, 2013, Chapter 1); "The statuesque brunette, with her exotic features and designer wardrobe, always looked like she'd walked out of a Calvin Klein ad" (Lennox, 2012, 182).

All in all, it seems that just like a saturation of ordinary language with psychological concepts was observed to be indicative of the omnipresence of psychology in the 20th century (Jovanovic, 2003, 11; see Chapter 1 of this book), the ordinary language becoming saturated with advertisement-laden content is symptomatic of the omnipresence of advertising in the life of individuals who live in the 21st century.

References

Primary References

The Main Section

Alexander, J., Crompton, T., Shrubsole, G. (2011). *Think of Me as Evil? Opening the Ethical Debates in Advertising*, Public Interest Research Centre (PIRC), Machynlleth, and WWF-UK, Godalming.

Alhadeff, A. C. (2015). "Numb to the World: Degradation Desensitization and Environmentally Responsible Behavior," *Tropical Resources* 34.

Alton, J. (1976). "Does the Right to Privacy Include a 'Right Not to Be Spoken To,'" http://www.johnalton.com/johnalton-malpractice-attorney/ [11.08.2017].

American Academy of Pediatrics, Council on Communications and Media. (2009). "Media Violence," *Pediatrics* 124(5): 1495–1503.

Anderson, J. (2014). "Autonomy and Vulnerability Entwined," [in:] C. Mackenzie, W. Rogers, S. Dodds (eds.), *Vulnerability: New Essays in Ethics and Feminist Philosophy*, Oxford University Press, Oxford.

Arendt, H. (1951/1962). *The Origins of Totalitarianism*, Meridian Books, Cleveland.

Arnold, D. G., Bowie, N. E. (2003). "Sweatshops and Respect for Persons," *Business Ethics Quarterly* 13(2): 221–242.

Arrington, R. L. (1982). "Advertising and Behaviour Control," *Journal of Business Ethics* 1(1): 3–12.

Atkins, K. (2006). "Autonomy and Autonomy Competencies: A Practical and Relational Approach," *Nursing Philosophy* 7(4): 205–215.

Ayres, I., Funk, M. (2003). "Marketing Privacy," *Yale Journal on Regulation* 20(1): 77–137.

Baier, A. (2009), "Sympathy and Self-Trust," [in:] *Reflections on How We Live*, Oxford University Press, Oxford.

Baier, A. (1986), "Trust an Antitrust," *Ethics* 96(2): 231–260.

Barclay, L. (2000), "Autonomy and the Social Self," [in:] C. Mackenzie, N. Stoljar (eds.), *Relational Autonomy: Feminist Perspectives on Autonomy, Agency, and the Social Self*, Oxford University Press, New York.

Bartholow, B. D., Bushman, B. J., Sestir, M. A. (2006). "Chronic Violent Video Game Exposure and Desensitization to Violence: Behavioral and Event-Based Brain Potential Data," *Journal of Experimental Social Psychology* 42: 532–539.

Bauer, L., Lieber, R., Plag, I. (2015). *The Oxford Reference Guide to English Morphology*, Oxford University Press, Oxford.

Beard, F. K. (2017), "The Ancient History of Advertising: Insights and Implications for Practitioners," *Journal of Advertising Research* 57(3): 239–244.

Benson, P. (2005). "Feminist Intuitions and the Normative Substance of Autonomy," [in:] J. S. Taylor (ed.), *Personal Autonomy: New Essays on Personal Autonomy and Its Role in Contemporary Moral Philosophy*, Cambridge University Press, Cambridge.

Black, C. (1953). "He Cannot Choose but Hear: The Plight of the Captive Auditor," *Columbia Law Review* 53(7): 960–972.

Bogost, I. (2007). *Persuasive Games: The Expressive Power of Videogames*, MIT Press, Cambridge, Mass.

Braybrooke, D. (1967). "Skepticism of Wants, and Certain Subversive Effects of Corporations on American Values," [in:] S. Hook (ed.), *Human Values and Economic Policy*, New York University Press, New York.

Brison, S. J. (1997/2018). "Outliving Oneself: Trauma, Memory, and Personal Identity," [in:] D. T. Meyers (ed.), *Feminists Rethink the Self*, Routledge, New York.

Brockmyer, J. F. (2012), "Media Violence, Desensitization, and Psychological Engagement," [in:] K. E. Dill (ed.), *The Oxford Handbook of Media Psychology*, Oxford University Press, Oxford.

Browne, M. N., Biksacky, L. F., Frondorf, A. (2009). "Advertising to Children and the Commercial Speech Doctrine: Political and Constitutional Limitations," *Drake Law Review* 58(1): 67–122.

Brudney, V. (2012). "The First Amendment and Commercial Speech," *Boston College Law Review* 53(4): 1153–1223.

Burman, E., Chantler, K. (2005). "Domestic Violence and Minoritisation: Legal and Policy Barriers Facing Minoritized Women Leaving Violent Relationships," *International Journal of Law and Psychiatry* 28(1): 59–74.

Buuren, Jasper van (2018). *Body and Reality: An Examination of the Relationships between the Body Proper, Physical Reality, and the Phenomenal World Starting from Plessner and Merleau-Ponty*, Transcript Verlag, Bielefeld.

Chantler, K., Bracewell, K., Baker, V., Heyes, K., Traynor, P., Ward. M. (2022). "An Analysis of Minoritisation in Domestic Homicide Reviews in England and Wales," *Critical Social Policy* 42(1): 1–24.

Cheng, J., Bernstein, M., Danescu-Niculescu-Mizil, C., Leskovec, J. (2017). "Anyone Can Become a Troll: Causes of Trolling Behavior in Online Discussions," [in:] *Proceedings of the 2017 ACM Conference on Computer Supported Cooperative Work and Social Computing, Portland.*

Christman, John, "Autonomy in Moral and Political Philosophy," [in:] E. N. Zalta (ed.), *The Stanford Encyclopedia of Philosophy* (Fall 2020 Edition), https://plato.stanford.edu/archives/fall2020/entries/autonomy-moral/ [01.01.2021].

Cohan, J. A. (2001). "Towards a New Paradigm in the Ethics of Women's Advertising," *Journal of Business Ethics* 33(4): 323–337.

Corbin, C. M. (2009). "The First Amendment Right Against Compelled Listening," *Boston University Law Review* 89(3): 939–1016.

Cowling, M. (2004/2016). "Rape, Communicative Sexuality and Sex Education," [in:] M. Cowling, P. Reynolds (eds.), *Making Sense of Sexual Consent*, Routledge, Abington.

Crisp, R. (1987). "Persuasive Advertising, Autonomy, and the Creation of Desire," *Journal of Business Ethics* 6(5): 413–418.

Cunningham, A. (2003). "Autonomous Consumption: Buying Into the Ideology of Capitalism," *Journal of Business Ethics* 48(3): 229–236.

Curry, W. C. (1957). Milton's Ontology, Cosmogony and Physics, University of Kentucky Press, Lexington.

Czyński, Ostrowski (2011). "Reklama w Przestrzeni Publicznej Miasta [Advertisement in Municipal Public Spaces]," *Przestrzeń i Forma* 16: 213–228.

De la Hera, T. (2019). *Digital Gaming and the Advertising Landscape*, Amsterdam University Press, Amsterdam.

Donchin, A. (2001). "Understanding Autonomy Relationally: Toward a Reconfiguration of Bioethical Principles," *Journal of Medicine and Philosophy* 26(4): 365–86.

Dreyfus, H. (2007). "Why Heideggerian AI Failed and How Fixing It Would Require Making It More Heideggerian," *Artificial Intelligence* 171(18): 1137–1160.

Durham, T. R. (1984). "Information, Persuasion, and Control in Moral Appraisal of Advertising Strategy," *Journal of Business Ethics* 3(3): 173–180.

Dworkin, A (1974). *Woman Hating*, E.P Dutton, New York.

Dworkin, A. (1987). *Intercourse*, Free Press, New York.

Ells, C. (2001), "Lessons about Autonomy from the Experience of Disability," *Social Theory and Practice* 27(4): 599–615.

Emerson, T. I. (1970). *The System of Freedom of Expression,* Random House, New York.

Ewen, S. (1988). *All Consuming Images: The Politics of Style in Contemporary Culture*, Basic Books, New York.

Fitzgerald, P. H. (1891), *The History of Pickwick,* Chapman and Hall, London.

Frankfurt, H. (1971). "Freedom of the Will and the Concept of a Person," *Journal of Philosophy* 68(1): 5–20.

Friedman, M. (1997/2018). "Autonomy and Social Relationships: Rethinking the Feminist Critique," [in:] D. T. Meyers (ed.), *Feminists Rethink the Self*, Routledge, New York.

Fromm, E. (1976/2008). *To Have or to Be*, Continuum, London.

Galbraith, J. K. (1952/1995). "The Dependence Effect," [in:] D.C. Colander, H. Lanreth (eds), *Classic Readings in Economics*, Maxi Press, New Haven.

Gehl, J. (2011). *Life Between Buildings: Using Public Space*, trans. J. Koch, Island Press, Washington.

Gehl, J. (2010). *Cities for People*, Island Press, Washington.

Gilligan, C. (1982). *In a Different Voice: Psychological Theory and Women's Development*, Harvard University Press, Cambridge, Mass.

Goering, S. (2008). "Postnatal Reproductive Autonomy: Promoting Relational Autonomy and Self-Trust in New Parents," *Bioethics* 23(1): 9–19.

Goldberg, L. (2008). "Embodied Trust Within the Perinatal Nursing Relationship," *Midwifery* 24(1): 74–82.

Goldberg, L. (2003), "In the Company of Women: Enacting Autonomy Within the Perinatal Nursing Relationship," *Nursing Ethics* 10(6): 580–587.

Goldstein, E. B. (2011), "Introduction to Cognitive Psychology," [in:] *Cognitive Psychology: Connecting Mind, Research, and Everyday Experience*, Third Edition, Wadsworth/Cengage Learning.

Gołębiewska, M. (2003). *Demontaż Atrakcji: O estetyce audiowizualności*, Słowo/Obraz Terytoria, Gdańsk.

Govier, T. (1993). "Self-Trust, Autonomy, and Self-Esteem," *Hypatia* 8(1): 99–120.

Grzegorczykowa, R. (2007). *Wstęp do językoznawstwa*, PWN, Warszawa.

Gyllensten, A. L., Skär, L. Miller, M., Gard, G. (2010), "Embodied Identity: A Deeper Understanding of Body Awareness," *Physiotherapy Theory and Practice* 26(7): 439–446.

Hartley, R. C. (2010). "Freedom Not to Listen: A Constitutional Analysis of Compulsory Indoctrination through Workplace Captive Audience Meetings," *Berkeley Journal of Employment & Labor Law* 31(1): 65–125.

Haiman, F. S. (1972). "Speech v. Privacy: Is There a Right Not to Be Spoken to?," *Northwestern University Law Review* 67(2): 153–199.

Held, V. (1993). *Feminist Morality: Transforming Culture, Society, and Politics*, The University of Chicago Press, Chicago.

Herman, B. (1993). "Could It Be Worth Thinking About Kant on Sex and Marriage?," [in:] L. Antony, Ch. Witt (eds.), *A Mind of One's Own: Feminist Essays on Reason and Objectivity*, Westview, Boulder.

Heyman, S. J. (2010). *Free Speech and Human Dignity*, Yale University Press, New Haven.

Hower, R. (1949). *The History of an Advertising Agency: N. W. Ayer & Son 1869–1949*, Harvard University Press, Cambridge.

Huxley, A. (1958). "The Arts of Selling," [in:] *Brave New World Revisited,* Harper & Row, New York.

Jaggar, A. (1989). "Feminist Ethics: Some Issues for the Nineties," *Journal of Social Philosophy* 20(1–2): 91–107.

Jones, K. (2012). "Trustworthiness," *Ethics* 123(1): 61–85.

Jovanovic, G. (2003). "Psychology at Sites of Crisis," [in:] N. Stephenson, H. L. Radtke, R. J. Jorna, H. J. Stam (eds.), Theoretical Psychology: Critical Contributions, Captus University Press, Concord.

Kant, I. (1924/1997). *Lectures on Ethics*, P. Heath, J. B. Schneewind (eds.), trans. P. Heath, Cambridge University Press, Cambridge.

Kant, I. (1788/1999). "Critique of Practical Reason" (CPR), [in:] M. J. Gregor (trans. and ed.), *Practical Philosophy: The Cambridge Edition of the Works of Immanuel Kant*, Cambridge University Press, Cambridge.

Kant, I. (1785/1999). "Groundwork of the Metaphysics of Morals" (GW), [in:] M. J. Gregor (trans. and ed.), *Practical Philosophy: The Cambridge Edition of the Works of Immanuel Kant*, Cambridge University Press, Cambridge.

Karpatkin, R. H., Holmes, A. (1995). "Making Schools Ad-Free Zones," *Educational Leadership: Journal of the Department of Supervision and Curriculum Development, N.E.A* 53(1): 72–76.

Kong, C. (2017), *Mental Capacity in Relationship: Decision-Making, Dialogue, and Autonomy*, Cambridge University Press, Cambridge.

Kukla, R. (2005). "Conscientious Autonomy: Displacing Decisions in Healthcare," *Hastings Center Report* 35(2): 34–44.

Langton, R. (2009). *Sexual Solipsism: Philosophical Essays on Pornography and Objectification*, Oxford University Press, Oxford.

Laub, D., Feldman, S. (1992), *Testimony: Crises of Witnessing in Literature, Psychoanalysis, and History*, Routledge, New York.

Lehrer, K. (1997). *Self-Trust: A Study of Reason, Knowledge, and Autonomy*, Oxford University Press, New York.

Lehu, J.-M. (2007). *Branded Entertainment: Product Placement and Brand Strategy in the Entertainment Business*, Kogan Page, London.

Lefebvre, H. (1974/1991). *The Production of Space*, trans. D. Nicholson-Smith, Blackwell, Oxford, UK/Cambridge, USA.

Lichtman, D. G. (2006). "Captive Audiences and the First Amendment," *University of Chicago Public Law & Legal Theory Working Paper* 118: 6–11.

Listwan-Franczak, K., Franczak, P. (2015). "Problematyka reklamy zewnętrznej na obszarach cennych przyrodniczo, przykład otoczenia Tatr, " *Prace Geograficzne* 142: 57–75.

Locke, J. (1694/1974). *An Essay Concerning Human Understanding*, A. D. Woozley (ed.), New American Library, New York.

MacKinnon, C. (1989). *Toward a Feminist Theory of the State*, Harvard University Press, Cambridge, Mass.

MacKinnon, C. (1987). *Feminism Unmodified*, Harvard University Press, Cambridge, Mass.

Maclean, A. R. (2002). "Consent, Sectionalisation and the Concept of a Medical Procedure," Journal of Medical Ethics 28(4): 249–254.

Marcuse, H. (1964/2007). *One-Dimensional Man: Studies in the Ideology of Advanced Industrial Society*, Routledge, London.

Martins, M. O. (2016). "An Ontology of Omnipresent and Omniscient Cameras: Changes to Telejournalism and the Ubiquity of Devices for Recording Reality," *Brazilian Journalism Research* 12(3): 98–113.

Mattelart, A. (1991). *Advertising International: The Privatisation of Public Space*, Routledge.

McGowan D. F. (1990), "A Critical Analysis of Commercial Speech," *California Law Review* 78(2): 359–448.

McLeod, C. (2002). *Self-Trust and Reproductive Autonomy*, The MIT Press, Boston.

McLeod, C, Sherwin, S. (2000). "Relational Autonomy, Self-Trust, and Health Care for Patients Who Are Oppressed," [in:] C. Mackenzie, N. Stoljar (eds.), *Relational Autonomy: Feminist Perspectives on Autonomy, Agency, and the Social Self*, Oxford University Press, New York.

Mendelová. D. (2018). "The Birth of American Advertising," *Communication Today* 9(2): 4–19.

Meyers, D. T. (2005). "Decentralizing Autonomy: Five Faces of Selfhood," [in:] J. Christman, J. Anderson (eds.), *Autonomy and the Challenges to Liberalism: New Essays*, Cambridge University Press, Cambridge.

Meyers, D. T. (2000). "Intersectional Identity and the Authentic Self? Opposites Attract!," [in:] C. Mackenzie, N. Stoljar (eds.), *Relational Autonomy: Feminist*

Perspectives on Autonomy, Agency, and the Social Self, Oxford University Press, New York.

Meyers, D. T. (1989). *Self, Society, and Personal Choice*, Columbia University Press, New York.

Meyers, D. T. (1987). "Personal Autonomy and the Paradox of Feminine Socialization," *The Journal of Philosophy* 84(11): 619–628.

Milton, J., Fenton. E. (1667/1821). *Paradise Lost*, J. Bumpus, Holborn Bars, London.

Moore, R. L., Murray, M. D. (2008). *Media Law and Ethics*, Taylor & Francis, New York.

Mráček, P., Mucha M. (2011). "Application of Knowledge in Advergaming as a Possible Source of Competitive Advantage," *Journal of Competitiveness* 3(3): 108–118.

Mrug, S., Madan, A., Windle, M. (2016), "Emotional Desensitization to Violence Contributes to Adolescents' Violent Behavior," *Journal of Abnormal Child Psychology* 44(1): 75–86.

Nedelsky, J. (1989). "Reconceiving Autonomy: Sources, Thoughts and Possibilities," *Yale Journal of Law and Feminism* 1(7): 7–36.

Nelson, P. (1978). "Advertising and Ethics," [in:] R. De George, J. Pichler (eds.), *Ethics, Free Enterprise, and Public Policy*, Oxford University Press, New York.

Newel, J., Salmon, C. T., Chang, S. (2006). "The Hidden History of Product Placement," *Journal of Broadcasting & Electronic Media* 50(4): 575–594.

Noddings, N. (2012). "The Caring Relation in Teaching," *Oxford Review of Education* 38(6): 771–781.

Noddings, N. (2005). *The Challenge to Care in Schools: An Alternative Approach to Education,* Second Edition, Teachers College Press, New York.

Noggle, R. (1995). "Autonomy, Value, and Conditioned Desire," *American Philosophical Quarterly* 32(1): 57–69.

Nussbaum, M. C. (1995). "Objectification," *Philosophy and Public Affairs* 24(4): 249–291.

O'Neill, O. (1989). *Constructions of Reason*, Cambridge University Press, Cambridge.

Oshana, M. (2014). "Trust and Autonomous Agency," *Res Philosophica* 91(3): 431–447.

Phillips, B. (1997). "In Defense of Advertising: A Social Perspective," *Journal of Business Ethics* 16(2): 109–118.

Pigliucci, M. (2017). How to Be a Stoic: Ancient Wisdom for Modern Living, Rider, London.

Pomeranz, J. L. (2012). "No Need to Break New Ground: A Response to the Supreme Court's Threat to Overhaul the Commercial Speech Doctrine," *Loyola of Los Angeles Law Review* 45: 389–434.

Post, R. (2000), "The Constitutional Status of Commercial Speech," *UCLA Law Review* 48(1): 1–57.

Presbrey, F. S. (1929), *The History and Development of Advertising*, Doubleday, New York.

Prosser, L. (1960). "Privacy," *California Law Review* 48(3): 383–423.

Ramos, D. M., Kamal, F., Wimmer, E. A., Cartwright, A. N., & Monteiro, A. (2006). "Temporal and Spatial Control of Transgene Expression Using Laser Induction of the *Hsp70* Promoter," *BMC Developmental Biology* 6: 55–61, https://bmcdevbiol.biomedcentral.com/articles/10.1186/1471-213X-6-55 [5.07.2018].

Rauschnabel, P. A., Felix, R., Hinsch, C. (2019). "Augmented Reality Marketing: How Mobile AR-Apps Can Improve Brands Through Inspiration," *Journal of Retailing and Consumer Services* 49(C): 43–53.

Rauschnabel, P. A. (2018), "Virtually Enhancing the Real World with Holograms: An Exploration of Expected Gratifications of Using Augmented Reality Smart Glasses," Psychology & Marketing 35(8): 557–572.

Rauschnabel, P. A., Ro, Y. K. (2016). "Augmented Reality Smart Glasses: An Investigation of Technology Acceptance Drivers," *International Journal of Technology Marketing* 11(2): 123–148.

Rauschnabel, P. A., Brem, A., Ro, Y. K. (2015). "Augmented Reality Smart Glasses: Definition, Conceptual Insights, and Managerial Importance," Unpublished Working Paper, The University of Michigan-Dearborn, College of Business.

Redish, M. H. (1982). "The Value of Free Speech," *University of Pennsylvania Law Review* 130(3): 591–645.

Rose, N. (1998). Inventing Our Selves, Cambridge University Press, Cambridge.

Ruane, K. A. (2014). "Freedom of Speech and Press: Exceptions to the First Amendment," Congressional Research Service, https://fas.org/sgp/crs/misc/95-815.pdf [Accessed 11.04.2017]

Sadurski, W. (1999). Freedom of Speech and Its Limits, Kluwer Academic Publishers, Dordrecht.

Sandel, M. J. (2010). *Justice: What's the Right Thing to Do?*, Farrar, Straus and Giroux, New York.

Sandel, M. J. (2013). *What Money Can't Buy: The Moral Limits of Markets*, Penguin, London.

Sartre, J. P. (1946/1973). *Existentialism and Humanism*, trans. P. Mairet, Eyre Methuen, London.

Schulze, V., Jöckel, S, & Will, A. (2007). *Grundlage der Werbewirkungsforschung für Ingame-Advertising: Theoretische Überlegungen anhand des Models der Wirkungspfade*, Ilmenau University of Technology, Ilmenau.

Sher, S. (2011). "A Framework for Assessing Immorally Manipulative Marketing Tactics," *Journal of Business Ethics* 102(1): 97–118.

Sherwin, S. (1998). "A Relational Approach to Autonomy in Healthcare," [in:] *The Feminist Health Care Research Network*.

Smith, M. W., Sun, W., Sutherland, J., & Mackie, B. (2014). "Game Advertising: A Conceptual Framework and Exploration of Advertising Prevalence," *The Computer Games Journal* 3(1): 94–123.

Sneddon, A. (2013). *Autonomy*, Bloomsbury, London.

Sneddon, A. (2006). "Equality, Justice, and Paternalism: Recentering Debate about Physician-Assisted Suicide," *Journal of Applied Philosophy* 23(4): 387–404.

Sneddon, A. (2001a). "What's Wrong with Selling Yourself into Slavery? Paternalism and Deep Autonomy," *Critica* 33(98): 97–121.

Sneddon, A. (2001b). "Advertising and Deep Autonomy," *Journal of Business Ethics* 33(1): 15–28.

Soja, E. W. (1996). *Thirdspace: Journeys to Los Angeles and Other Real-and-Imagined Places*, Blackwell, Cambridge, USA.

Spence, E., Van Heekeren, B. (2005). Advertising Ethics, Pearson, Upper Saddle River.

Spence, E. (2018). "Harm in Media Marketing: The Branding of Values," [in:], P. L. Plaisance (ed.), *Communication and Media Ethics*, Walter de Gruyter Inc., Boston.

Steiner, T. (2008). *Advertising in Online Games and EC Audiovisual Media Regulation*, NCCR Trade Working Paper No 2008/3, NCCR Trade Regulation Swiss National Centre of Competence in Research, University of Lucerne, https://www.unilu.ch/fileadmin/shared/Publikationen/steiner_advertising-in-online-games-and-ec-audiovisua-media-regulation.pdf [29.06.2018].

Stratton, J. (2001). *The Desirable Body: Cultural Fetishism and the Erotics of Consumption*, University of Illinois Press, Urbana/Chicago.

Strauss, M. (1991). "Redefining the Captive Audience Doctrine," *Hastings Constitutional Law Quarterly* 19(1): 85–122.

Taylor, C. (1985a). "Self-Interpreting Animals," [in:] *Human Agency and Language: Philosophical Papers 1*, Cambridge University Press, Cambridge.

Taylor, C. (1985b). "What is Human Agency?," [in:] *Human Agency and Language: Philosophical Papers 1*, Cambridge University Press, Cambridge.

Taylor, C. (1989). *Sources of the Self: The Making of the Modern Identity*, Harvard University Press, Cambridge.

Taylor, C. (1991). *The Ethics of Authenticity*, Harvard University Press, Cambridge.

Taylor, T. D. (2012). *The Sounds of Capitalism: Advertising, Music, and the Conquest of Culture*, University of Chicago Press, Chicago.

Todes, S. (2001). *Body and World*, The MIT Press, Cambridge, USA.

Vedrashko, I. (2006). *Advertising in Computer Games*, Thesis (M.A.), Submitted to the Department of Comparative Media Studies in partial fulfillment of the requirements for the degree of Master of Science in Comparative Media Studies at the Massachusetts Institute of Technology, *Gamesbrandsplay.com*, http://gamesbrandsplay.com/files/vedrashko_advertising_in_games.pdf [20.06.2018].

Villarán, A. (2017). "Irrational Advertising and Moral Autonomy," *Journal of Business Ethics* 16(2): 109–118.

Von Hayek, F. A. (1961). "The Non Sequitur of the 'Dependence Effect,'" *Southern Economic Journal* 27(4): 346–348.

Waide, J. (1987). "The Making of Self and the World in Advertising," *Journal of Business Ethics* 6(2): 73–79.

Warren, S., Brandeis, L. (1890. "The Right to Privacy," *Harvard Law Review*, 4(5): 193–220.

Welsch, W. (1997). *Undoing Aesthetics*, trans. A. Inkpin, Sage Publications, London.

Westlund, A. C. (2009). "Rethinking Relational Autonomy," *Hypatia* 24(4): 26–49.

Wright, R. G. (1997), *Selling Words: Free Speech in a Commercial Culture*, New York University Press, New York.

Zick, T. (2009). *Speech Out of Doors: Preserving First Amendment Liberties in Public Places*, Cambridge University Press, Cambridge.

Ziporyn, B. (2016). *Emptiness and Omnipresence: An Essential Introduction to Tiantai Buddhism*, Indiana University Press, Bloomington.

The Legal Acts Section (from the most recent to the earliest)

American Bar Association, Center for Professional Responsibility, "Rule 7.3, Direct Contact With Prospective Clients," [in:] *Model Rules of Professional Conduct. Hill v. Colorado*, 530 U.S. 703 (2000).

44 Liquormart, Inc. v. Rhode Island, 517 U.S. 484 (1996).

Rosenberger v. University of Virginia, 515 U.S. 819 (1995).

Florida Bar v. Went For It, Inc., 515 U.S. 618 (1995).

Davis v. Barking, Havering and Brentwood Health Authority (1993) 4 *Medical Law Rev* 85.

United States v. Edge Broadcasting Co., 509 U.S. 418 (1993).

Hustler Magazine, Inc. v. Falwell, 485 U.S. 46 (1988).

Frisby v. Schultz, 487 U.S. 474 (1988).

Carey v. Brown, 447 U.S., 471 (1987).

Zauderer v. Office of Disciplinary Counsel, 471 U.S. 625 (1985).

Penthouse International, Ltd. v. Koch, 599 F. Supp. 1338 (S.D.N.Y. 1984).

Bolger v. Youngs Drug Products Corp., 463 U.S. 60 (1983).

Central Hudson Gas and Electric Corp. v. Public Service Commission, 477 U.S. 557 (1980).

First National Bank v. Bellotti, 435 U.S. 783 (1978).

Bates v. State Bar of Ariz, 433 U.S. 350 (1977).

Virginia State Board of Pharmacy v. Virginia Citizens Consumer Council, Inc., 425 U.S. 748 (1976).

Erznoznik v. City of Jacksonville, 422 U.S. 205 (1975).

Lehman v. City of Shaker Heights, 418 U.S. 298 (1974).

Pittsburgh Press Co. v. Pittsburgh Commission on Human Relations, 413 U.S. 376 (1973).

Kleindienst v. Mandel, 408 U.S. 753 (1972).

Rowan v. U.S. Post Office Department, 397 U.S. 728 (1970).

Public Utilities Commission v. Pollak, 343 U.S. 451 (1952).

Breard v. City of Alexandria, 341 U.S. 627 (1951).

Kovacs v. Cooper, 336 U.S. 77 (1949).

Thomas v. Collins, 323 U.S. 516 (1945).

Murdock v. Pennsylvania, 319 U.S. 105 (1943).

Valentine v. Chrestensen, 316 U.S. 52 (1942).

Secondary References: Non-Academic

The Main Section (in alphabetical order)

Adi771 (10 August 2005), "Uważajcie na paczki rozdawane po porodzie!," *Forum. gazeta.pl*, https://forum.gazeta.pl/forum/w,585,27579026,27579026,uwazajcie_na_paczki_rozdawane_po_porodzie_.html [10.05.2020].

AirSign, "Why Aerial Advertising," *Airsign.com*, http://www.airsign.com/compare-advertising.php [5.07. 2018].

Alt Terrain, "Bicycle Billboard," *Altterrain.com*, http://altterrain.com/bicycle-billboard-mobile-bike-outdoor-advertising-green-eco-friendly-ads-html/ [10.07.2018].

American Association of Advertising Agencies (2015), "How many advertisements is a person exposed to in a day?," https://ams.aaaa.org/eweb/upload/faqs/adexposures.pdf [22.07.2015].

American Bar Association, Center for Professional Responsibility, "Rule 7.3, Direct Contact With Prospective Clients," [in:] *Model Rules of Professional Conduct.*

America's Media Usage and Ad Exposure 1945–2014 (2014), Media Dynamics Inc.

Amnesty International, "This is consent: How to talk (and think) about consent," *Amnesty.org*, https://www.amnesty.org/en/latest/campaigns/2021/06/ltay-toolkit-blog-how-to-talk-and-think-about-consent/ [2.02.2022].

A Night To Remember, "Corporate Sponsor Options," *Anighttoremember.com*, http://anighttoremeberprom.com/sponsors/sponsor-options/ [1.05.2018].

Anonymous Reporter (8 Apr 2011), "Want Someone Else to Pay Your Mortgage? Just paint an Ad over the Entire Front of Your House," *Daily Mail*, http://www.dailymail.co.uk/news/article-1374489/Adzookie-pay-mortgage-allow-logo-painted-house.html [9.07.2018].

Anonymous Reporter (23 Mar 2018), "No Hoardings in Parks after Thousands Back Campaign," *South Bristol Voice*, https://www.southbristolvoice.co.uk/park-adverts [9.07.2018].

Baker, R., Smith, K. (12 Feb 2001). "Stealth TV," *American Prospect* 12(3).

Blue Line Media, "Taxi Advertising," https://www.bluelinemedia.com/taxi-advertising [10.07.2018].

Bonner, J. L. (25 Mar 2009). "Idaho Teacher Sells Advertising Space on Tests," *Campaign for a Commercial-Free Childhood*, http://www.commercialexploitation.org/news/2009/03/idahoteacher.html [20.04.2018].

Branson, R. (25 Jan 2017). "London's Air Ambulance Turns 28," *Virgin.com*, https://www.virgin.com/richard-branson/londons-air-ambulance-turns-28 [17.06.2018].

Brashares, A. (2001), *The Sisterhood of the Traveling Pants*, Delacorte, New York.

Brezeky, C. (28 Feb 2013). "Japon: Les Cuisses des Jeunes Filles, le Nouvel Eldorado Publicitaire," http://www.puretrend.com/article/japon-les-cuisses-des-jeunes-filles-le-nouvel-eldorado-publicitaire_a73905/1, *Puretrend.com*, [30.12.2018].

Brown, D. (2003). *The Da Vinci Code*, Doubleday, New York.

Brownrigg, S. (4 Nov 2001). "Your Ad Here: The Bulgari Connection By Fay Weldon," book review, *New York Times*, https://www.nytimes.com/2001/11/04/books/your-ad-here.html [26.06.2018].

Brueggeman, S. (4 Jan 2015). "5 Reasons to Market to Waiting Room Audiences," *EPPG: EBSCO Professional Partnership Group*,

https://www.ebscoppg.com/5-reasons-market-waiting-room-audiences/ [18.06.2018].

Burge, K. (14 Feb 2006). "Ad Watch: Police Sponsors Put Littleton Cruiser on the Road," *Boston Globe*, http://archive.boston.com/news/local/articles/2006/02/14/ad_watch_police_sponsors_put_littleton_cruiser_on_the_road/ [7.06.2016].

Butler, K. (23 Aug 2011). "The Battle Heats up over Billboards in Los Angeles City Parks," *Pacific Swell: Southern California environment news and trends*, https://www.scpr.org/blogs/environment/2011/08/23/3291/battle-heats-over-billboards-los-angeles-city-park/ [11.09.2018].

Byrd, R. (2013). *Take Me Under*, Penguin Books, New York.

Cabvertising, http://www.cabvertising.eu/ [12.11.2019].

Campaign For a Commercial-Free Childhood, http://www.commercialfreechildhood.org/ [22.06.2018].

Chansikar, A. (2020). *Love You Two*, Notion Press, Chetpet.

Chapman, P. (15 Dec 2011). "Virgin Mary Billboard Sparks Outrage in New Zealand," *Telegraph*, https://www.telegraph.co.uk/news/worldnews/australiaandthepacific/newzealand/8957667/Virgin-Mary-billboard-sparks-outrage-in-New-Zealand.html [9.07.2018].

Chen, X. (2 May 2012). "Ads To Appear on Book Covers," *China Daily*, http://en.people.cn/90882/7805027.html [26.06.2018].

Clancy, T. (2003). *The Teeth of the Tiger*, G.P. Putnam's Sons, New York.

Davies, S. (2019). *The Montessori Toddler: A Parent's Guide to Raising a Curious and Responsible Human Being*, Workman Publishing, New York.

Delbo, C. (1995). *Auschwitz and After*, trans. R.C. Lamont, Yale University Press, New Haven.

DeNisco, A. (16 Mar 2015). "School Advertising Goes Digital: Digital Billboards that Resemble Large Touch-Screen Tablets Placed in Schools in Two Arizona Districts," *District Administration Magazine*, https://www.districtadministration.com/article/school-advertising-goes-digital [29.04.2018].

Design Swan (20 Jan 2010). "15 Creative Washroom Advertising," *DesignSwan.com*, https://www.designswan.com/archives/15-creative-washroom-advertising.html [11.09.2018].

Dickens, C. (1837). *The Pickwick Papers*, Chapman & Hall, London.

Dobbin, B. (26 Dec 2011). "Some Police Agencies Sold on Sponsorship Deals," *Boston Globe*, https://www.bostonglobe.com/news/nation/2011/12/26/some-police-agencies-sold-sponsorship-deals/UnV86WKh5ObLs32p7qLk5L/story.html [7.06.2018].

Duck, B. (10 Aug 2010). "California Ambulances Advertising for Non Profits on Vehicles–Moving Billboards," *The Medical Quack: Health Care Blog from Barbara Duck*, http://ducknetweb.blogspot.com/2010/08/california-ambulances-advertising-for.html [16.06.2018].

Dudek, M. (24 Apr 2015). "Baseball and Advertising," *Britteninc.com*, https://britteninc.com/2015/04/24/baseball-and-advertising/ [15.05.2018].

Duffin, C. (2 May 2013). "Police Commissioner Wants Private Firms To Sponsor Cars and Stations," *Telegraph*, https://www.telegraph.co.uk/news/uknews/crime/10031215/Police-commissioner-wants-private-firms-to-sponsor-cars-and-stations.html [4.06.2018].

EAM 1, "Inflight Advertising," *Theairport.org*, http://www.theairport.org/inflight-advertising.html [11.07.2018].

EAM 2, "Airport Advertising," *Theairport.org*, http://www.theairport.org/airport-advertising.html [11.07.2018].

Falk, A. (30 Jun 2005). "Mom Sells Face Space for Tattoo Advertisement," *Desert Morning News*.

Ferbrache, C. (28 Oct 2015). "Ambulances as Billboards: The Pros & Cons," *EMSWORLD*, https://www.emsworld.com/article/12131984/ambulances-as-billboards-the-pros-cons [17.06.2018].

FireRescue1 Staff (30 Nov 2017). "Should Fire Departments Sell Ad Space on Fire Trucks?," *FireRescue1*, https://www.firerescue1.com/apparatus/articles/365958018-Should-fire-departments-sell-ad-space-on-fire-trucks/ [10.06.2018].

Funtic. (15 Jun 2011). “Креативная реклама на дверях лифтов,” *Copypast.ru*, https://copypast.ru/2011/07/15/kreativnaja_reklama_na_dverjakh_liftov_12_foto.html [10.07.2018].

Gapminder, “The World Has Reached Peak Number of Children!,” *Gapminder.org*, https://www.gapminder.org/news/world-peak-number-of-children-is-now/ [16.12.2021].

Giantasio, D. (16 Dec 2011). “St. Matthews in the City Strikes Again,” *Adweek*, https://www.adweek.com/creativity/mary-gets-positive-pregnancy-test-churchs-christmas-billboard-137166/ [9.07.2018].

Gibson, D. K. (24 June 2016). “How Bicycle Advertising Will Save the World,” *BBC*, http://www.bbc.com/autos/story/20160624-how-bicycle-advertising-will-save-the-world [10.07.2018].

Graham, D. T. (24 Mar 2014). “Palatine Rural Fire District Sells Ad Space on Truck, Ambulance,” *Daily Herald*, http://www.dailyherald.com/article/20140324/news/140329315/ [10.06.2018].

Greenland, S. (2018). *Watching You*, Entangled Publishing, Fort Collins.

Gutierrez, K. (26 March 2018). “Ashley High student sings his way to Hollywood,” *Wwaytv3.com*, https://www.wwaytv3.com/2018/03/26/ashley-high-student-sings-his-way-to-hollywood/ [8.06.2020].

Hamati, D. (Apr 2012). “Paint My House,” *Saturated Space @ the Architectural Association School of Architecture*, http://www.saturatedspace.org/2012/04/paint-my-house.html [9.07.2011].

Hankinson, J. (1989, written under the pseudonym ‘Lawrence St. Clair’). *Isabelle and Veronique: Four Months, Four Cities*, Blue Moon Books, New York.

Hardy, D. (16 Oct 2011). “To Balance Budgets, Schools Allow Ads,” *Philadelphia Inquirer*.

Highfield, R. (21 Nov 2006). “Ads Could Knock Spots off Butterfly Wings,” *Telegraph*, https://www.telegraph.co.uk/news/uknews/1534721/Ads-could-knock-spots-off-butterfly-wings.html [5.07.2018].

Hoag, C. (19 Sep 2010). “Schools Seek Extra Cash Through Campus Ads,” *Associated Press*.

Holz, J. (9 Feb 2003). “To Serve and Persuade,” *New York Times*, https://www.nytimes.com/2003/02/09/nyregion/to-serve-and-persuade.html [7.06.2018].

Hsieh, A. (5 Aug 2010). “Advertising on Ambulances: A Slippery Slope?,” *EMS1 (Emergency Medical Services)*, https://www.ems1.com/ambulances-emergency-vehicles/articles/863528-Advertising-on-ambulances-A-slippery-slope/ [16.06.2018].

IEG Sponsorship Report 2014. (30 Jan 2014 I). "Inside The Evolving World of Municipal Marketing," *Sponsorship.com*, http://www.sponsorship.com/iegsr/2014/02/03/Inside-The-Evolving-World-of-Municipal-Marketing.aspx# [12.09.2018].

IEG Sponsorship Report 2014. (30 Jan 2014 II). "Cities Look To Follow NYC Lead In Securing Sponsorship For Bike Share Programs," *Sponsorship.com*, http://www.sponsorship.com/IEGSR/2014/02/03/Inside-The-Evolving-World-of-Municipal-Marketing/Cities-Look-To-Follow-NYC-Lead-In-Securing-Sponsor.aspx [12.09.2018].

IFBB Pro Roxie Beckles, "How to Build a Coke Bottle Body With Muscle and Curves," *Roxstarfitness.com*, https://www.roxstarfitness.com/coke-bottle-body-3/ [07.06.2020].

Jail Advertising Network, http://www.jailadvertisingnetwork.com/ [22.06.2018].

IQ.screen, AI Advertising Platform, https://iqscreen.pl/ [12.11.2019].

Jain, N., "Ambulance Access for All," *Changemakers.com*, https://www.changemakers.com/disruptive/entries/ambulance-access-all [22.06.2018].

Jarvis, W. (14 Jul 2017). "Follow the Money: Ads on NBA Jerseys Open the Doors for Other Top Sports," *AdAge*, http://adage.com/article/advertising/big-thing-ads-nba-jerseys-china/309744/ [1.06.2018].

Johnson, C. (17 Sep 2006). "Cutting Through Advertising Clutter," *CBS News*, http://www.cbsnews.com/news/cutting-through-advertising-clutter/ [31.07.2016].

Johnson, S. B. (11 May 2012). "Advertising on Book Covers and Inside Books," *Explorations: Writing, Culture, Life*, https://sarahblakejohnson.blogspot.com/2012/05/advertising-on-book-covers-and-inside.html [26.06.2018].

Johnson, S. (29 Sep 2014). "New Research Sheds Light on Daily Ad Exposures," *Sjinsights.net*, https://sjinsights.net/2014/09/29/new-research-sheds-light-on-daily-ad-exposures/ [31.07.2016].

Kalb, I. (10 Apr 2013). "Putting Brand Names On Stadiums Can Be Extremely Valuable," *Business Insider*, http://www.businessinsider.com/name-that-venue-and-collect-billions-of-brand-impressions-2013-4?IR=T [19.05.2018].

Lauletta, T. (17 Oct 2017). "Here Are the New Nike Uniforms for All 30 NBA Teams," *Business Insider*, http://www.businessinsider.com/new-nike-nba-uniforms-2017-7?IR=T [23.05.2018].

Lea, R. (3 May 2012). "Don't Judge a Book by the Ad on Its Cover," *The Guardian*, https://www.theguardian.com/books/booksblog/2012/may/03/book-cover-advertising [26.06.2018].

Lennox, K. (2012). *Hidden Agenda*, Harlequin, New York.

Les Associés d'EIM. (2004). *Les Dirigeants Face au Changement: Baromètre 2004*, Huitième Jour, Paris.

Levi, P. (1993). *Survival in Auschwitz*, Macmillan, New York.

Lewin, T. (26 Jan 2006). "In Public Schools, the Name Game as a Donor Lure," *New York Times*, https://www.nytimes.com/2006/01/26/education/in-public-schools-the-name-game-as-a-donor-lure.html [1.05.2018].

Mackay, A. (2004). The Practice of Advertising, Butterworth-Heinemann, London.

Mahdawi, A. (12 Aug 2015). "Can Cities Kick Ads? Inside the Global Movement to Ban Urban Billboards," *The Guardian*, https://www.theguardian.com/cities/2015/aug/11/can-cities-kick-ads-ban-urban-billboards [26.12.2018].

Massive Media Experiential Agency, "Sand + Sea Marketing and Advertising," *Massivemediainc.com*, https://www.massivemediainc.com/sand-and-sea-marketing-and-advertising-massivemedia/ [11.09.2018].

Masuda, K. B. (15 Nov 2012). "A Sure-fire Domain for Advertising: Where the Eye Goes, the Ad Goes," *Soranews24.com*, https://soranews24.com/2012/11/15/a-sure-fire-domain-for-advertising-where-the-eye-goes-the-ad-goes/ [30.12.2018].

Matrix Media Outdoor Advertising Experts. (7 Jan 2013). "Health & Wellness Marketing: Doctor Office Marketing," *Matrixmediaservices.com*, https://www.matrixmediaservices.com/doctor-office-advertising/ [18.06.2018].

Media Dynamics Inc. (2014). "America's Media Usage and Ad Exposure 1945–2014."

Medical Practice Consulting, "In-Hospital TV Advertising Solution," *Mpconsulting.co.za*, https://www.mpconsulting.co.za/compliance-management/in-hospital-tv-advertising [20.09.2021].

Miejskie Przedsiębiorstwo Komunikacyjne Łódź Sp. z o.o., *Cennik (Price List)*, *Mpk.lodz.pl*, www.mpk.lodz.pl/files/r_zal_cennik.pdf [10.07.2018].

Moran, C. (6 Feb 2014). "20 Years Ago, Only 1 Baseball Stadium Had A Corporate Sponsor: Now All But 9 Do," *Consumerist*, https://consumerist.com/2014/02/06/20-years-ago-only-1-baseball-stadium-had-a-corporate-sponsor-now-all-but-9-do/ [02.05.2018].

My Free Car, www.myfreecar.com [6.07.2018].

M. F. (31 Aug 2016). "Why Advertising on Football Shirts Is More Expensive Than Ever," *The Economist*, https://www.economist.com/the-economist-explains/2016/08/31/why-advertising-on-football-shirts-is-more-expensive-than-ever [25.05.2018].

Newman, A. A. (27 Aug 2007). "Your Ad Here, on My S.U.V.? and You'll Pay?," *New York Times,* https://www.nytimes.com/2007/08/27/business/media/27wrap.html [6 Jul 2018].

Newman, A. A. (18 Feb 2009). "The Body as Billboard: Your Ad Here," *New York Times,* https://www.nytimes.com/2009/02/18/business/media/18adco.html [4 Apr 2018].

Nowicka, H. (8 Sep 1996). "A Police Car Is on Its Way… But First a Word from Our Sponsors," *Independent,* https://www.independent.co.uk/news/a-police-car-is-on-its-way-but-first-a-word-from-our-sponsors-1362314.html [4.06.2018].

PatientPop. (23 May 2017). "6 Ways to Ensure Your Patients Love Your Waiting Room," *Patientpop.com,* https://www.patientpop.com/blog/running-a-practice/6-strategies-turn-waiting-room-asset/ [18.06.2018].

Pelargos Family Service "Paczki samplingowe," Pelargos.pl, https://www.pelargos.pl/oferta/sampling/paczki-samplingowe/ [10.05.2020].

Penner, M. (7 May 2004). "Baseball Cancels Plans for Movie Ad on Bases," LA Times, http://articles.latimes.com/2004/may/07/sports/sp-penner7 [1.06.2018].

Pennington, B. (18 Oct 2004). "Reading, Writing and Corporate Sponsorships," *New York Times,* https://www.nytimes.com/2004/10/18/sports/othersports/reading-writing-and-corporate-sponsorships.html [30.04.2018].

Pinion-Whitt, M. (4 Aug 2010). "Calif. Ambulances to Become 'Moving Billboards,'" *EMS1 (Emergency Medical Services),* https://www.ems1.com/ambulances-emergency-vehicles/articles/862153-Calif-ambulances-to-become-moving-billboards/ [16.06.2018].

Pitts, L. Jr. (10 Nov 2002). "Don't Let Cop Cars Become Billboards," *Baltimore Sun.*

PlayMyAd, "Medical Offices," *Playmyad.com,* http://www.playmyad.com/venues/medical-offices [18.06.2018].

Present Service Marketing Communication, "Samplingi," *Present-Service.pl,* http://www.present-service.pl/oferta-mamaklub.html#samplingi-00 [10.05.2020].

Prosperous Parks, "Funding Opportunities," *ProsperousParks.com,* https://prosperousparks.com/funding_opps.html?r=1&h=&w= [10.09.2018].

Publicité Ascension, http://www.pubascension.com/ [10.07.2018].

Rallo, J., Ma, M. (2012). *My Son, Yo-Yo,* The Chinese University Press, Hong Kong.

Rampell, C. (15 Apr 2011). "On School Buses, Ad Space for Rent," *New York Times,* https://www.nytimes.com/2011/04/16/business/media/16buses.html [10.07.2018].

Rape, Abuse & Incest National Network, "What Consent Looks Like," *Rainn.org*, https://www.rainn.org/articles/what-is-consent [2.02.2022].

Reed, P. (10 May 2017). "Is Advertising on Professional Sports Teams' Jerseys Going Too Far?," *The Spectator*, https://www.spectatornews.com/sports/2017/02/01/is-advertising-on-professional-sports-teams-jerseys-going-too-far/ [29.05.2018].

Rubenstein, S. (14 Apr 1999). "$5.8 Million Tattoo: Sanchez Family Counts the Cost of Lunch Offer," *San Francisco Chronicle*.

Sanya, A. (26 Jul 2018). "Japanese Company Uses Young Ladies' Armpits as Advertising Space," *Lailanews.com*, https://lailasnews.com/japanese-company-uses-young-ladies-armpits-as-advertising-space/ [30.12.2018].

Schoettle, A. (9 Jan 2010). "City's Plan to Raise Money with Sponsorships Takes Wing with KFC," *Indianapolis Business Journal*, https://www.ibj.com/articles/15609-city-s-plan-to-raise-money-with-sponsorships-takes-wing-with-kfc [10.06.2018].

Shay, J. (1994). *Unchained Memories*, HarperCollins, New York.

Spina, A. (27 Mar 2011). "Advertising Company Putting Ads in County Jail," *Buffalo News*.

Statista (2021). "Advertising Spending Worldwide from 2000 to 2023," https://www.statista.com/statistics/1174981/advertising-expenditure-worldwide/. [16.12.2021]

St Matthew-in-the-City, "Our Billboards," *Stmathews.nz*, https://www.stmatthews.nz/billboards [9.07.2018].

Story, L. (15 Jan 2007). "Anywhere the Eye Can See, It's Likely to See an Ad," *New York Times*, https://www.nytimes.com/2007/01/15/business/media/15everywhere.html [9.07.2018].

Sydney Trains, "Advertise with Sydney Trains," *Transport.nsw.gov.au*, https://www.transport.nsw.gov.au/sydneytrains/advertise-sydney-trains [11.07.2018].

TDI India, "Tree Guard," *TDIIndia.com*, https://www.tdiindia.com/TreeGuard.htm [10.09.2018].

Tendler, S. (6 Jan 1997). "Police Look to Private Firms for Sponsorship Cash," *Times*, London.

Tice, C. (15 Oct 2009). "Marketing to a Captive Audience," *Entrepreneur Europe*, https://www.entrepreneur.com/article/203714 [18.11.2019].

u/Zippo16. (4 Jul 2012). "Uncle Sent Me This Pic, This Is a Real Life Cow Used to Advertise a Deli in Kentucky," *Reddit.com*, https://www.reddit.com/r/WTF/comments/w1n8s/uncle_sent_me_this_pic_this_is_a_real_life_cow/ [30.12.2018].

Van Mensvoort, K. (2007). "Papilio Nike Ulysses: Branded Butterfly," *Mensvoort.com*, https://www.mensvoort.com/work/papilio-nike-ulysses/ [5.07.2018].

Van Mensvoort, K. (17 Dec 2006). "Branded Butterfly Wings," *Nextnature.net*, https://www.nextnature.net/2006/12/branded-butterfly-wings/ [5.07.2018].

Van Wagner, leaflet 1, "Train wrap specification sheet," *Caltrain.com*, http://www.caltrain.com/about/doingbusiness/Advertising/trainads.html [11.07.2018].

Van Wagner, leaflet 2, "San Francisco station domination specification sheet," *Caltrain.com*, http://www.caltrain.com/about/doingbusiness/Advertising/trainads.html [11.07.2018].

Villa, L. (24 Apr 2015). "Heidi Klum burns up lingerie campaign video featuring Sia's 'Fire Meet Gasoline,'" *AXS.com*, https://www.axs.com/news/heidi-klum-burns-up-lingerie-campaign-video-featuring-sia-s-fire-meet--50363 [29.06.2018].

Villeneuve, A. (2011). "Advertising in Jail Is a Branding Crime," *Beneath the Brand*, http://www.talentzoo.com/beneath-the-brand/blog_news.php?articleID=9829 [15.04.2018].

Wall, M. (11 May 2018). "Would You Pay for an Ad-Free Internet?," *BBC.com*, https://www.bbc.com/news/business-44066077 [26.12.2018].

Watson, J. (Feb 2013). "New York Jail Profits from TV Ads," Prison Legal News, https://www.prisonlegalnews.org/news/2013/feb/15/new-york-jail-profits-from-tv-ads/ [15.04.2018].

Weldon, F. (2001). *The Bulgari Connection*, Atlantic Monthly Press, New York.

Wikipedia, *List of Sports Clubs Named after a Sponsor*, https://en.wikipedia.org/wiki/List_of_sports_clubs_named_after_a_sponsor [1.06.2018].

William. (1 Oct 2017). "Reverse Graffiti Legality. Is 'Clean Advertising' Legal in the UK?," *Digital Refresh*, https://www.digitalrefresh.uk/reverse-graffiti-legality-clean-advertising-legal-in-the-uk/ [10.09.2018].

Wolfson, B. (17 Feb 2015). "How Many Advertisements Is Enough?," *Soccer Politics*, https://sites.duke.edu/wcwp/2015/02/17/how-many-advertisements-is-enough/ [29.05.2018].

Wood, D. B. (3 Oct 2002). "Your Ad Here: Cop Cars As the Next Billboards," *Christian Science Monitor*, https://www.csmonitor.com/2002/1003/p01s01-ussc.html [5.06.2018].

Worldometer, "Current World Population," and "Growth," [in:] *World Population*, https://www.worldometers.info/world-population/ [18.12.2021].

(13 Nov 1995), "See And Don't Call Back," *ADWEEK—W. EDITION*.

(6 Nov 2002), "To Protect and To Sell," editorial, *Toledo Blade*.

(29 Nov 2002), “Reject Police-Car Advertising,” editorial, *Charleston (South Carolina) Post and Courier.*

(29 Nov 2002), “A Badge, a Gun—And a Great Deal on Vinyl Siding,” editorial, *Roanoke (Virginia) Times & World News.*

(28 Jan 2003), “A Creepy Commercialism,” editorial, *Hartford Courant.*

(15 Feb 2007), “Our Rising Ad Dosage: It's Not as Oppressive as Some Think,” *Media Matters.*

The Dictionary Entries Section

“Ad-free,” [in:] *Cambridge Dictionary*, Cambridge University Press. https://dictionary.cambridge.org/dictionary/english/ad-free [06.08.2021].

Shawtybad555 (5 Dec 2010). “Body like a coke bottle,” [in:] *Urban Dictionary*, https://www.urbandictionary.com/define.php?term=body%20like%20a%20coke%20bottle [06.06.2020].

“Duracell-bunny,” [in:] *Your Dictionary*, https://www.yourdictionary.com/duracell-bunny#wiktionary [06.06.2020].

“High culture” (2011), [in:] D. Chandler, R. Munday (eds.), *A Dictionary of Media and Communication*, First Edition, Oxford University Press, Oxford.

Films, Television Series, Shows, Songs, and Videogames Referred to in the Thesis (from the most recent to the earliest)

Primeminibeats, Gypsy (2020), “Body Like a Coke Bottle” [song], non-album single, no record label, released on iTunes, Apple Music, Amazon.

Selling Sunset (2019–) [show], Adam DiVello (creat.), Done and Done Productions, Lionsgate, United States.

Anon (2018) [film], Andrew Niccol (dir.), K5 International, Sierra/Affinity, Road Pictures. Scythia Films, Inc., Cutting Edge Group, Sky Cinema Original Films, United Kingdom.

YCee, Maleek Berry (2017), “Juice” [song], *The First Wave*, Tinny Entertainment.

GAB, SouthBoyz (2017), “Coca Cola Body” [song], non-album single, Rhythmic Music Records.

Sia (2015), “Fire and Gasoline” [song], *1000 Forms of Fear*, Inertia, Monkey Puzzle, RCA.

Street of Dreams (2013) [film], Martin Scorsese (dir.), Dolce & Gabbana, Grey Advertising Global, United States.

Once Upon a Time (2013) [film], Karl Lagerfeld (dir.), Channel, Cité du Cinéma, France.

Lou Bega (2010), "Sweet Like Cola" [song], *Free Again*, Syndicate Musicproduction.

The Real Housewives of New York City (2008–) [show], Scott Dunlop (creat.), Ricochet, United States.

London Taxi: Rush Hour (2006) [game], Microsoft Windows, Metro3D Europe, United Kingdom.

Frankie J, Mannie Fresh, Chamillionaire (2006), "That Girl" [song], *Priceless*, Columbia.

Goal! (2005) [film], Danny Cannon (dir.), Milkshake Films, Touchstone Pictures, United Kingdom.

The Sisterhood of the Traveling Pants (2005) [film], Ken Kwapis (dir.), Alcon Entertainment, Di Novi Pictures, Debra Martin Chase Productions, Alloy Entertainment, United States.

L.A. Rush (2005) [game], Microsoft Windows, Zoo Digital Publishing, United Kingdom.

Football Manager (2005–2021) [game], Microsoft Windows, Sega, United Kingdom.

The Terminal (2004) [film], Steven Spielberg (dir.), Amblin Entertainment, DreamWorks Pictures, Parkes/MacDonald Productions, United States.

Cellular (2004) [film], David Ellis (dir.), Electric Entertainment, United States.

Goldie Lookin' Chain (2004), "You Knows I loveS You Baby" [song], non-album single, Atlantic.

Darkened Skye (2002) [game], Microsoft Windows, Simon & Schuster, United States.

Busta Rhymes, Sean P Diddy Combs (2002), "Pass the Courvoisier" [song], *Genesis*, J Records/Legacy.

American Idol (2002–) [show], Simon Fuller (creat.), FremantleMedia, 19 Entertainment, United States.

Sting (2000), "Desert Rose" [song], *Brand New Day*, A&M Records.

Neopets (1999) [web game], Cross-platform, Adam Powell and Donna Williams, Viacom, JumpStart Games, United Kingdom.

Will Smith (1997), "Just cruising" [song], *Men in Black - The Album*, Columbia.

Star Trek Generations (1994) [film], David Carson (dir.), Paramount Pictures Studios, United States.

NYPD Blue (1993–2005) [television series], Steven Bochco, David Milch (dirs.), Steven Bochco Productions, 20th Century Fox Television, United States.

MC Nas-D, DJ Freaky Fred (1992), "It's My Cadillac (Got That Bass)" [song], *It's My Cadillac (Got That Bass)*, Pandisc Records.

The Ford Simulator (1987) [game], MS-DOS, Ford Motor Company, United States.

Index

Polish Contemporary Philosophy and Philosophical Humanities

Edited by Jan Hartman

Vol. 1 Roman Murawski: Logos and Máthēma. Studies in the Philosophy of Mathematics and His- tory of Logic. 2011.

Vol. 2 Cezary Józef Olbromski: The Notion of lebendige Gegenwart as Compliance with the Tem- porality of the "Now". The Late Husserl's Phenomenology of Time. 2011.

Vol. 3 Jan Woleński: Essays on Logic and its Applications in Philosophy. 2011.

Vol. 4 Władysław Stróżewski: Existence, Sense and Values. Essays in Metaphysics and Phenome- nology. Edited by Sebastian Kołodziejczyk. 2013.

Vol. 5 Jan Hartman: Knowledge, Being and the Human. Some of the Major Issues in Philosophy. Translated by Ben Koschalka. 2013.

Vol. 6 Roman Ingarden: Controversy over the Existence of the World. Volume I. Translated and annotated by Arthur Szylewicz. 2013.

Vol. 7 Jan Hartman: Philosophical Heuristics. Translated by Ben Koschalka. 2015.

Vol. 8 Roman Ingarden: Controversy over the Existence of the World. Volume II. Translated and annotated by Arthur Szylewicz. 2016.

Vol. 9 Tomasz Kubalica: Unmöglichkeit der Erkenntnistheorie. Leonard Nelsons Kritik an der Erkenntnistheorie unter besonderer Berücksichtigung des Neukantianismus. 2017.

Vol. 10 Renata Ziemińska: The History of Skepticism. In Search of Consistency. 2017.

Vol. 11 Jan Woleński: Logic and Its Philosophy. 2018.

Vol. 12 Wielslaw Gumula: On Property and Ownership Relations. 2018.

Vol. 13 Andrzej Zaporowski: Action, Belief, and Community. 2018.

Vol. 14 Andrzej Bator / Zbigniew Pulka (eds.): A Post-Analytical Approach to Philosophy and Theory of Law. 2019.

Vol. 15 Krzysztof Śleziński: Towards Scientific Metaphysics. Volume 1: In the Circle of the Scientific Metaphysics of Zygmunt Zawirski. Development and Comments on Zawirski's Concepts and their Philosophical Context. 2019.

Vol. 16 Krzysztof Śleziński: Towards Scientific Metaphysics. Volume 2: Benedykt Bornstein's Geo- metrical Logic and Modern Philosophy. A Critical Study. 2019.

Vol. 17 Jan Felicjan Terelak: Eustress and Distress: Reactivation. 2019.

Vol. 18 Roman Murawski: Lógos and Máthēma 2. Studies in the Philosophy of Logic and Mathema- tics. 2020.

Vol 19 Andrzej J. Noras: Geschichte des Neukantianismus. Übersetzt von Tomasz Kubalica. 2020.

Vol. 20 Tomasz Jarmużek: Tableau Methods for Propositional Logic and Term Logic. Translated by Sławomir Jaskólski. 2020.

Vol. 21 Marta Kudelska: Why Is There I Rather Than It? Ontology of the Subject in the Upaniṣads. 2021.

Studies in Philosophy, History of Ideas and Modern Societies

Edited by Jan Hartman

Vol. 22 Georg Schmid: The Treachery of the Elites. On Political Discontent. 2021.

Vol. 23 Hanna Urbańska: The Philosophical System of Śiva Śatakam and Other Śaiva Poems by Nārāyaṇa Guru. In Relation to Tirumandiram by Tirumūlar. 2022.

Vol. 24 Marcin Krasnodębski: Green Chemistry. A Brief Historical Critique. 2022.

Vol. 25 Artur Przybysławski: Thales and the Beginnings of European Reflection. 2023.

Vol. 26 Krzysztof Krenc: Can Machines Have Free Will? Analysis of the Concept of Free Will in Relation to the Psychophysical Problem. 2023.

Vol. 27 Joanna Iwanowska: Omnipresence of Advertising. 2024.

www.peterlang.com

www.ingramcontent.com/pod-product-compliance
Ingram Content Group UK Ltd.
Pitfield, Milton Keynes, MK11 3LW, UK
UKHW041826031026
15587UKWH00002B/588

9 783631 905838